Voices

Plays for Studying the Holocaust

Janet E. Rubin

The Scarecrow Press, Inc.
Lanham, Maryland, and London
1999

SCARECROW PRESS, INC.

Published in the United States of America
by Scarecrow Press, Inc.
4720 Boston Way, Lanham, Maryland 20706
http://www.scarecrowpress.com

4 Pleydell Gardens, Folkestone
Kent CT20 2DN, England

Copyright © 1999 by Janet E. Rubin

All rights reserved. No part of this publication may be reproduced, stored in a retrieval system, or transmitted in any form or by any means, electronic, mechanical, photocopying, recording, or otherwise, without the prior permission of the publisher.

British Library Cataloguing in Publication Information Available

Library of Congress Cataloging-in-Publication Data

Voices : plays for studying the Holocaust / [edited by] Janet E. Rubin.
    p. cm.
    Includes bibliographical references and index.
    ISBN 0-8108-3655-6 (alk. paper)
    1. Holocaust, Jewish (1939-1945) Drama. 2. Holocaust, Jewish (1935-1945)--Study and teaching. 3. Holocaust, Jewish (1939-1945), in literature--Study and teaching. 4. Drama--20th century.
    I. Rubin, Janet.
    PN6120.H73V65   1999
    812'.5409358--dc21   99-20979
                                                                                  CIP

∞™ The paper used in this publication meets the minimum requirements of American National Standard for Information Sciences—Permanence of Paper for Printed Library Materials, ANSI/NISO Z39.48–1992.
Manufactured in the United States of America.

Dedicated with love to my brother and sister, Harvey M. Rubin and Shirley R. Friedland, and to the memory of my parents, Frieda and Benjamin A. Rubin.

Contents

ACKNOWLEDGMENTS ix

COPYRIGHTS xi

PART ONE

    Chapter 1   Background on the Holocaust   3
        Introduction   3
        Meeting the Challenge   4
        The Holocaust   6
            Chronology   7
        How to Use This Book   16

PART TWO

    Chapter 2   Plays and Activities: Beginning Study   21
        Can You Hear Them Crying?   21
            The Playwright: Virginia Burton Stringer   21
            The Play   22
            Information about the Play and the Holocaust   22

Can You Hear Them Crying?	23
Production Notes	38
Set Design	39
Costumes	40
Props	40
Biographies	40
Teaching Activities	42
Angel in the Night	49
The Playwright: Joanna H. Kraus	49
The Play	50
Information about the Play and the Holocaust	50
Angel in the Night	52
Synopsis of Scenes	86
Production Notes	87
Teaching Activities	90
Chapter 3 Plays and Activities: Intermediate Study	95
Kindertransport	95
The Playwright: Diane Samuels	95
The Play	96
Information about the Play and the Holocaust	97
Synopsis of Act One, scene one	99
Kindertransport	100
Teaching Activities	118
T-Money & Wolf	122
The Playwrights: Kevin Willmott & Ric Averill	122
The Play	123
Information about the Play and the Holocaust	123
T-Money & Wolf	126
Production Notes	162
Teaching Activities	163
Chapter 4 Plays and Activities: Advanced Study	169
The Man in the Glass Booth	169
The Playwright: Robert Shaw	169
The Play	170
Information about the Play and the Holocaust	171
Synopsis	174
The Man in the Glass Booth	174
Teaching Activities	186

A Bright Room Called Day	191
The Playwright: Tony Kushner	191
The Play	192
Information about the Play and the Holocaust	193
Synopsis of the Second Interruption	196
Second Interruption	197
Synopsis of Scene Seventeen	197
Scene Seventeen	198
Synopsis of Scene Twenty-Three	201
Scene Twenty-Three	202
Synopsis of Scene Twenty-Four	205
Scene Twenty-Four	205
Teaching Activities	207
"*Voice*" in *Remnants*	210
The Playwright: Hank Greenspan	210
The Play	210
Information about the Play and the Holocaust	211
Synopsis	213
"*Voice*" in *Remnants*	213
Teaching Activities	215
Hitler's Childhood	217
The Playwright: Niklas Rådström	217
The Translator: Frank Gabriel Perry	217
The Play	218
Information about the Play and the Holocaust	219
Hitler's Childhood	221
Teaching Activities	277

PART THREE

Bibliography		285
Appendix A	Plays, Playwrights, and Publishers	293
Appendix B	Resource References	297
Appendix C	Other Works by Contributors	305
INDEX		309
ABOUT THE AUTHOR		313

Acknowledgments

Jaime Monllor and the United States Holocaust Memorial Museum
Anna Dadlez
Lib Segal
Katherine Falk Fehrman
Saginaw Valley State University Foundation
Saginaw Valley State University
Saun Strobel
Jan Kimmel and Scott Mellendorf of the Melvin J. Zahnow Library at
    Saginaw Valley State University
Congress of Jewish Culture, New York City
Janet Martineau
Ric Averlll
Virginia Stringer
Hank Greenspan
Frank Perry
Susan Schulman, A Literary Agency
Orlin Corey and the Anchorage Press

Copyrights

Can You Hear Them Crying?
CAUTION: All rights, including professional, amateur, motion picture, recitation, lecturing, performance, public reading, radio broadcasting, and television are strictly reserved. Inquires on all rights should be addressed to Meriwether Publishing Ltd., Permissions Dept., 885 Elkton Drive, Colorado Springs, CO 80907.

Angel in the Night
copyright MCMXCV
Joanna Halpert Kraus
Printed in the United States of America
All Rights Reserved
(*Angel in the Night*)
The play printed in this anthology is not to be used as an acting script. All inquiries regarding performance rights should be addressed to Dramatic Publishing Company, 311 Washington St., Woodstock, IL 60098. Phone: (815) 338-7170. Fax: (815) 338-8981.

Kindertransport
Copyright © 1995
Diane Samuels
Used by permission of Dutton, a division of Penguin Putnam Inc.
CAUTION: Professionals and amateurs are hereby warned that *Kindertransport* is subject to a royalty. It is fully protected under the copyright laws of the United States of America, the British Commonwealth, including Canada, and all other countries of the Copyright Union. All rights, including professional, amateur, motion picture, recitation, lecturing, public reading, radio broadcasting, television, and the rights of translation into foreign languages are strictly reserved. Reprinted by permission of Susan Schulman, A Literary Agency, 454 W. 44th Street, New York, NY 10036. Email: schulman@aol.com

T-Money & Wolf
copyright MCMXCIV
Kevin Willmott and Ric Averill
Printed in the United States of America
All Rights Reserved
(*T-Money & Wolf*)
The play printed in this anthology is not to be used as an acting script. All inquires regarding performance rights should be addressed to Dramatic Publishing Company, 311 Washington St., Woodstock, IL 60098. Phone: (815) 338-7170. Fax: (815) 338-8981.

The Man in the Glass Booth
The Man in the Glass Booth by Robert Shaw
Copyright © 1969 by Robert Shaw
Renewed 1996, Deborah and Colin Shaw (Executors)
CAUTION: Professionals and amateurs are hereby warned that "The Man in the Glass Booth" being fully protected under the copyright laws of the United States of America, the British Commonwealth countries, including Canada, and the other countries of the Copyright Union, is subject to a royalty. All rights, including professional, amateur, motion picture, recitation, public reading, radio, television and cable broadcasting, and the rights of translation into foreign languages, are strictly reserved. Any inquiry regarding the availability of performance rights, or the purchase of individual copies of the authorized acting edition, must

be directed to Samuel French Inc., 45 West 25th Street, New York, NY 10010, with other locations in Hollywood and Toronto, Canada.

A Bright Room Called Day

All rights reserved. Except for brief passages in newspaper, magazine, radio, or television reviews, no part of this book may be reproduced in any form or by any means, electronic or mechanical, including photocopying or recording, or by an information storage and retrieval system, without permission in writing from the publisher.

Professionals and amateurs are hereby warned that this material, being fully protected under the copyright laws of the United States of America and all other countries of the Berne and Universal Copyright Conventions, is subject to a royalty. All rights, including but not limited to professional, amateur, recording, motion picture, recitation, lecturing, public reading, radio and television broadcasting, and the rights of translation into foreign languages are expressly reserved. Particular emphasis is placed on the question of readings and all uses of these plays by educational institutions, permissions for which must be secured from the author's agent: Joyce P. Ketay, 1501 Broadway, Suite 1910, New York, NY 10036. Phone: (212) 354-6825.

Voice

"*Voice*" is excerpted from *Remnants* by Hank Greenspan. © Copyright 1991 by Hank Greenspan. All Rights Reserved. Reprinted by permission of the author. Particular caution is given regarding all performance rights including public readings or recitations, as well as all reproduction of the work including photocopying, videotaping, or sound recording. All inquiries concerning "Voice" or *Remnants* should be addressed to Hank Greenspan, 369 Hilldale Drive, Ann Arbor, MI 48105.

Hitler's Childhood

Translation © Frank Gabriel Perry 1995
Original text © Niklas Rådström 1983
Copyright agent: Alan Brodie Representation Ltd.
211 Piccadilly
London W1V 9LD
England
Tel: +44-171-917 2871
Fax: +44-171-917 2872

Part One

Chapter 1

Background on the Holocaust

The Holocaust: the systematic slaughter of eleven million people, six million of whom were Jews, by the Nazis during World War II.

Introduction

Voices screaming. Voices shouting. Voices whispering. Voices quivering. Voices sobbing. These are the voices of the Holocaust, compelling and compassionate human instruments communicating experiences and events so dark, defiant, disturbing, and deeply personal that they echo in memory. Some of the voices produce remarkable stories; others are strikingly ordinary. Voices of victims, perpetrators, heroes, villains, rescuers, and survivors *are* the voices of the Holocaust.

Whose voices will continue to tell the human stories of this tragic and terrifying period? Holocaust survivors today are senior citizens. Events that occurred half a century ago and that so remarkably shaped both individual lives and world history risk being diminished and fading from our minds as these elderly pass from us. Will their deaths produce the silence the Nazis failed to achieve? Will their narratives, whether recounting acts of unspeakable horror or steadfast courage, quietly depart from our thoughts?

Or, might it be playwrights who can give lasting expression to these stories through voices that come from the stage? Through plays, the pain of violence, the accounts of risk and resistance, the anguish of separation and loss, and the hope and determination of survival become real once more. Plays make active partners of those who see or read them. Students using scripts and related activities think, feel, and imagine as they make connections to dramatic and historic events. Long after the final line of dialogue, the characters, stories, and experiences portrayed remain powerful in the mind. Scripts provide unique opportunities for students studying the Holocaust to research, recount, reflect, and remember. Because of their inherent vibrancy, intimacy, and empathy, plays can make certain that the voices of the Holocaust are never stilled.

Clearly, the stories of the Holocaust, of human experiences and the lessons inherent in them, must be preserved. Recent events bring into focus the pressing necessity of instilling this knowledge in young people. When, in America, churches are burned, hate groups like the Ku Klux Klan rally, and Holocaust deniers publish their claims, the need to bring this past into sharp scrutiny takes on renewed urgency. By providing Holocaust education to young people, we insure that the voices of those who experienced the atrocities committed by the Nazis in their program of the Final Solution are not quieted.

Even when studied or performed in a classroom rather than in a theatre, and even when the artists are students rather than professional actors, directors, and designers, the ability of scripts to communicate, to make real, and to make a lasting impression earns respect. Educating by entertaining and enlightening, the words and actions that the playwright shares have the power to transport learners to different times and places. By asking students to join them in sharing their stories, dramatic characters assist young people in merging the past, present, and future. This synthesis is vital to insuring that hatred can never again be allowed such free reign.

Meeting the Challenge

Teaching young people about the Holocaust and helping them to understand the complexity of this human tragedy is, without question, challenging. There are numerous issues to be addressed. How can this historic event be made relevant to today's youth? How can they be helped to comprehend such massive destruction and its causes? How can hatred, so unbridled and intense, be explained? How is today's world different from the world of more than a half century ago? How should concerned adults deal with the level of intellectual and emotional discomfort that this material often produces in both teacher and student? To what extent should balance be achieved between emotional response and factual accuracy? What does it feel like to be the victim of intense racial, ethnic, or political hatred? How can oversimplification, weak symbolism, and trivialization of content be avoided? How can the carnage and abhorrently graphic details that are a part of the Holocaust be kept in perspective? What content should be covered and to which educators do these curricular responsibilities fall? What, if any, psychological risks do young learners face in contemplating this material?

Plays offer both an artistic and an educational resource, bringing a unique perspective to studying the Holocaust. As an instructional tool, they help educators to meet the challenges associated with some of the difficult issues this subject raises pedagogically. As an example, consider the ability of a play to make these events of the past relevant to today's students. Many of the young people who will see or study the plays in this anthology are the same age (adolescents and teens) as survivors would have been when they were captured. Many of those exterminated were in the early years of life. Between one and a half and two million children were lost to horrible deaths. Through dramatic characters like the children in *Can You Hear Them Crying?* and Pawlina in *Angel in the Night*, students are introduced to characters who, in many respects, are like them. In other plays or excerpts from them, such as *T-Money & Wolf* and "*Voice*" from *Remnants*, they meet those with whom they may or may not have common interests and experiences. Dramatic literature does more than illustrate the similarities between fictional characters and young readers and audiences; it invites comparisons that envelop the Holocaust in real-life experiences that contemporary students can understand. They see that ordinary people, indeed, can be denied normal lives because of extraordinary times and events.

In addition, because of the breadth and scope of subject matter, settings, and themes found in plays, studying about the Holocaust in this way expands opportunities for integrating curriculum. Dramatic literature has a natural home in language arts, but plays about the Holocaust invite curricular partnerships with history, sociology, social studies, psychology, fine arts, science, comparative religion, and technology. Holocaust study typically encompasses an examination of topics such as the Jewish people; stereotyping and anti-Semitism; Hitler and his rise to power; life in the Ghetto; deportations and displacement; World War II and the Nazi desire for world conquest; the camps; the Final Solution, personal responses of resisting, rescuing, or failing to act; as well as contemplation of the aftermath and freedom. These topics can be examined from various curricular perspectives given the diversity of characters and stories in Holocaust plays. Given substantiative treatment through dramatic form, the full scope of the issues and events encompassing this terrible time can be better analyzed and understood. Further, plays prompt students to investigate issues of personal responsibility and to do so within a range of dramatic and historical contexts. The actions, decisions, and emotions of characters such as victims, villains, rescuers, and survivors offer divergent avenues for academic exploration.

Plays give students opportunities to identify with characters and events and to empathically experience the content they are learning. They put human faces on people and places, sparking insights into things that have happened and their short- and long-term influence. Young learners are helped to understand that, whether fictional or true, the human stories of the Holocaust are stories from which to remember and learn.

The Holocaust

Defined both as complete devastation and destruction and as a sacrifice by fire, *Holocaust* has come to mean the systematic annihilation of Jews by the Nazis during the Second World War. A historical first, the Holocaust symbolizes the Nazi's planned and purposeful strategy for destroying an entire people. Jews, however, were not the only victims. Eleven million lives, six million of those Jewish, were lost to this genocidal regimen. Among those murdered were Gypsies, Poles, Serbs, homosexuals, those labeled by the Nazis as political enemies, the physically challenged, and the mentally impaired. While this book is not intended to provide a comprehensive description of the Holocaust, an overview is provided.

It also should be remembered that the impact of the Holocaust did not end in 1945. Although students most commonly study 1933–1945 as the years of the Holocaust, the foundation for this genocide was laid long before the twentieth century. Anti-Semitism, dating back to the time of Jesus Christ and firmly established when Jews were blamed for his murder, made them attractive targets when Germany needed a scapegoat after suffering defeat in World War I. Severe economic problems and political unrest following that conflict paved the way for Adolf Hitler to assume political power. Hitler brought with him a hatred of Jews and the slogans, *One People, One Reich, One Leader* and *Today Germany, Tomorrow the World*, left little doubt that there would be no place for them and other so-called undesirables in Hitler's Third Reich. Further, to insure that the words of the slogans came to pass, Hitler used fear, intimidation, and inspiration to bring the German people into line and to crush opposition to his world view.

Topics given less attention in Holocaust curricula must also be considered relative to this unprecedented example of organized hatred and killing. They include displaced persons camps, the goal of refugees to get to Palestine, the problems associated with finding loved ones after the war and often with beginning new lives in foreign countries, the creation of the Jewish state of Israel, the psychological effects of the suffering on survivors and their families in particular and on the Jewish population in general, the difficulties of non-Jewish victims in rebuilding and resuming their lives, and current examples of genocide in various parts of the world. A generation had been lost but those who did emerge from the camps did not simply return home and resume life as they had once known it. Understanding the unabated drive toward ethnic cleansing as nations watched, what life was like after liberation, the physical and psychological devastation of the Holocaust, and the motivations of the perpetrators are a part of this study, as is how its effects are evidenced in today's complex world.

How did the Holocaust happen? What follows provides a look at the milestones resulting in the development and demise of the Third Reich as ruled by Adolf Hitler. The chronology is intended to help students understand how and why this program of raw hatred, harassment, suffering, and extermination occurred.

Chronology

1914-1918
World War I. Germany is defeated, setting the stage for economic and political strife. Germans feel victimized by the terms of the Treaty of Versailles. Among the German people, this feeds a renewed sense of nationalism and belief in their natural superiority.

Brainwashing (the *Ubermenschen* syndrome) begins to shape German thinking.

Hitler, born in Austria, serves in the German army and becomes a German nationalist. During his service, he is awarded the Iron Cross, First Class. Temporarily blinded by mustard gas, Hitler ends his military career but becomes taken with the idea that he is destined to save Germany.

1919-1923
Hitler joins the German Workers Party, which becomes the *Nationalsozialistische Deutsche Arbeiterpartei* (NSDAP). Hitler drafts, and the organization adopts, a program that includes early indications that Jews and others, such as foreigners and Gypsies, will not be a part of the new Germany. "Only members of the nation (*Volksgenosse*) can be citizens of the state. Only those of German blood, regardless of denomination, can be members of the nation. Jews, therefore, cannot be members of the nation" (Holocaust Education and Memorial Centre 5). This party is the forerunner of the Nazi party and Hitler becomes its leader in 1921. During this time, the Nazi flag, salute, and swastika, brownshirted storm troopers, and the chants *Sieg Heil* and *Heil Hitler* are created and adopted.

The NSDAP attempts to overthrow the Weimar Republic but fails. Hitler is imprisoned. While in jail he writes his biography, *Mein Kampf* (*My Struggle*), in which he articulates his philosophical doctrine.

1932
Hitler is defeated by Paul von Hindenburg in the German Federal Republic presidential election.

1933
Between this year and 1939, more than 400 laws are created to "define, segregate, and impoverish German Jews" (United States Holocaust Memorial Museum exhibit).

In January, Hindenburg appoints Hitler Chancellor of Germany. Through manipulation of the law and terror tactics such as the "temporary" suspension of civil rights, which are never restored, Hitler restricts freedoms and moves to decimate opposition. The Gestapo or Special State Police, the SA or Storm Troopers, and the SS or Security Police crush Hitler's political enemies.

The Reichstag burns. Hitler uses the fire as an opportunity to create what is, for all intents and purposes, a police state. Dissension is equated with treason and is a capital crime.

Hitler takes control of the Republic and the Enabling Act gives him dictatorial powers. Dachau Concentration Camp is founded by Heinrich Himmler and 200 Communists are the first internees.

Jewish businesses are nationally boycotted and trade unions closed. Jewish children are banned from most schools and adults are prohibited from holding positions as civil servants, public high school teachers, and National Health Service physicians.

Books whose content has been deemed offensive or threatening to Nazi ideology are publicly burned.

As an organization, Jehovah's Witnesses are banned.

1934
Hitler becomes *Führer* of Germany by consolidating the positions of President and Chancellor.

1935
Membership in Hitler Youth numbers six million.

Laws define who is a Jew. Intermarriage or extramarital relationships with Aryans are prohibited. Jews are stripped of citizenship. The criminal code is expanded. *J* is stamped in Jewish passports. Sara and Israel are names Jews are forced to add to their own. Economic measures against Jews make life increasingly difficult for them.

Persecution, including being taken to concentration camps, worsens for other groups such as Jehovah's Witnesses, Romanies (Gypsies), political dissidents, and homosexuals.

1936

Sachsenhausen Concentration Camp is established.

Signs ostracizing Jews from public places and events are removed as Germany hosts the Olympic Games.

Germany and Italy form an alliance, the Rome-Berlin Axis.

1937

Between this year and 1939, Jews are forced to turn over their property and businesses or to sell them at ridiculously low prices.

1938

German Jews, for the first time, are exiled to Poland, among them the parents of Hershel Gynszpan. The young Gynszpan shoots and kills German representative Ernst vom Rath in Paris.

Kristallnacht, or the "Night of Broken Glass," takes place in November as retaliation for vom Rath's assassination. Storm Troopers, the SS, and Hitler Youth, mobilized by Paul Joseph Goebbels, orchestrate what is labeled a spontaneous public outburst against Jews. Seven thousand Jewish businesses are vandalized, synagogues are set afire, Jews are slain or injured, and 25,000 are taken into custody and deported to Dachau and Sachsenhausen Concentration Camps.

Austria is annexed by the Germans. Throughout Austria, riots and violence against Jews take place.

Public schools in Germany and Austria prohibit Jewish children from attending.

1939

Germany seizes Czechoslovakia. World War II begins. At 4:45 a.m. on September 1, German troops invade Poland and on September 17, the Soviets enter from the east. By the end of September, Poland is totally occupied. Although Poland resists Nazi aggression, the Ribbentrop/Molotov Treaty of Friendship makes simultaneous invasion of the country from both sides possible. Polish leaders, academics, artists, politicians, priests, and others are slaughtered, imprisoned, or resettled to minimize opposition and to accommodate those of "superior" German stock.

Hitler orders that the mentally and physically handicapped be killed. Those so doomed are taken to gas chambers in Austria and Germany where they are slain. In 1941, public protests force this program to continue in secret.

Jews must wear yellow stars or armbands.

The first Jewish ghetto, Piotrków Trybunalski, is established in Poland.

1940

Germany invades Denmark, Norway, Luxembourg, Holland, Belgium, and France.

The concentration camp at Auschwitz is established.

Jews are forced into ghettos.

Japan joins Germany and Italy in a Tripartite alliance.

1941

Germany invades Greece, Yugoslavia, and the Soviet Union.

In June, mass shootings of Jews begin in conquered portions of the Soviet Union. Ultimately, more than 1.2 million Jews are murdered by mobile killing squads (*Einsatzgruppen*) in the occupied Soviet territories.

In September, 33,771, men, women, and children are slain at Babi Yar in the Soviet Union over two days, constituting the single biggest massacre of the Holocaust. In the ensuing months, an estimated 100,000 Jews, Gypsies, and Soviet prisoners of war are executed there. Also in this year, massacres are staged at Riga, Odessa, and Rovno killing 25,000–28,000, 39,000, and 21,000, respectively.

Throughout the Reich, Jews are forced to wear the Star of David.

Jewish emigration stops and mass deportation to concentration camps begins. In Poland, the first methodical gassings of Jews begins on December 8 at the death camp town of Chelmno.

Pearl Harbor is bombed and the United States enters the war. Germany, supporting its Japanese ally, declares war upon the United States.

1942

The Final Solution, a plan to exterminate all European Jews, becomes state policy at the Wannsee Conference. Efforts to solve the "Jewish problem" justify Nazi atrocities throughout the Holocaust. The Final Solution refers to a last program of genocide that would eliminate the Jews forever.

The Majdanek, Sobibor, Treblinka, Belzec, and Auschwitz-Birkenau death camps begin operating in Poland. By this year, most Eastern European Jews are confined to ghettos. Many are forced from ghettos to the camps. By March, 20 to 25 percent of the Jewish population who will perish in the Holocaust already have done so.

By summer, German-occupied Europe houses 400 ghettos. More than two million Jews and 8,000 Gypsies endure horrid living conditions.

The United States government learns about the Final Solution seventeen months prior to establishing the War Refugee Board. Information from the German industrialist Eduard Schutte to World Jewish Congress representative Gerhart Riegner reveals Hitler's plan to annihilate European Jews. Riegner cables this information to the president of the World Jewish Congress, Rabbi Stephen S. Wise, in New York but the American State Department intercepts and withholds the cable. When, in August, Wise receives the information from another source, the State Department pressures him to remain silent. Even after verifying the information in November, the United States government takes no action.

1943

The Warsaw ghetto uprising takes place and for almost a month Jews are able to resist the Germans. Seven hundred to 750 ghetto residents resist 2,000 heavily armed soldiers and police officers. Ultimately, however, the rebellion is defeated and, by May, the Warsaw ghetto is no more.

With assistance from Belgium's underground, Jews escape from a transit train going from the Mechelen Camp (Transport No. 20) to Auschwitz.

At Stalingrad, the German army surrenders to the Soviets.

At the Bermuda Conference on Refugees, the Allies fail to produce an agreement.

In Denmark, 95 percent of the Jewish population are spared from Hitler's death decree as locals and members of the Danish resistance engineer a boatlift escape to Sweden.

1944

With Germany moving into Hungary and Hitler successfully installing an occupationalist government there, 12,000 Jews are taken daily to Auschwitz and murdered. Adolf Eichmann supervises the gassing deaths of nearly a half million Hungarian Jews.

June 6 marks D-Day as the Allies land at Normandy, France.

July marks the first major death march. More than 4,000 prisoners from a camp established on the site of the Warsaw ghetto ruins are moved eighty-one miles to Kutno. Twenty-five percent of those forced to march perish.

Thousands perish in additional death marches during the period of 1944–1945.

An assassination attempt against Hitler by dissident German officers and politicians fails. Many of the plotters are executed.

Paris is liberated in August.

At Auschwitz-Birkenau, prisoners destroy Crematorium IV.

1945

On May 7, Germany surrenders. World War II ends with Hitler's defeat and the liberation of the death camps.

1946

Nazi leaders go on trial in Nuremberg for crimes against humanity and for war crimes.

Numbers, almost too large to comprehend, also tell the story of the Holocaust. As students consider some of the following statistics, their recognition of human behaviors and sense of the magnitude of destruction grows. As they comprehend the scope of this human tragedy, students can be guided toward envisioning how some people lived, some died, and some prospered in a time of unspeakable cruelty, suffering, and sorrow.

- On May 10, 1933, in Berlin alone more than 25,000 books are burned in the effort to rid Germany of ideas contrary to those of the Nazis. Jewish and non-Jewish authors from both within and outside of Germany are targeted.

- By 1939, 300,000 of the 500,000 Jews living in Germany have fled. Few of those remaining survive the war.

- By the end of World War II in France, 25 percent of the Jewish population has perished; in the Netherlands, the figure is more than 75 percent. In total, 73 percent of the European Jewish population is lost by war's end.

- Between 1942 and 1944, 25,500 Jews are deported from the Breendonck and Mechelen transit camps in Belgium to Auschwitz.

- More than 1.2 million Jews are killed in the occupied Soviet territories by mobile killing squads.

- Between June 1941 and May 1945, more than 3.3 million Soviet prisoners of war die.

- As many as 10,000 per day are killed at the Auschwitz-Birkenau Concentration Camp. As this was both a slave labor camp and an extermination center, pregnant women, children, the elderly, Gypsies, and Jews are among the dead.

- On May 14, 1946, the commandant at Auschwitz attests that during his tenure, two million Jews there die by gassing and 500,000 others are annihilated through other means; his account of those gassed, however, is overestimated by approximately one million.

- The largest single mass deportation to Auschwitz during the Holocaust involved 437,402 Hungarian Jews.

- As many as 100 people are crowded into each railroad car taking victims to their deaths in concentration camps; trains average 1,000–2,000 doomed passengers per trip.

- Children living outside of Germany who are not Jewish and whose physical characteristics are those of the Nazi ideal are separated from their parents for adoption within Germany; some are later rejected and sent to camps.

- Before Romania's surrender, 350,000 Romanian Jews die.

- Examples of the number of Jewish refugees other nations accepted between 1933 and 1945:
    United States — 200,000
    Palestine — 125,000
    Argentina — 50,000
    Brazil — 27,000
    Britain — 70,000
    Canada — fewer than 5,000
    China — 25,000
    Bolivia — 14,000
    Chile — 14,000

- Estimated number of deaths at killing centers:

Camps Designated as Killing Centers	Duration of Executions	Number Killed
Chelmno	Beginning December 8, 1941, and lasting 32 months	150,000–320,000
Belzec	From March to December 1942	552,000–600,000+
Sobibor	Lasting 16 months	200,000–250,000+
Treblinka	Beginning July 1942 and lasting 14 months	750,000–870,000
Majdanek	Beginning early in 1942 and lasting to summer 1943	360,000–500,000
Auschwitz-Birkenau	Lasting 3 years	1.1 million–1.25 million
San Sabba	Beginning October 1943 through May 1945	5,000

Given the vastness of the numbers, it may be tempting to forget that each one stands for a person, an individual life. When the Holocaust is examined and understood at this level, however, it becomes more difficult to dismiss impressions that emerge from learning about physical, psychological, and material mayhem and butchery on an unimaginable scale.

How to Use This Book

This anthology has been designed for continuous usage as students pass from introductory through intermediate and advanced levels of Holocaust study. Appeal of the works to upper elementary, middle, and high school age students is predicated upon issues and circumstances to which young people can relate. Following this introductory portion, Part II of the book is comprised of several complete plays and segments from additional scripts. Each play is briefly introduced with information about the playwright. Noteworthy material relative to the play, such as awards garnered, a synopsis, or historical significance of content that facilitates placing the piece in context, is shared with the reader. Activities for teaching and learning about the Holocaust follow each script or excerpt.

Appendices provide resource information. Appendix A furnishes the contact names and addresses for playwrights and publishers whose work is included in this volume. Appendix B gives reference information for resources mentioned in Part II of the text. Appendix C lists other plays by contributors.

The plays have been selected based upon the ability of the characters and stories to create empathy, insight, and understanding. They are the works of award-winning playwrights, are themselves award-winning plays, or are of historical or dramatic significance. Each has been selected because of its power to help personalize and develop an understanding of the events, people, and times that are a vital part of Holocaust study. The playwrights represent past and present voices addressing the same broad topic.

It is hoped that the contents herein offer unique insights and educational possibilities. Bringing together scripts, activities, and resources, this book has been compiled so as to offer intellectual and emotional experiences that students will long remember. The voices echoing dramatically from these scripted pages ring with both true and fictional stories of the Holocaust that we should not fail to hear.

For the dead and *the living we must bear witness.*
(United States Holocaust Memorial Museum)

Part Two

Chapter 2

Plays and Activities: Beginning Study

Can You Hear Them Crying?

The Playwright: Virginia Burton Stringer

Virginia Burton Stringer is founder and Artistic Director of *WINGS theatre by young people*. She directed the original production of *Can You Hear Them Crying?* and she and her company have been featured at the University of Central Florida 1995 Summer Writing Institute. Stringer's comprehensive theatre education program, *Theatre Curriculum For Elementary Through High School Students*, is currently used by the City of St. Petersburg, Florida, Department of Leisure Services as a means of offering drama classes in community centers.

    Stringer's professional acting credits include stage, commercials, and industrial films. Her teaching experiences, ranging from elementary school through high school and including community education, cover more than twenty years. A graduate of the University of North Carolina at Charlotte, she also studied theatre at Virginia Commonwealth

University. Stringer is active as a director in the St. Petersburg, Florida, area and continues to write.

The Play

Can You Hear Them Crying? was originally produced in November 1994 at the Carrollwood Playhouse in Tampa, Florida, by the Color Performance Theatre, a division of the Carrollwood Players, Inc. It has subsequently been performed at a variety of institutions, including universities, synagogues, senior citizens centers, and, in 1997, at the American Alliance for Theatre and Education national conference.

Information about the Play and the Holocaust

Theresienstadt, first established as a ghetto on November 24, 1941, and later functioning as a concentration camp and a way station to Auschwitz, was created to be a model of deception. Intended to show the outside world how well Jews were treated by the Nazis, the camp was showcased as an example of thriving Jewish cultural life that included theatre, orchestra, and opera performances, a 60,000 book library, opportunities for education and religious study, and lectures. Internees arrived steadily from 1941 through 1945 and were kept together as families. In June of 1944, when workers from the International Red Cross visited the camp, they saw cafés, flowers, shops, and a bank. A propaganda film entitled *The Führer Presents the Jews with a City* was even made to emphasize the benevolent treatment given to those resettled there.

All of this belied the facts that, of the approximately 140,000 Jews who were transferred to Theresienstadt, nearly 33,000 died there and another 90,000 were deported to Auschwitz. The death rate in 1942, for example, was 54.4 percent as disease, starvation, and dehumanization took their toll. Even those who were seen in the propaganda film were not spared; they were sent to their deaths upon completion of the motion picture.

Of the 15,000 children under the age of fifteen who entered the Theresienstadt prison, only 100 survived. The artwork and poetry they secretly created, however, has become their legacy. *Can You Hear Them Crying?* is both a description of how children lived in this camp and a tribute to the strength of their imaginations and spirits. Their experiences, as revealed in *I Never Saw Another Butterfly*, are recounted here. The playwright describes her one act as a work of remembrance for all of the young victims of the Holocaust, including the children of Theresienstadt.

Can You Hear Them Crying?

SETTING: The Ghetto Theresienstadt
TIME: Then and Now

LIST OF CHARACTERS:
(Age range, 8 to 17; males or female, as indicated)
    Alena Synkova
    Alesa (Alexander)
    Alicia (Pavel)
    Butterfly Dancers (male or female)
    Ela (Peter)
    Elizabeth Spiegel
    Ellen (Noah)
    Eva Pickova
    Franta Bass (male or female)
    Friedl Dicker-Brandeis
    Helka
    Liliane
    Lizea
    Nina (Gideon)
    Ruth
    Sarah Spiegel

BUTTERFLY BALLET: *There may be one to any number of "Butterflies." Dancers may be of any age, up to late teens, and with any level of dance training and proficiency. In other words, the director/choreographer has much creative latitude in this presentation. In any case, the theme should be a beautiful summer's day in a garden filled with fragrant flowers and much activity and life! The music should be lively (see production notes for selection suggestions) and the dancers cheerful! There should be one or two (no more than three) central* BUTTERFLY *characters who will move throughout the play and weave the storyline together. One lead* BUTTERFLY *is the "last, the very last..." at the end, so this dancer should be competent. As the opening music ends, all of the butterflies scatter and disappear very quickly.*

The house lights go to black with the end of the ballet. In blackout, children's voices can be heard playing games, laughing, singing nursery rhymes. As the lights fade up, children enter in groups doing various activities. Some paint, some listen to a reader, some play tag, others play marbles. Their voices are typical of children chattering and playing. The children freeze and fall silent as the music begins (see production notes for selection suggestions) and the central butterfly(ies) enter. The butterfly(ies), wanting to play, too, move through the children happily as if trying to elicit their attention. The tone becomes serious as, one by one, the children leave the stage when approached by a butterfly, never taking notice of her (him). The butterfly(ies) is/are saddened with each exit. Only one child is left, ALICIA (PAVEL). She/He sees the butterfly(ies) and they all play together. The choreography, from this point, tells the story of the poem The Butterfly *by Pavel Friedmann. During the dance, the child and the butterfly(ies), while playing hide and seek around the three set pieces, manage to turn the faces of the set one by one, to reveal the "camp" set. The child must "hide" offstage and make a fast change into the tattered pinafore (or in the case of a male actor, the tattered shirt) during this game. The dance should end with the butterfly(ies) disappearing, leaving the child alone in a freeze position, as the music fades. The narrator enters from stage right. The lights dim and the narrator is picked up by a spot.*

ALESA: This is Theresienstadt, as the Gestapo renamed it. It is a ghetto in northern Czechoslovakia. Built by Emperor Josef II in 1780, the original name of this stone encircled garrison was Terezin, after his mother, Empress Maria Theresa. Ironically, this fortress town at the foot of a mountain and in the fork of two rivers was built as a strategic buffer to protect Czechoslovakia from German invasion. In March of 1939, that defense failed and German occupation of Czechoslovakia began. From 1941 to 1945, at the order of Adolf Eichmann, this dark, walled city became a transit camp for one hundred forty thousand Jews, including fifteen thousand children. This is their story.

As narrator exits spot to the right, ALICIA enters from left. Lights fade up to half, slowly.

ALICIA: Longing For Home,* March 1943. *(anonymous)*
Already over a year, I've lived in this ghetto,
In Terezin, in this blackish town,
And when I remember my home,
It now means more to me than ever before.

You, home, my home,
Why did they pull me from you?
Here the weak, die, so light, as a feather,
And when they die, they return, never.

I'd like to return home again,
For me, home is like spring flowers.
When I lived at home, before,
It never seemed so sweet.

Now remembering those golden days...
I'll soon return there, perhaps.
Along the street, people are walking,
On every one, you immediately see
That Terezin is a ghetto here,
With awful tragedy and fear.
Little food and poverty, here,
Living slowly in horror.
But no one must surrender!
The world turns and time changes.

We all hope a time will come,
When we'll return home, again.
I know, now, how dear home was,
And I often remember it.

As ALICIA (PAVEL) exits, one of the butterflies enters from the other side. Short musical interlude (same music as when the butterfly first found the child in the opening scene; choreography should mimic their movement) with butterfly searching for the child. The butterfly finds nothing, is saddened and exits. LILIANE enters.

LILIANE: The Nazis unexpectedly found themselves with an awkward problem...what to do with certain...special categories of Jews.

There were the World War I veterans who had fought valiantly, side by side, with Aryan Germans to defend the Fatherland. There were the high profile musicians, writers, actors, artists and spiritual leaders known throughout the world who would surely be missed if they suddenly disappeared. Hitler could not risk public scrutiny. The answer was Theresienstadt. In the words of Heinrich Himmler, *(mockingly)* "...make Terezin a 'model ghetto.' Exhibit it as a town inhabited by Jews and governed by them, and in which every manner of work is to be done!" A model ghetto...a town built for eight thousand residents, at times, housed more than sixty thousand deprived, starving and sick human beings.

During the last of the NARRATOR'S monologue, three children, ELA (PETER), HELKA and ELLEN (NOAH) enter. They meet center to form a triangle, ELA, down center facing up center, HELKA left and ELLEN right, facing in toward center and all looking down. As LILIANE exits, ELA turns to face front, as do HELKA and ELLEN.

ALL: Terezin*
    That bit of filth on soiled walls,
    And all around, barbed wire,
    And thirty thousand souls who sleep
    Souls who wake
    And souls who see
    Their own blood spilled.

ELA: *(takes one step forward. Other two turn upstage)*
    I was a child, once,
    Three years before,
    That youth longing for different worlds.
    I am no longer a child
    I have learned hatred.
    Now I am already an adult,
    I have known fear.

ALL: *(facing downstage)* Bloody words and dead days then,
    That's quite different than bogeymen!

In one step, all three rotate positions. ELA turns to stage right and up facing upstage, HELKA turns stage left and moves down center facing down and ELLEN *moves stage left still facing upstage. They move simultaneously, to maintain the triangle. This move should be crisp, almost military like, with little upper body movement.*

HELKA: But I do believe that today, I only sleep,
  That I'll awake and return to childhood.
  That childhood, sweet, like a briar rose,
  Like a bell which awakens from a slumber,
  Like a mother who cares for an ailing child
  Loves him with aching woman's love.
  How terrible is youth which still lives
  With enemies, for gallows ropes,
  How horrible for those children on your lap
  To say: this one for the good, this one for the vicious.

(The triangle rotates as before with ELLEN *down center.)*

ELLEN: There, far away, where childhood sweetly lies,
  On a pathway, among the trees,
  There within that home
  That was once my contentment,
  There, somewhere, in a little garden and in its flowers,
  Is where my mother gave birth to me onto this earth
  Only for me to cry...

  In the blaze of a candle, I sleep
  And once perhaps I will understand
  That I was such a tiny creature,
  Just so small, like this poem.

(ALL turn to face front)

ALL: These thirty thousand souls, asleep
    there in the forest awaken,
    Open an eye
    And because of
    What they see,
    They'll fall asleep again... *(all exit)*

NINA *enters from opposite side.*

NINA: With extreme overcrowding and poor sanitation, disease was rampant. The very old and the very young were hit hardest by a deadly typhus epidemic. By the time the camp was liberated in May of 1945, a combination of disease, starvation and despair had claimed thirty-three thousand, four hundred fifty-six individual human beings inside the stone walls and barbed wire. Another eighty-eight thousand, two hundred and two human beings had been transported to their deaths in the extermination camps. *(exit)*

EVA PICKOVA enters and takes a moment to look at the "Camp."

EVA: Fear*
   Today, new fears arose in the ghetto,
   An evil illness brings terror in its path.
   While Death tightly holds an icy scythe,
   The victims in its wake weep and writhe.

   Today a father's heartbeat forecasts his fear,
   And mothers lay their heads onto their hands.
   Now children cough and die with typhus here.
   A heavy toll is taken from their bands.

   Today hearts still beat inside their breasts,
   While friends on their deathbeds lie.
   Should we not follow, is it not best,
   Rather than watch — and then also die?

   Oh, no...My God, please bless our lives,
   We can not watch our numbers fade away.
   We yearn for a better world,
   We must see our work completed — We must not die! *(exit)*

SARAH SPIEGEL enters and crosses hurriedly with ELIZABETH SPIEGEL close behind. They mime carrying suitcases. ELIZABETH stops center stage as if to turn and go back.

ELIZABETH: Oh, Mama! I forgot my sweater!

SARAH: We have no time to go back. They will see us. We must hurry on. *(Removes her coat, in mime, of course, and puts it on ELIZABETH'S shoulders.)* Here, take my coat.

ELIZABETH: But, Mama, you'll get so cold!

SARAH: It's all right, my darling. You see? I have my sweater to keep me warm. Now come, we must hurry. Hurry!

SARAH exits leaving ELIZABETH onstage. Lights dim, spot picks up child.

ELIZABETH: I found her sweater today. It was in the pile of clothes we had to sort. I know it was hers...it still smells like her. When I touched it, I knew right away. It's soft and warm, like her. I thought about keeping it so I could give it back to her when I see her again. But the others warned me that I might be punished if THEY found it. So I left it there, on the pile. I held it for a long time remembering how she looks and smells and feels...poor Mama. She must be cold without her sweater. *(exit)*

(NINA enters)

NINA: Beyond the wall,
above the sky.
A life, perhaps,
perhaps to die.

A train at night.
Then gone, no trace.
Human cargo,
each tiny face. *(exit)*

(ALESA enters from opposite side.)

ALESA: The word TRANSPORT sent a wave of fear throughout Theresienstadt each time it was uttered. That word meant more people coming in...or...going out. Either way, it meant death. In the summer of 1943, twelve hundred Jewish children were brought into camp by transport. It was learned, later, that they were from the Bialystok ghetto in Poland. They were the remnants of an uprising against the Nazis which left the ghetto burned to the ground. The children were covered with dirt and crawling with lice. Once inside the walls, the children were isolated from the rest of the population, along with fifty-three doctors and nurses chosen from the "residents" to care for them. About six weeks later, in the middle of the night, all twelve hundred children, and the fifty-three doctors and nurses, were loaded like cattle into railroad cars and transported to their deaths in Auschwitz.

During the NARRATOR'S monologue, a group of children begins to assemble on the stage, one at a time. They arrange themselves as if they are all trying to look through the same keyhole or over each other's shoulders. The size of the group may vary from two to eight.

VOICE 1: Can you see their faces?

VOICE 2: Do they have faces?

VOICE 3: They are such tiny frames.

VOICE 4: Bones sticking out of sleeves.

VOICE 5: Where are they from?

VOICE 6: Twelve hundred of them!

VOICE 7: Or more!

VOICE 8: Where will they put them?

VOICE 6: Twelve hundred of them!

VOICE 7: Or more!

VOICE 1: They all look so frightened.

VOICE 2: They all look alike under the dirt!

VOICE 3: What are their names?

VOICE 4: Franta.

VOICE 5: Walter.

VOICE 6: Helka.

VOICE 7: Peter.

VOICE 8: Can they see us looking?

VOICE 2: We dare not get caught.

VOICE 1: Can you hear them crying?

VOICE 3: I'm afraid to listen.

VOICE 4: The doctors and nurses...surely, they will help!

ALL: *(together but not in unison)* Surely, surely, surely...

VOICE 5: Where did they go?

VOICE 6: Gone in the night!

VOICE 7: A transport, I think. *(exit, right)*

VOICE 8: In the dead of the night. *(exit, left)*

VOICE 1: Twelve hundred, or more...all gone, in the night. *(exit, right)*

VOICE 2: Bones sticking out of sleeves. *(exit, left)*

VOICE 3: All alike...under the dirt. *(exit, right)*

VOICE 4: Can you hear them crying? *(exit, left)*

VOICE 5: Can you see their faces? *(exit, right)*

VOICE 6: *(Turns to exit, pauses, looks at audience.)* Did they have faces...? *(exit)*

(LILIANE enters)

LILIANE: Incredibly, amid the squalor and suffering, culture thrived at Theresienstadt. There were sixty thousand books in the library! The population included Jewish composers, scholars, singers, diplomats, actors, engineers, artists...the "cream of the crop" of European intellectuals. One such person, a painter, by the name of Friedl Dicker-Brandeis, gave the children art lessons. They eagerly, quietly anticipated each of her visits. Small, fragile and highly sophisticated, Ms. Dicker-Brandeis managed to make life bearable for countless children by giving them an outlet for their tortured inner worlds. In all, about five thousand drawings and collages were created. A suitcase full survived the war. There were also classes in creative writing and poetry contests.

During the last few lines of NARRATOR'S monologue, poetry class quietly moves onstage.

FRIEDL: Franta Bass?

FRANTA: *(stands)* The Old House,* by Franta Bass.
Abandoned here, the old house
stands quiet and asleep.
The old house that once was lovely,
standing there, before,
it was quite lovely.
Now it stands alone,
quietly rotting —
Such a wasted house,
and wasted hours. *(Sits)*

FRIEDL: Very nice, Franta. You are becoming quite the poet. Alena Synkova, we've not heard from you today.

ALENA: *(She stands, shyly)* I'd Like To Go Alone,* by Alena Synkova.
I'd like to go away alone
Where other, nicer people live,
Far away into the unknown,
Where no one kills each other.
Perhaps there are more,

One thousand strong,
Who'll reach this goal
Before too long. *(sits quickly)*

FRIEDL: Perhaps, indeed...thank you, Alena.

FRANTA: I have another, Teacher!

FRIEDL: All right, Franta. But this is the last one for you today.

FRANTA: *(stands)* The Garden,* by Franta Bass.
A small garden,
Full of sweet-smelling roses.
On a narrowing pathway
A little boy takes a stroll.

A little boy, a darling.
Like that flower bud blooming.
Until the flower blooms,
The little boy can still be.

FRIEDL: It's getting late. We must end our lesson for today. Go now, all of you. You must be in by curfew. Go now, hurry. HURRY! *(Mimes gathering up books and papers and "shoos" the children offstage. All exit, quickly, except one teenage girl.)*

RUTH: Dusk*
In flew the dusk on the wings of evening...
For whom do you greet me?
Will you give my mouth a kiss for him?
Oh, how I wish for the place of my birth!

Perhaps you alone, quiet dusk,
have seen the teardrops shed in your lap
from eyes that beg to see
the shadow of palm and olive trees
in Israel.

Perhaps you, alone, will understand
Zion's daughter,

who cries
for her tiny home beside the Elbe
and but for fear, would go back to it. *(she exits)*

ELIZABETH *enters miming the writing of a letter. She stops in the pool of light, center and reads the letter.*

ELIZABETH: Dear Papa, Frau Dicker-Brandeis gave us another art lesson today. She says that I have great potential! She says that my use of color is very...mature! I look forward to her visits to our group. She is so lively, she almost makes us forget...we are not at home. I saw the full moon last night. It was our only light. We are not allowed to use the electricity and we have no more candles. This does not seem a very privileged place to me. I have not seen Mama for two days. I am afraid she is sick. Do you remember that you told me, "The full moon is very special. If you look at it, you will see the face of God"? Well, it's true, Papa! I saw God's face last night! It was very late and everyone else was asleep. I woke up and right there, through the cracks, I saw the moon as big as anything. Do you remember that you said, no matter how far apart we are, if we both look at the full moon, we will see each other's face? I saw your face, Papa. Did you see mine? I miss you, Papa. I want to come back home soon. I love you. Tell my kitten, "hello." Love, your Lizbeth. *(exit)*

LIZEA: *(Enters from opposite side)* Communication with the outside world was strictly forbidden. In January of 1942, a group of people was arrested on charges of smuggling out a letter. In all, sixteen people were executed for the "crime." The Nazis were particularly concerned with the appearance of Theresienstadt to the outside world. In June of 1944, the International Red Cross sent a committee to "inspect" the camp. Great pains were taken to prepare for their arrival. Buildings were painted, street signs erected, flowers planted, all to show the world the "model Ghetto"! *(Remains onstage, turns to watch activity.)*

The children enter from both sides on cue, "the International Red Cross...." Some sweep, some paint the walls, some plant flowers. Much activity "preparing" the camp. All done in mime to lively orchestra music. (See production notes for music suggestions.) Each of the set pieces is turned to reveal the signs and window boxes of flowers. The butterflies also dance merrily among the children and then abruptly disappear as the music ends and the children pull off the tattered pinafores and hide them behind their backs while lining up with "cheesy" grins on their faces to greet the committee. The committee enters one side, heads up in a pompous position. They move in a straight line, never looking at the camp. They talk and move in unison and rhythm across the stage and exit on the last line.

COMMITTEE 1: How lovely!

COMMITTEE 2: How charming!

COMMITTEE 3: How quaint!

COMMITTEE 4: How glorious!

ALL: Why, Mr. Hitler! Why so notorious?

LIZEA: *(Turns to audience)* A propaganda film was even made, shortly after the visit, to show the world how well the Jews were living under the Nazis. A few days later, Kurt Gerron, a well-known German actor who had played a leading role in the film, was transported to Auschwitz, where he died in the gas chamber. Things in the camp quickly returned to "normal."

During LIZEA's monologue, children put the pinafores back on and slowly move in silence to turn the set back to the camp. Children then freeze in various groupings of two or three as if comforting each other. However, they never actually touch and it is obvious to the audience. They maintain this posture throughout the rest of the scene. The principal BUTTERFLY enters with music and moves in among the children for the last time. Choreography should be that of finality and sadness. She/He finds a "living" child, ALICIA (PAVEL), who comes to life, at this point. This should be choreographed to very somber music. The BUTTERFLY is trying to take the child, but the child, while willing to go, cannot. Finally, the BUTTERFLY must leave because she/he can no longer live in the ghetto. Music ends when BUTTERFLY exits. ALICIA (PAVEL) is left downstage of the other children reaching for the BUTTERFLY. She moves down center into spotlight.

ALICIA: The Butterfly* by Pavel Friedmann
    She was the last. Truly the last.
    So full, so dazzling, so blazing yellow.
    Like the sun's tears shattered
        against a white stone...

    Such a bright yellow,
    whimsically up to the sky.
    She went away, surely to
        kiss the world good-bye.

    I've lived in here for seven weeks,
    trapped inside this ghetto.
    Yet I found loving here.
    The dandelions call to me
    And the white tree branches in the chestnut court.
        But I haven't, since, seen a butterfly here.

    She, then, was the last one.
    Butterflies don't live now,
        in this ghetto. *(ALICIA moves upstage to join the tableau.)*

LILIANE enters, takes downstage position.

LILIANE: In the four years of terror at Terezin, fifteen thousand children were processed in and out of Theresienstadt. Of those, less than one hundred survived, not one of them under fifteen years old.

During this speech, the children who are offstage enter and join the frozen tableau.

ALL: *(All turn to face front in a straight line)* I am the children.
    I am the future of yesterday.
    I am fifteen thousand, not yet fifteen.
    I am the missing generation.
    Do you know me?
    Can you hear me crying?

All children except LILIANE return to original tableau positions, actually touching. ALL FREEZE.

LILIANE: In the not so distant future, there will be no one left to tell the story, firsthand. When my children study the Holocaust, there may be no one left with a number tattooed on his or her arm. Shall we allow these children to die, forgotten? Shall we allow the doctors, the writers, the painters, musicians, mothers, teachers, who never were, to fade into the history books as mere numbers? *(Turns to go upstage to join the tableau. Stops and turns back to audience.)* Oh, if you think it isn't real, that it never happened...you are wrong! If you think it can never happen again, go home...turn on the television...watch the news. Pick up your newspaper and read. Then find a quiet place, close your eyes, and tell me...Can you hear them crying? *(She takes her place in the tableau and the principle* BUTTERFLY(ies) *join the tableau.)*

The scene is dimly lit. We hear the song, "The Lonely Child"* (see Production Notes) sung in Yiddish with English words spoken over music. Lights slowly fade to black as the last words are spoken.

OPTIONAL ENDING: *Instead of the Yiddish ballad above, original poetry and/or music may be heard as the lights fade very slowly to black.*

Production Notes

Casting

The original cast was twelve females ranging in age from nine to seventeen years old, but cast size may vary. Roles which may be assigned to males are Alesa (Alexander); Alicia (Pavel); Ela (Peter); Ellen (Noah); and Nina (Gideon). Franta Bass may be male or female. The butterflies, also, may be male or female and vary in number from two to several (*little* butterflies, which appear only in the beginning dance, can give small children in the group the chance to participate). There is one butterfly that is the principal butterfly and appears throughout the script.

Text

The poems indicated by an asterisk (*) are among the "suitcase full that survived." They are poems written by children while in the ghetto, Theresienstadt. The original works are archived at the Jewish Museum in Prague, Czech Republic. The translations in this script are from the original language texts and were translated by Izabela Zalewski Bishop. Similar English translations of these and other writings are in *I Never Saw Another Butterfly*, published by Schocken Books, a division of Random House. All other work is original and historically accurate.

Music

In the original production, the Butterfly Ballets are choreographed to the first four movements of *String Quartet No. 1* by Ervin Schulhoff, himself a victim of the Holocaust (please see "Biographies"). The interval music is by Gideon Klein, also a victim (please see "Biographies"), who was imprisoned at Theresienstadt. This music is available on the *Silenced Voices: Victims Of The Holocaust* CD by The Terezin Chamber Music Foundation, on the Northeastern Label. The ballad, *Dos Elnte Kind (The Lonely Child),* lyrics by Shmerke Kaczerginski, music by Yankl Krimski, is on the CD and audiocassette *remember the children: Songs for and by Children of the Holocaust*, National Holocaust Museum, Washington, DC, and is performed by Adrienne Cooper.

Please Note: Original music or other authentic music of the period may be substituted for the above selections without fear of losing the intent of the piece. In fact, there is opportunity for much latitude in creating a production that uses the best talents available in many areas of art, music, and theatre!

Set Design

The stage is bare and black is the recommended color. There should be entrances right and left. The set consists of three triangular "kiosks" on wheels, to which are attached the pieces of art that represent each scene. The scenes are "Butterflies" (opening); "Ghetto" (prior to the narrator's entrance); "The Red Cross Inspection" (appears during LIZEA'S monologue).

Art for the opening scene

Large yellow butterflies of finger paint, construction paper, pastels, and watercolors; various sizes.

Art for the Ghetto Theresienstadt

Pictures should represent children's interpretation of the script and research information.

Art for the Red Cross inspection

Poster board painted to look like window boxes with flowers. Signs that say:
    School
    Hospital
    Concert Tonight
    Poetry Contest Tomorrow
    Holiday
    Closed for Repairs

All pictures and signs should be attached in random positions that are always askew.

Costumes

Girls

White blouse, black skirt, white pinafore; tattered and "dirty" pinafore with bright yellow Star of David (use burlap for star)

Boys

White shirt, black trousers; tattered and "dirty" shirt with bright yellow Star of David

bare feet

Butterflies

Black opaque tights and long sleeved leotard are the basics. Wings are of bright yellow flowing material (attached at center back and wrists to give wing effect.)

Props

None should be added! Everything (brooms, paintbrushes, flower pots, sweater, coat, pencils, paper, etc.) should be pantomimed.

Biographies

Eva Pickova *(Fear*)* was born in Nymburk on May 15, 1929. She was deported to Terezin on April 16, 1942. She died in Auschwitz on December 18, 1943. She was 14 years old.

Alena Synkova *(I'd Like To Go Away Alone*)* was born in Prague on September 24, 1926. She was deported to Terezin on December 22, 1942. She survived and returned to Prague.

Franta (Frantisek) Bass *(The Old House,* The Garden*)* was born in Brno on September 4, 1930. He was sent to Terezin on December 2, 1941, and died in Auschwitz on October 28, 1944. He was 14 years old.

Hanus Hachenburg (*Terezin**) was born in Prague on July 12, 1929. He was deported to Terezin on October 24, 1942. He died in Auschwitz on December 18, 1943. He was 14 years old.

Pavel Friedmann (*The Butterfly**) was born in Prague on January 7, 1921. He was sent to Terezin on April 26, 1942. He died in Auschwitz on September 29, 1944. He was 23 years old.

Friedl Dicker-Brandeis was born in Vienna. She was a Bauhaus-trained painter of portraits and landscapes, a designer, a teacher. She became a "resident" of Terezin in December of 1942. Through her regular art classes, she saw to it that children had a way to moderate the chaos in their lives through artistic expression. She was deported to Auschwitz on October 6, 1944. Friedl Dicker-Brandeis died at Birkenau.

Gideon Klein was born on December 6, 1919, in Prerov, Czechoslovakia. His brilliant and promising career in music was cut short by his transport to Theresienstadt in December of 1941. Gideon Klein was sent first to Auschwitz then to Furstengrubbe, where he died in January 1945.

Ervin Schulhoff was born on June 8, 1894, in Prague. He took an interest in the Communist Party and the combination of his political views and his Jewish background meant an early end to his career and life. He was imprisoned in the Wulzburg concentration camp where he died on August 18, 1942.

Longing For Home, *March 1943** and *Dusk** were written by children whose names are not known and are published anonymously.

Teaching Activities

- Students can learn what happened to those whose work is found in this script by reading the Biographies section immediately following the play. Ask them to select one of these people and create an identification card, such as the one from the United States Holocaust Memorial Museum pictured below, for him or her.

IDENTIFICATION CARD

For the dead and the living we must bear witness

United States
Holocaust Memorial Museum

This card tells the story of a real person who lived during the Holocaust.

Name: **Nanny Gottschalk Lewin**
Date of Birth: **March 13, 1888**
Place of Birth: **Schlawe, Germany**
Nanny was the oldest of four children born to Jewish parents in the small town of Schlawe in northern Germany, where her father owned the town's grain mill. Nanny was given the Hebrew name Nocha. She grew up on the mill grounds in a house surrounded by orchards and a big garden. In 1911 Nanny married Arthur Lewin. Together, they raised two children, Ludwig and Ursula.

Please turn page at end of 4th floor.

1933–39: My widowed mother and I have moved to Berlin. We feared the rising antisemitism in Schlawe and hoped, as Jews, to be less conspicuous here in a large city. We live downstairs from my sister Kathe who is married to a Protestant and has converted. Shortly after we got settled, the Germans restricted the public movements of Jews, so that we no longer feel safe when we're out of our apartment.

Please turn page at end of 3rd floor.

1940–44: My mother and I have been deported to the Theresienstadt ghetto in Bohemia. We've been assigned a room on the second floor of a house that is dirty, crowded and infested with lice. The stove is fueled with sawdust. As the youngest in our room — and I'm 56 — I've been lugging in the bags of sawdust on my back. I've been getting increasingly weaker, am now hard of hearing and need a cane to walk. Early this morning I learned that I'm on a list of people to go to another camp. I don't want to go but have no choice.

Please turn page at end of 2nd floor.

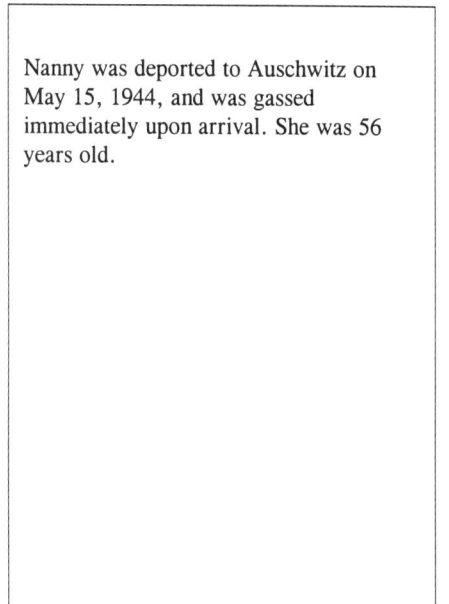

Nanny was deported to Auschwitz on May 15, 1944, and was gassed immediately upon arrival. She was 56 years old.

To learn more about the places and events described on this ID card, visit the Wexner Learning Center, located on the second floor.

This is card #2795.

- Adults as well as children were sent to Theresienstadt. One such deportee was Nanny Gottschalk Lewin. Divide the class into groups and make each responsible for one phase of her life. Groups should do research to determine what Lewin's life would have been like during that time and at that place. They should use the information they gather to create a dramatization that is shared with the class.

    Phase #1: Nanny Gottschalk Lewin was born in Schlawe, Germany, on March 13, 1888. She was the oldest of four children. Her father owned the grain mill in the northern German town of Schlawe. Nanny, whose Hebrew name was Nocha, grew up on land surrounded by orchards and a garden. She married Arthur Lewin in 1911 and they had two children, Ludwig and Ursula.

    Phase #2: From 1933 to 1939, Nanny lived with her widowed mother in Berlin. They had fled Schlawe in the wake of mounting anti-Semitism and lived downstairs from Nanny's sister Kathe, who had married a Protestant and had converted. Not long after Nanny arrived in Berlin, public movements of Jews were restricted and so she still did not feel safe.

    Phase #3: Between 1940 and 1944, Nanny and her mother were deported to Theresienstadt and housed on the second floor of a dirty, lice-infested dwelling. At fifty-six years old, she was the youngest in her room and had to carry sawdust for the stove on her back. By the time she was deported to Auschwitz on May 5, 1944, she was using a cane to walk and was hard of hearing. She was sent to the gas chamber upon arrival at Auschwitz.

- Assign students to read the book, *I Never Saw Another Butterfly* as well as the full length and one-act scripts of that work. Compare and contrast these versions with *Can You Hear Them Crying?*

- As a craft project, provide an opportunity for students to make butterflies for display in the classroom. Directions for constructing butterflies are readily found in arts and crafts books.

- Using improvisation, students should develop scenes showing the reality of camp life at Theresiendstadt and scenes showing the ideal life that the Nazis wanted the outside world to see. Videotape the scenes.

- Provide opportunities for students to write poems about life in a concentration camp for a classroom creative writing contest. Couple this assignment with one in which students imagine that they are residents of a camp and write letters that they hope to smuggle out to others. Using readers theatre format, compile a script of these poems and letters and create a performance to which other classes are invited.

- Encourage students to locate music created by those who experienced the Holocaust and to invent their own choreography for some of these pieces.

- Ask students to select music and to choreograph a butterfly dance for the opening of the play. If possible, costume the dancers as butterflies.

- The character, Alesa, opens the play by recounting the history of Theresienstadt. Ask students to research and expand upon this chronology. Next, invite them to apply their knowledge by constructing a time line detailing the history of Theresienstadt from garrison to death site. This time line can be framed with students' drawings and pictures of butterflies and displayed in the classroom.

- Choral reading is a form of oral interpretation in which musical qualities are assigned to the spoken word. Typically, pieces are interpreted for solo or grouped voices. Techniques include speaking in unison, echoing, or solo performance. Using the keyhole scene (pages 29–31), ask students to render this passage as a choral reading and perform it for classmates.

- With the students, develop a list of things that would have to be done to prepare the camp for the Red Cross visit. State each item in a sentence to pantomime, making certain that verbs are active and children are in character. As an example, *You are a child residing in Theresienstadt. Show how you paint the walls of your dormitory* — can be effectively pantomimed.

- In the final speech of the play, Liliane calls attention to current events fraught with death and destruction. Ask students to identify some of these present-day conflicts and to research the parties involved, the natures of the disputes, and the histories of the conflicts. Invite them to identify the countries involved on a map or globe and to give an oral report on the causes and results of the fighting.

- As a class, create original poetry and music for the ending of the play.

- Learn the lullaby, *Dremlen Feygl Oyf Di Tsvaygn*, which was written for an infant victim of the Holocaust. Next, select one of the poems from *Can You Hear Them Crying?* and set it to music. Compare the compositions.

DREMLEN FEYGL OYF DI TSVAYGN
WORLD WAR II LULLABY

Drem - len fey - gl oyf___ di tsvay - gn,
Sh... mayn tay - er___ kind. Bay___ dayn vi - gl
oyf a na - re, Zitst a frem - de un zingt.
Bay___ dayn vi - gl oyf a na - re,. Zitst a frem - de un
zingt. Lyu - lu, Lyu - lyu. Lyu.___

Dremlen feygl oyf di tsvaygn,	Birdies slumber on the branches
Sholf, mayn tayer kind,	Sleep, my precious child,
Bay dayn vigl oyf dayn nare	At your cradle in the dugout
Zitst a fremde un zingt.	Sits a stranger crooning: hushabye.
Lyulyu, lyulyu, lyu.	
S'iz dayn vigl vu geshtanen	Your cradle once did stand
Oysgeflochtn fun glik,	Woven out of happiness,
Un dayn mame, oy dayn mane	And your mother, oh, your mother
Kumt shoyn keynmol nit tsurik.	Never will return. Hushabye.
Lyulyu, lyulyu, lyu.	
Ch'ob gezen dayn tatn loyfn	I saw your father running
Unter hogl fun shteyn,	Under a hail of stones,
Iber felder iz gefloygn	And across the fields there echoed
Zayn faryosemter geveyn.	His mournful cry. Hushabye.
Lyulyu, lyulyu, lyu.	

As found in the Pennsylvania Holocaust Curriculum Guide.
Courtesy of the Congress of Jewish Culture.

Angel in the Night

The Playwright: Joanna H. Kraus

The American Alliance for Theatre and Education first honored Joanna H. Kraus in 1971 by bestowing the Charlotte B. Chorpenning Cup, its highest award for playwriting, upon her. In 1996, *Angel in the Night* received that organization's Distinguished Play Award in Category A — scripts for upper grades and secondary school age children. Kraus has been the recipient of numerous commissions, grants, fellowships, and awards, including the Lifetime Achievement Award of the New York State Theatre Education Association. In 1989, she garnered first prize for *The Devil's Orphan*, later retitled *Remember My Name*, at the Indiana University Purdue University Indianapolis (IUPUI) National Playwriting Competition (now called the Waldo M. and Grace C. Bonderman National Youth Theatre Playwriting Symposium). Her residencies and workshops include affiliations with, among others, the Raleigh Little

Theatre, North Carolina Museum of History, Enloe Performing Arts High School, and the Leighton Studios at Banff Centre for the Arts in Alberta, Canada. Her writing credits include numerous plays, books, articles, and reviews. Kraus is a member of the Dramatists Guild and resides in California. She is retired from the State University of New York College at Brockport.

The Play

Angel in the Night is based upon the life of Marysia Pawlina Szul. The play combines fact and fiction to tell how a young Polish-Catholic girl hid four Jews during the Holocaust and, by taking this personal risk, saved their lives. This required great courage because when World War II began, Poland fell immediately to the Nazis. Hitler and his minions not only hated Polish Jews and wanted to destroy them, but saw all Polish people as sub-human and fit only for slave labor. Both Jews and non-Jews suffered under Nazi rule. Szul's heroism has been acknowledged with a medal and trees planted in her honor and, in both Jerusalem and Chicago, she has been recognized as a Righteous Person.

Marysia Szul, Mania Birnberg, and Frieda Saperstein were interviewed by the playwright for development of *Angel in the Night*. The script has won the American Alliance for Theatre and Education's Distinguished Play Award. In affiliation with the Avenue of the Righteous and under the direction of National Louis University, Evanston, Illinois, the play was commissioned by the Honors of Humanity Project.

Information about the Play and the Holocaust

Righteous Person is the name given to a non-Jew who saved Jewish lives during the Holocaust. These rescuers, often ordinary citizens, helped those targeted by the Nazis to survive. Many Righteous Persons, after having their deeds verified, have been honored for their efforts at Yad Vashem, a Holocaust museum in Jerusalem. An avenue lined with carob trees leads to the entrance to the museum. Each tree has been planted to honor one such protector.

For non-Jews in German-occupied areas, the decision to safeguard a Jew was a difficult one as penalties were severe. To be caught meant that a person might be shot immediately or publicly hanged. Further, an entire family or community might be punished for the actions of a single rescuer. In addition to the risks, the incentives for turning in Jews were attractive. These included maintaining personal safety, bounties of goods that were difficult to obtain such as liquor, cigarettes, or sugar, and reward money. Benefactors also had to share scarce food, living spaces, and other necessities with those they were hiding. Most non-Jews neither helped nor hindered in these efforts. When, however, local citizens did act to assist others, they contributed to the survival of the Jewish population in their countries.

Who were these rescuers and what motivated their actions? The answers are as diverse as the men and women who endangered themselves for others. In general, these were independent, principled people who acted upon what they believed to be right, even if this meant personal peril. Decisions were often based less upon rational thinking than upon reaction to injustice. As these rescuers had routinely engaged in doing good deeds, they saw little that was extraordinary in their lifesaving ventures. These defenders, it should be noted, were not always proponents of particular racial, ethnic, or political points of view. Often, the decision to rescue had to be made immediately and would be based solely upon the value assigned to human life.

Predicting who might become a rescuer was, at best, perilous and difficult. Those who denounced Hitler might decline in fear; those who denounced Jews might agree to help. Those who declined might be driven by anti-Semitism or simply a desire to avoid involvement; those who agreed might be guided by humanitarianism, money paid to them for their protection, or a desire to take part in resistance efforts. In many cases, the Jews saved were strangers to these guardians until the time came to harbor them.

It is estimated that about one percent of the non-Jewish population of Europe, including Righteous Persons like Marysia Pawlina Szul, hid Jewish children during the Holocaust. Jewish adults and youth were hidden in all manner of places, including city dwellings and rat-infested sewers. The countryside location depicted in *Angel in the Night* also is authentic. Rural areas and farms were appealing hiding places because of the belief that Nazis were less likely to be found in such locales. Even in these more isolated areas, however, rescuers faced the risk of discovery by small military units, detection by civilian fighters, or denunciation by neighbors. Whether in urban or rural settings, both those in hiding and their protectors faced peril.

Angel in the Night

SETTING: The Epilogue and Prologue occur in a Chicago suburb. The action occurs in southeast Poland near the city of Zoborow.
TIME: The Epilogue and Prologue occur in the present. The Play takes place during World War II, 1942-1944.

LIST OF CHARACTERS:
four men, four women, one girl, minimum with doubling (may be expanded to nine men, seven women, and one girl)
    Mania (in the present) — mid-60s
    Marysia Pawlina (in the present) — late 60s
    Friedza (in the present) — late 50s
    Marysia Pawlina (in the past) — a young Polish woman, 18
    Domicela — her mother, 48
    Golda — a Jewish fugitive, 27
    Friedza (in the past) — her daughter, 8
    Mundek — her baby son
    Hanka — her former Polish neighbor
    Henryk — her husband
    Tadeusz — a Polish neighbor, 22
    Mania (in the past) — a Jewish fugitive, 14
    Bruno — a German soldier, 37
    Ernst — a German captain, 23
    Otto — a German officer
    Luther — a German soldier
    Kurt — a German prison guard
    Waldo — a German prison guard
    Stanislaus — a Polish guard in a German prison, 50s

AUTHOR'S NOTE: At the edge of the city of Jerusalem in Israel there is a center for research on the Nazi Holocaust and a memorial to the lives lost. Yad Vashem was established in 1953.

    Beyond its somber walls is a tree-lined avenue commemorating the bravery of those who helped to save others. They were called Righteous Persons. Among them were leaders of nations and menial laborers. Each Righteous Person had to be recommended by survivors and proof presented. A tree was then planted to honor the individual and a medal presented with the following inscription, "Whoever saves a single soul, it is as if he had saved the whole world."

Outside of Chicago there is a similar Avenue of the Righteous Park located in Evanston, Illinois. It was dedicated in 1987.

In both parks a tree was planted in Marysia Pawlina Szul's honor.

Prologue

SCENE: *Mania's living room. An affluent Chicago suburb. The present. The tea table is set with a fresh linen cloth, silver tea service, tall glasses in metal holders and a banquet of Polish pastries.*

AT RISE: *MANIA is adjusting her centerpiece of fresh flowers. PAWLINA appears in the interior doorway.*

PAWLINA *(from the doorway)*. Stop fussing!
MANIA *(without turning)*. But I haven't seen her in years. She's...so...successful.
PAWLINA *(enters room and parades in her new outfit)*. How do you like it?
MANIA *(turns, inspects and impulsively hugs her)*. Perfect! Pawlina, the blouse is perfect on you. It goes with your suit. It goes with your eyes —
PAWLINA *(breaks in laughing)*. You picked it out. But, Mania, are you sure this is what they wear to plant a tree?
MANIA. You don't have to plant it. You just have to stand there. Someone else will do the digging. You're our celebrity, remember?
PAWLINA. I'd rather do the digging. *(They look at each other. SOUND: Doorbell. MANIA crosses, glances in the mirror and stops to fix her hair.)* Answer the door!
MANIA. She's here. Oh, I wish I hadn't gained so much weight. *(SOUND: Doorbell again.)*
PAWLINA. Go! (MANIA *exits to open the front door.* PAWLINA *crosses to the table.*) (In Polish.) Ummmmm. *Herbatniki!*[1] *(PAWLINA takes a tiny pastry from the pyramid.) Bezy!*[2] *(She swallows it*

---

1. Tea cakes.
2. Similar to a meringue.

appreciatively and selects another.) Piernik Wyborny![3] *(She savors the taste of the tea cake.)*
MANIA'S VOICE *(offstage)*. Friedza!
FRIEDZA'S VOICE *(offstage)*. Mania!
BOTH VOICES *(offstage)*. You look WONDERFUL!

(FRIEDZA and MANIA enter. PAWLINA and FRIEDZA look at one another, then embrace.)

FRIEDZA. Panna Pawlina.
PAWLINA. Little Friedza. *(They sit.)*
MANIA. Did you have trouble finding the house?
FRIEDZA. No. I had a long-distance conference call. A buyer from Tokyo. It's hard with the time difference.
MANIA. Sure.
FRIEDZA *(looks at tea table, astonished)*. Mania, who's coming?
MANIA. I want there should be enough. In my house there should be enough.
FRIEDZA. If the whole city of Chicago comes, you've got enough. What'd you do, buy out the Polish bakery?
MANIA. I made them! *(Rising.)* Come. It's a long drive.
FRIEDZA. Relax. They can't dedicate the park without the star.
PAWLINA. Star! I'm not a star. Mania, why such fancy cakes? We only had those at Christmas — or christenings.
MANIA. We wouldn't be here without you. There's no name for what you did.
FRIEDZA. There's a name *(Takes newspaper from briefcase.)* Right here on the front page. "Righteous Person."
PAWLINA. Friedza, Mania. What does that mean? I only did what was right.
FRIEDZA. It means most people didn't.
PAWLINA. You know the proverb. It was my mother's favorite. *(In Polish.)* Przyjaciel w domu yest bóg w domu. A guest in the home is God in the home.
FRIEDZA *(slowly)*. We weren't exactly guests. And your mother didn't want us. *(Rises.)* No one wanted us. No one in the whole country wanted us.
MANIA. Friedza, it's late. We really should go.

---

3. Similar to a fruitcake.

FRIEDZA. I remember running through the hayfields trying to hide. It was autumn.
PAWLINA. It was spring, Friedza.
FRIEDZA. No. Fall. Harvest time. The hayfields were taller than I was.
PAWLINA. What do you know? You were eight years old.

> (*LIGHTING: fades on women as they exit. SOUND: Polish folk music. OTHER ACTORS set up haystack and a suggestion of Domicela's house and barn. When the stage is set, a young FRIEDZA dashes on anxiously looking around. It is May 1942. FRIEDZA tears off her white armband with the blue Star of David, flings it aside and darts into the haystack. SOUND: Rifle shots in the distance, bloodhounds howling.)*

Act One

SCENE: *A field in rural southeast Poland. It is late afternoon, towards the end of May 1942. At the edge of the field is a high mound of hay. SOUND: Distant church bells.*

AT RISE: *PAWLINA sings to herself, filling her apron with wildflowers (poppies, daisies). She crosses to put them in the water pail. Suddenly the haystack moves. PAWLINA stops in her tracks. She crosses herself. A pair of frightened eyes are now visible. Then a hand grabs PAWLINA'S skirt. A desperate face follows.*

GOLDA has lost her husband, her home and all that they owned. She has fled from the ghetto with two small children. Her Polish has a Yiddish accent.

GOLDA *(softly)*. Don't be frightened, Panna Pawlina.
PAWLINA *(looks closer)*. Paniusia Schachterova!!!
GOLDA. Sh-h. We escaped.
PAWLINA. From the ghetto?
GOLDA *(nods)*. Friedza's with me too. *(FRIEDZA's scared face appears.)*
PAWLINA. Hello, Friedza. Is your husband with...
GOLDA. No. Murdered.
PAWLINA. Oh, my God!

GOLDA. We've been hiding for three days.
PAWLINA. You have to get away from here. It's not safe. *(FRIEDZA's face disappears.)*
GOLDA. Nowhere is safe, Panna Pawlina. I have to talk to you.
PAWLINA. It's too dangerous. Someone might see us.
GOLDA. Just keep picking flowers. *(PAWLINA bends down near the haystack and picks wildflowers.)* My baby's going to die if we don't get some water. He's only a few weeks old. Please, just some water.
PAWLINA *(demeanor changes)*. A baby. I didn't know. I didn't see him. *(She reaches down and touches the baby's head in the haystack.)* He's burning up!
GOLDA. Mundek's been like that all day.
PAWLINA *(sings softly)*. Hello, Mundek.
GOLDA. Just some water, Panna Pawlina. Water. Please.
PAWLINA. As soon as it's dark, slip around to the barn. I'll bring you water. And bread. And then, Paniusia Schachterova, go where they don't know you.
GOLDA. Bless you, Panna Pawlina. Bless you. *(Her face disappears. PAWLINA starts to run off forgetting her flowers. She runs back to scoop them up and drops one by the haystack.)*
PAWLINA *(whispers)*. For you, Mundek. *(Haystack is silent.)*

SCENE TWO

SCENE: *Outside DOMICELA's thatched-roof farmhouse. Twilight.*

AT RISE: *A soldier attaches a notice to the side of the barn. PAWLINA is pumping water. On the ground is a yoke with buckets. Under her apron is a round loaf of dark bread.*

DOMICELA. Why so much water?
PAWLINA. For the animals.
DOMICELA *(looks at her suspiciously)*. One horse! One cow! And there's a bread missing.
PAWLINA *(innocently)*. Maybe a neighbor came in.
DOMICELA. Tadeusz would have told me.
PAWLINA. Was Tadeusz here?

DOMICELA. Repairing the roof. He hung around waiting to see you all afternoon.
PAWLINA. When did he leave?
DOMICELA. When I had to get dinner for your brother and sister. Why were you so late? *(DOMICELA crosses to PAWLINA, pulls the bread from her apron and waits for an explanation.)*
PAWLINA. It's for Paniusia Schachterova...from the next village.
DOMICELA. Are you crazy? What good do you think one loaf of bread will do?
PAWLINA. It's terrible what they're doing...behind that barbed wire fence.
DOMICELA. Who told you to look? When you take the cart to market, go a different way!
PAWLINA. Mamusia! I could hear the women screaming. And then...I saw a baby...at the end...of a bayonet. You wouldn't kill a sick animal like that.
DOMICELA. There's a war going on, Pawlina. Stay away from there. It's not safe. Not with all those soldiers around. For a pretty girl like you, there's worse things than being killed. You can't save Paniusia Schachterova.
PAWLINA *(quietly)*. She's in our barn.
DOMICELA. Mother of God! Do you know what they'll do if they catch you helping a Jew? *(Crosses to poster and reads.)* "Anyone caught helping or hiding Jews will be punished by death." *(PAWLINA doesn't answer.)* They'll shoot you, Pawlina. And then they'll shoot me. And then your brother and sister. And then maybe they'll throw in Krasula the cow for luck!
PAWLINA. What if we were in trouble, Mamusia?
DOMICELA. We're not Jews. We're Poles. Pawlina, I have nothing against Paniusia Schachterova. But it's her neck or mine. Her family or mine.
PAWLINA. Mamusia, you always said we're all the same. In the eyes of God we're all the same.
DOMICELA. It's not his eyes I'm worried about! It's the eyes of those Nazi soldiers. They took most of our food.
PAWLINA. Mundek's so tiny he doesn't eat solid food.
DOMICELA. Who's Mundek?
PAWLINA. Her brand new baby. He's ill.
DOMICELA. Ill! Mother of God, what if he cries? Tiny, sick babies have strong lungs. There's no sure way to keep a baby quiet.

PAWLINA. The Nazis found a way.
DOMICELA. Marry Tadeusz and have your own baby. Forget about this one. *(Sighs.)* To be oorn into a world like this.
PAWLINA. Mamusia, just let them hide in the barn until he's better.
DOMICELA. No!
PAWLINA. Then at least until they're rested. They're worn out.
DOMICELA. I know you! When you were little you brought in birds with broken wings and fussed over them until they flew. Who else is out there?
PAWLINA. Her little girl, Friedza. Mamusia, she hasn't eaten in three days!
DOMICELA *(pause. Sighs and gives her bread).* Here! When you milk Krasula, give them half. *(PAWLINA looks at her still waiting.)* All right, all right. Let them rest in the barn. Oh my God, I wouldn't want to be in her shoes with one in her arms and one at her skirt. *(Firmly.)* But before sunrise, Pawlina, they go! *(PAWLINA kisses her mother. She places the yoke across her shoulders.* SOUND: *In the distance, soldiers shouting excitedly — in unintelligible German. Howl of bloodhounds.)*

SCENE THREE

SCENE: *The storage barn that night by the dim light of a kerosene lamp.*

AT RISE: *GOLDA, the baby MUNDEK and FRIEDZA are visible. PAWLINA ladles milk from the pail into earthenware cups. FRIEDZA gulps hers down.*

PAWLINA. I told Krasula the milk was for you. *(Gives her more.)*
FRIEDZA *(impressed).* Can you talk to Krasula?
PAWLINA. I sing to her. She understands.
FRIEDZA. Could you teach me how to milk her?
PAWLINA *(uncomfortably to GOLDA).* My mother says you have to leave.
GOLDA *(startled).* When?
PAWLINA. Before dawn. So the neighbors don't see.
GOLDA. But the baby's still sick.
PAWLINA. I'll give you some food to take with you.
GOLDA *(distraught).* Where can we go? How many haystacks can we hide in?

PAWLINA. There are so many people around at planting time. She's afraid they'll hear the baby cry. And the German police are everywhere.
GOLDA. Hunting for Jews! Panna Pawlina, I want to save my children! Help me! Please help me! *(SOUND: MUNDEK wakes up and starts to cry.)* Sh-h! Sh-h! *(Instantly GOLDA sings a Yiddish song softly, MUNDEK quiets down.)* If he starts to cry, I'll sing to him. He won't make a sound.
PAWLINA *(quoting)*. We're a poor family, Paniusia Schachterova. There's no food.
GOLDA *(interrupts)*. But we'll pay for our food and pay you to stay! My husband — *(Starts to cry.)* they beat him up. With clubs. The men who used to work for him in the wheat fields. They beat him up and left him in a ditch to die. And when I found him, I couldn't recognize his face. The police just laughed. But once upon a time, Panna Pawlina, we were respected people in the village.
PAWLINA. I know.
GOLDA. Just before the Nazis took our home, my husband buried my jewelry in the garden. He hid our silver tea service up in the attic. Panna Pawlina, it's all yours if you'll let us stay. *(PAWLINA doesn't answer.)* Friedza, you remember where Tateh hid everything, don't you? *(FRIEDZA nods.)* I don't dare leave Mundek alone. But Friedza, you could show Panna Pawlina where we hid our valuables.
PAWLINA *(tries to explain)*. My mother's frightened.
GOLDA. Who isn't? Night and day I'm frightened. But one day this war will end and God will bless you. What good are all my things? It's the children that matter! *(PAWLINA thinks. GOLDA removes MUNDEK's diaper and from the seam removes a gold bracelet. Puts it on PAWLINA's wrist.)* Here. My husband gave me this gold bracelet when Mundek was born. Now, maybe it can keep him alive.
PAWLINA *(hesitates)*. It's beautiful!
GOLDA. Wear it, Panna Pawlina. Or sell it. But let us stay here.
PAWLINA. For how long?
GOLDA. How long can this war last? Three weeks? Two months at the most. Just keep us here until it's over, and you can have all that I own.
PAWLINA. I'd like to help you, but...

GOLDA *(distraught)*. My husband murdered, my house taken, my baby ill. What's next?
FRIEDZA. I'm here, Mameh.
GOLDA *(hugs her)*. Yes! Yes! *(SOUND: MUNDEK starts to fret.)*
PAWLINA *(picking up baby)*. Sh-h, Mundek. Sh-h. *(PAWLINA softly sings a Polish lullaby. Instantly the baby is quiet, transfixed.)* Oh, so you like Polish singing too! *(GOLDA watches.)*
GOLDA. Go. Go now. Take everything you can. We gave some neighbors our best winter clothes. They promised to keep them safe. Panna Pawlina, you can give your mother my fur coat.
PAWLINA. No! Wherever you are you'll need it.
GOLDA. Ask her again. Please. We could hide in your barn. There's room.
PAWLINA. I want to help you, Paniusia Schachterova; but my mother said you had to leave. It's a terrible risk.
GOLDA. Maybe if you tell her we can pay, she'll change her mind. Try.
PAWLINA *(looks down at MUNDEK sleeping in her arms)*. Look, Paniusia Schachterova! He's sleeping quietly now. And there's a little tiny smile. He's getting better.
GOLDA. Panna Pawlina, our lives are in your hands!
PAWLINA *(struggling)*. I don't want to hurt anyone. Not you. Or me. Or my family.
GOLDA. We could dig a hole.
FRIEDZA. And cover it up with straw.
PAWLINA *(crosses thoughtfully with MUNDEK still in her arms to place where bunker will be)*. Maybe...a bunker...
FRIEDZA. No one will ever know we're here.
GOLDA. Hide us. Please. Don't send us out there to die! *(SOUND: MUNDEK whimpers.)*
PAWLINA *(kisses him)*. Sh-h-h. *(Hums refrain. LIGHTS: fade.)*

SCENE FOUR

SCENE: *A wooded area near HANKA's thatched-roof farm. A moonless night.*

AT RISE: *PAWLINA and FRIEDZA are cutting through the woods.*

FRIEDZA. Why are we going this way?

PAWLINA. Better to stay off the road.
FRIEDZA. I never saw my house like that, all empty. They took everything. Everything except the staircase.
PAWLINA. We were too late, Friedza.
FRIEDZA. But Tateh said no one would ever find Mameh's jewelry. I helped him cover the hole with grass and leaves. When we were done you couldn't tell it was there.
PAWLINA. Somebody dug up the whole garden.
FRIEDZA. Even my rose bush. I planted it all by myself. In the ghetto — *(PAWLINA covers FRIEDZA's mouth. FRIEDZA whispers.)* We couldn't have flowers. Mameh's going to blame me. She'll say that I didn't hunt hard enough.
PAWLINA. I'll tell her we both hunted. Now, let's get the clothes. You can't spend a Polish winter in a summer dress!
FRIEDZA. Will you go to the door with me?
PAWLINA. No. You have to go alone.
FRIEDZA. You're not supposed to help us, are you?
PAWLINA. That's what the Nazis say. *(SOUND: Owl hooting. Night wind in the trees.)*
FRIEDZA. Can you hold my hand until we get there?
PAWLINA *(holds her hand)*. Just tell them that your mother sent you to collect the clothes she left, that she needs them. That's all. Don't tell them anything else.
FRIEDZA. Some kids smuggled food in, sugar and flour, and one boy, littler than me, he brought in two eggs. He climbed the wall with two eggs, and the guards never caught him. *(They approach the door to the thatched-roof farm.)*
PAWLINA. I'll wait for you in the woods over there. Go on.

(PAWLINA pushes her gently. FRIEDZA knocks timidly at the door. Then boldly, she knocks louder. HANKA, a stern-faced farm woman, answers the door, peering out into the night. She looks down and sees FRIEDZA.)

HANKA. Jesus, Maria! Will you look who's here. I thought you were...Well, what is it?
FRIEDZA. I came for my mother's things.
HANKA. What things?
FRIEDZA. Our clothes. The two wool dresses, her black fur coat and my rabbit muff.

HANKA. What are you talking about?
FRIEDZA *(insisting and taking a step in)*. We need our clothes. She sent me.
HANKA *(slaps her face)*. It's against the law to keep Jewish property. *(Calls.)* Henryk.

(A huge man stands in the doorway.)

HANKA. The little Jew wants her rabbit muff! She says her mother left a fur coat with us.
FRIEDZA. She did! She did! I know she did.
HENRYK *(removing his leather belt)*. When children lie, there's only one way to cure them. *(Whacks her.)*
FRIEDZA. I'm not lying! She sent me! *(SOUND: Offstage, German soldiers marching and chanting.)*
HENRYK *(calls)*. Hey, over here! Here's a Jewish brat! *(SOUND: Soldiers continue singing. HANKA has a firm hand on FRIEDZA.)*
HANKA. Get them, I'll hold her.
HENRYK *(hollering)*. Hey, over here. Come over here. *(exits.)*

(FRIEDZA kicks HANKA hard. In surprise, HANKA lets go. FRIEDZA flees to the woods. HENRYK reenters with the SOLDIERS.)

HANKA *(points)*. That way. Hurry!
LUTHER. Halte! *(SOUND: A shot rings out in the air.)*
OTTO. Halte! *(SOUND: Another shot. FRIEDZA hides, crouching under a tree trunk in the woods. In the dark, the SOLDIERS run right over the tree trunk.)*
LUTHER. Halte! *(SOUND: Another shot. FRIEDZA is terrified.)*
HENRYK. Why didn't you hold her?
HANKA. Why didn't you come faster?
HENRYK. They need a higher fence around that ghetto!
HANKA. We lost the money, Henryk. Fifty zlotys. Even if they do catch her, we won't get it now.
PAWLINA *(whispers)*. Friedza. Quick. We'll cut through the birch trees. *(FRIEDZA crawls to meet PAWLINA.)*
FRIEDZA. Panna Pawlina, are you going to kick us out now? *(LIGHTING: There is moonlight on them both. PAWLINA wipes away a tear on*

FRIEDZA's face. Pause. PAWLINA *takes* FRIEDZA's *hand and they dart through the trees, alert to any sound.)*

SCENE FIVE

SCENE: *Domicela's kitchen. The next day.*

AT RISE: DOMICELA *is sweeping.* PAWLINA *is at the table kneading bread dough.*

DOMICELA. No! I said one night, and now it's the next day. We can't have her here. I have two little ones.
PAWLINA. So does she! What if you were being hunted and killed?
DOMICELA. If they stay here, we will be! The only way a Pole survives is to stay out of the enemy's way, plant your potatoes and keep your mouth shut.
PAWLINA. No one will know. We can dig a bunker. Tonight.
DOMICELA. No.
PAWLINA. Tadeusz will help.
DOMICELA. Tell them to go somewhere else. Let someone else hide them. They can do it better than we can.
PAWLINA. Who, Mamusia? Her old neighbors told the soldiers to shoot. To shoot a child!
DOMICELA. If the moon had been out, the soldiers would have shot you too!
PAWLINA. Please, Mamusia.
DOMICELA. Take them some food, and send them away. Tell them that's all we can do. *(PAWLINA doesn't move.)* Fast! Go!
PAWLINA. I can't. Mamusia, they didn't do anything wrong. They're not criminals.
DOMICELA. They're Jews. That's enough. For the Nazis that's more than enough.
PAWLINA. Mamusia, they're people!!
DOMICELA. So are we!
PAWLINA. She has such a sweet baby. He smiles when I sing Polish to him. Just let them stay until he's better. *(Slowly brings out bracelet.)* Paniusia Schachterova gave me this bracelet, Mamusia, to pay us.

64   Voices: Plays for Studying the Holocaust

DOMICELA *(astonished, bites it)*. Gold! Pawlina, this is real gold. Do you know what I could buy with this? *(Pause.)* Give it back. If I try to use that, fifteen soldiers will be firing questions at me and then their rifles.
PAWLINA. Then I'll give it to Tadeusz. He'll know what to do. One week, Mamusia. Maybe then the war will be over.
DOMICELA. Maybe then Krasula the cow will talk! Why is it so important?
PAWLINA. Because I keep thinking what if it were you and me? And Jurek and Bronia? *(Pause.)*
DOMICELA *(decides)*. Leave your brother and sister out of this. They're too young. They'll talk.
PAWLINA. Mamusia!!
DOMICELA. Just until the baby's strong enough to travel.
PAWLINA *(hugs her)*. Oh, Mamusia, thank you. Thank you.
DOMICELA. Pawlina, I don't want to see them. I don't want to hear them. I don't want anything to do with them. If the German soldiers come knocking at the door, I don't want to know anything about it.
PAWLINA *(hugs her)*. You won't even know they're here! I promise!
DOMICELA. Yesterday, I saw the captain wipe his boots on the Polish flag. *(Spits in disgust.)* When the mushroom season starts, we'll send him a basket — some of those large, shiny ones that look so good. *(Winks at PAWLINA.)*
PAWLINA. The poisonous ones?
DOMICELA *(presenting an imaginary basket)*. A little present from the Polish people! *(They laugh.)* As for that family out there, you're on your own! *(DOMICELA exits and returns a few seconds later with precious flour, which she plunks down on the table.)* Here's the last of the flour. You better bake another bread!

SCENE SIX

SCENE: *The storage barn, just before dawn. The next day. There are mounds of fresh earth. In the background are piles of hay.*

AT RISE: *TADEUSZ and PAWLINA finish digging out a narrow bunker. They have been working all night.* SOUND: *The shovels hitting the dirt. TADEUSZ smooths the sides with his shovel, checks their work and then gestures to PAWLINA to bring the fugitives out.* PAWLINA *leads the frightened* FUGITIVES *from the haystacks to the bunker, where there is only enough room to sit in a row.* TADEUSZ *and* PAWLINA *help them climb in. They stare out terrified, as* TADEUSZ *and* PAWLINA *cover the opening with straw.*

FRIEDZA. Mameh!!
GOLDA. Sh-h. (PAWLINA *and* TADEUSZ *complete the camouflage. Exhausted,* PAWLINA *sinks to the ground.* TADEUSZ *lifts her up. Wearily, they start loading the earth into baskets.)*
TADEUSZ *(low voice).* We've got to get rid of it now, before the sun comes up.
PAWLINA *(low voice).* I didn't think it would take all night. I'm so tired, Tadeusz, I could fall asleep standing up.
TADEUSZ. Me too. Remember, not too much dirt in any one place. Hurry, Pawlina.
PAWLINA. Can we go together?
TADEUSZ. No. Better not. *(Kisses her cheek.)* The Underground could take lessons from you.
*(*TADEUSZ *exits with a basket of earth.* PAWLINA *struggles with a heavy basket of earth and lumbers out with her load.* SOUND: *Music to indicate passage of time.* PAWLINA *brings in* MANIA. MANIA *has just escaped from the ghetto. Her blonde hair is in two braids worn down the front fastened with two small ribbons at the bottom.* PAWLINA *helps others out of bunker to stretch.)*

PAWLINA *(introducing her).* Mania, this is Paniusia Schachterova and her daughter, Friedza.
GOLDA *(Yiddish). A gezunt af dir.* [Translation. Health be unto you that you're with us.] *(*GOLDA *hugs her.* MANIA *doesn't answer.)* You don't speak Yiddish?
MANIA *(proudly).* We only spoke Polish at home, and I went to a Polish school.
GOLDA *(suspicious).* What kind of Jewish girl doesn't speak any Yiddish?
MANIA *(admits).* I understand it.
GOLDA. You look like a little Polish girl. Such pretty hair.
MANIA. My sister Regina's hair was beautiful. It was so long, she could sit on it. She looked just like a painting before...*(Cries.)* They "liquidated" her section yesterday.

FRIEDZA *(wanting attention)*. Do you have a brother? *(Pause.)*
MANIA. I used to, Friedza. A little brother. Then they said, "We can't feed little children who can't do anything." They took their rifles...they made us watch.
GOLDA *(a deep sigh. Yiddish)*. Oy vay. When does it stop? *(Shakes her head. FRIEDZA, jealous, brings MUNDEK over.)*
FRIEDZA. I have a little brother. His name is Mundek. *(MANIA reaches out to touch him and FRIEDZA pulls him away.)* You can't touch him. He's *my* brother.
GOLDA. Friedza!
FRIEDZA. It's our hiding place. We were here first. Panna Pawlina, how long have we been here?
PAWLINA. A month.
FRIEDZA *(whispers subversively to Mania)*. Panna Pawlina can kick you out too.
PAWLINA. Shake hands, right now, and say you're sorry. *(They shake hands and FRIEDZA mumbles that she is sorry.)* That's better. *(Brings bucket over.)* I've brought you dinner — potatoes and milk. *(Gives bowl to MANIA first, who devours it. GOLDA and FRIEDZA take food.)* I'll bring you food whenever I can. But if the Nazis ever catch you, swear you never saw me. You don't even know what I look like. Say you found this empty storage barn and hid here. Promise?
MANIA *(nods)*. I promise.
GOLDA. I promise.
FRIEDZA. I'll never tell them anything.
PAWLINA. And if I see them coming anywhere near you, I'll yell my brother's name twice.
MANIA. What's his name?
PAWLINA. Jurek.
FRIEDZA *(to MANIA)*. How'd you escape?
MANIA. Yesterday, I woke up early. I don't know why. When I peeked out the window, it was still dark; but I saw hundreds of soldiers. They were very quiet like they were waiting for something. I knew something awful was going to happen. *(Shows amber ring.)* My mother gave me this. A year ago. She said, "Amber protects you." So, I crawled through a secret hole in the attic, and then I lay down and inched along the roof gutters, until I reached the other side. I was so scared I'd fall, so scared they'd shoot me. But it was dark, and the soldiers never saw me.

FRIEDZA *(mesmerized)*. It was the amber ring. Can I try it on?
MANIA. Just for a minute.
FRIEDZA *(puts ring on)*. It looks like firelight. Is it really magic?
MANIA *(shakes her head)*. Some people say so. On the first day of school Regina would always say, "Every bead of my amber necklace is a different story." When the children were good, she'd tell them one. She was...such...a...good...teacher. *(Cries inconsolably. PAWLINA puts an arm around her.)*
FRIEDZA *(solemnly returns the ring)*. If I'm good, will you tell me one of her stories? *(MANIA nods.)* What happened to the necklace?
MANIA. Our maid took it. She said, "Now I'll be something; and you'll be nothing." She had Regina's necklace on and a meat cleaver in her hand. When my mother couldn't get her wedding band off, she lifted the cleaver up in the air and screamed, "Get it off or I'll use this."
FRIEDZA. How come she didn't take the amber ring?
MANIA. It was lost. But it was in my pocket the whole time.
FRIEDZA. See, it did save you. *(PAWLINA has helped them all back into the bunker.)*
GOLDA *(crosses to MANIA)*. Mania, from now on, you'll be with us. Whatever happens...will happen to all of us. *(They stare into the dark.)*

SCENE SEVEN

SCENE: *The kitchen, Domicela's farmhouse. Mid-June 1943, the day of the Corpus Christi celebration. There is a hallway and a ladder that leads to the attic.*

AT RISE: *PAWLINA is singing as she arranges spring leaves on the mantle of the stove, decorating for Corpus Christi Day. On the table are bottles of vodka, mineral water, tumblers, and a plate of Polish sausage. She removes a freshly-baked bread from the baking compartment of their old wood-burning stove and sets it, with a sharp knife, on the table. DOMICELA rushes in.*

DOMICELA. I see them. They're coming here. I told you this would happen. Leave that and get out of here.
PAWLINA. Here! You're sure?

DOMICELA. I sent your brother and sister on ahead. Hurry, Pawlina. It's that baby!
PAWLINA. Mamusia, they've been here over a year. No one knows. Let me think.
DOMICELA. There's no time.
PAWLINA. We have to warn them!
DOMICELA. Soldiers, Pawlina!
PAWLINA *(points to attic)*. Oh, God, the baby's diapers are up there drying.
DOMICELA. I'm going!
PAWLINA. Mamusia, when you run past the barn, yell Jurek's name — twice. They'll understand.

(DOMICELA exits. PAWLINA grabs her broom and rushes to the ladder and scrambles up. SOUND: Soldiers knocking at the door. They knock again, insistently. PAWLINA scrambles down, as the door opens and two German SOLDIERS enter. BRUNO and ERNST, the captain. Both speak with a slight German accent.)

ERNST. When you deal with these Polish pigs, use your rifle. Either end, Bruno. Either end.
BRUNO *(spies PAWLINA's comely legs coming down the ladder)*. Do I have your permission, Captain.
ERNST *(claps him on the shoulder)*. We didn't teach you Polish to play with the ladies.
BRUNO *(slyly)*. But the Führer wants children too. *(They laugh.)*
ERNST. Either women or drink will be your downfall, Bruno.
BRUNO *(too familiar)*. But a pleasant way to go, Herr Captain. A pleasant way to go.
ERNST *(sternly)*. Do your job first. For the Führer and the fatherland. I'll look outside. Heil Hitler. *(Gives Nazi salute.)*
BRUNO. Heil Hitler. *(Returns salute. ERNST exits. SOUND: In the distance DOMICELA yells, "Jurek! Jurek!")*
PAWLINA *(all smiles and charm)*. Your friend is leaving?
BRUNO. He'll be back. What were you doing up there?
PAWLINA *(holding broom)*. What do you think? Sweeping. My mother told me to.
BRUNO *(alert)*. Where is she now?
PAWLINA. At church. It's Corpus Christi Day. Didn't you know?

BRUNO. Why aren't you there?
PAWLINA. I've got one more loaf of bread in the oven. *(With an ingratiating smile.)* And now there's a handsome soldier in my kitchen.
BRUNO *(poking her with his rifle but not very hard).* You're hiding Jews, aren't you?
PAWLINA. Jews! Are you kidding? There aren't any left! They took them all to the city and killed them. *(BRUNO is appraising her. PAWLINA points to his rifle.)* That could go off and ruin my bread. Sit down and have some vodka. It's a holiday. *(BRUNO is torn.)*
BRUNO. I'm going up that ladder.
PAWLINA. There's nothing up there but spiders.
BRUNO. I'll look for myself...*(Looking at PAWLINA.)* in a minute.
PAWLINA *(flirts).* You're a good-looking soldier. *(Tosses her long blond hair.)* Or maybe it's just the uniform.
BRUNO *(grabs her).* Or maybe it isn't. We could find out.
PAWLINA. What would your girlfriend back home say?
BRUNO *(a wave of homesickness).* You look almost like a German fräulein...with that long blond hair.
PAWLINA. Why don't you put your rifle down? Have some vodka.
BRUNO. I'm on duty. If you're hiding anyone, they'll hang you.
PAWLINA *(lightly).* It's too hot a day to talk about hanging.
BRUNO. In Germany, we drink beer on a day like this. *(Sits down, nostalgic.)* A tall stein of beer.
PAWLINA. You're in Poland now. *(Pours two glasses.)* Here! Polish men drink it in one gulp. But Polish men are pretty strong.
BRUNO. So am I. *(They clink glasses and toast each other. The drink hits him.)* What kind of vodka is this?
PAWLINA. The best. Homemade. Invite your friend. *(PAWLINA pours him more and gives it to him. They toast each other again. BRUNO is getting warmer, puts his rifle down and opens his collar.)*
BRUNO. On a day like this, we'd sit in the beer garden and eat sausages and dance the polka. *(BRUNO bangs the table and hums a polka tune. PAWLINA passes him the small plate of sausage.)*
PAWLINA. This is kielbasa, Polish sausage. Try it.
BRUNO *(tasting it).* Not as good. But it'll do. It'll do. *(He eats all that's there, while PAWLINA refills his glass with vodka. BRUNO downs it. She takes mineral water.)*

PAWLINA. There'll be plenty of dancing tonight. A handsome man like you won't have any problem finding girls to dance the polka with. *(PAWLINA pours more vodka. BRUNO notices her empty glass.)*
BRUNO *(thickly)*. You have some more, too. I'll teach you how we do the German polka and maybe a few other things. *(Laughs and puts an arm around her.)* What's your name?
PAWLINA. Pawlina.
BRUNO. I'm Bruno. *(Pours himself more vodka and refills her glass.)* To my Polish Pawlina!
PAWLINA. Careful, that's strong stuff, if you're not used to it.
BRUNO *(drunk)*. I'm a strong man. Pawlina, Pawlina, pretty soon you'll find out just how strong I am.

(ERNST enters.)

ERNST. Heil Hitler! *(Gives Nazi salute.)*
BRUNO *(struggles to his feet)*. Heil Hitler! *(Returns salute. The cordial, drunken host.)* We're having a party. This is Pawlina. My Polish Pawlina. Give him some vodka, *liebchen*.
ERNST *(smashes BRUNO's glass to the ground)*. You're a disgrace. Get drunk on your own time. And with a German girl, not a Pole.
BRUNO. She's very nice. Pawlina's very nice, Herr Captain.
ERNST. I've done the outside. All the haystacks. They crawl in there sometimes. Did you check the house — before you started drinking?
BRUNO. Sure I did. There's no one here. It's...What's the name of that holiday again?
PAWLINA. Corpus Christi Day.
BRUNO. It's one of their holidays. Her mother's out. C'mon, Captain. I'm going to teach her the German polka.
ERNST *(walks into hallway)*. Where's that ladder go?
BRUNO. Upstairs! *(Laughing at his own joke.)*
ERNST. Bruno! Get over here.
BRUNO. I'll be back, Pawlina. Don't go away. *(BRUNO, with difficulty, starts up the ladder. PAWLINA crosses, ready to crash it.)*
ERNST. Stand back. That's an order.
PAWLINA. I was just going to hold it steady. It's rickety.
ERNST *(with disgust)*. You Poles don't know how to do anything right. Not even how to build a ladder. *(PAWLINA starts to hold it. ERNST*

strikes her arm off.) Leave it alone. *(Pause, while BRUNO drunkenly searches.)*
BRUNO. Nothing up here, Captain. Ow! Nothing but spiders. *(BRUNO comes down nursing a finger.)* One bit me. What do you feed those spiders.
PAWLINA. Polish vodka!
BRUNO. Polish vodka! *(Laughing at her joke.)* Polish vodka! You and I are going to get along just fine!
ERNST. You're going back to the barracks. *(ERNST roughly pushes BRUNO out the door.)*
BRUNO. See you later, Pawlina.

(BRUNO and ERNST leave. PAWLINA sinks into a chair overwhelmed by the narrow escape. SOUND: TADEUSZ whistling the same song PAWLINA was singing earlier. TADEUSZ knocks and enters.)

TADEUSZ. Pawlina? *(PAWLINA rushes towards him.)*
PAWLINA. They were here!
TADEUSZ. Is everyone all right?
PAWLINA. I don't know yet. *(PAWLINA is trembling. TADEUSZ holds her.)* I'm frightened. Tadeusz, I'm frightened. What if they come again? What if next time we're not so lucky? I thought I could protect them. But now...I'm not so sure. What if I can't go through with it? What if in the end...Tadeusz, I'm frightened!!
TADEUSZ *(calming her)*. I'll stay with you.
PAWLINA. No. No! I have to check the barn.
TADEUSZ *(crosses to the door)*. I left some tools in the barn anyway. You wait here.

(TADEUSZ exits. Momentary silence, then...SOUND: A shot. PAWLINA screams. ERNST and BRUNO re-enter with TADEUSZ, who is holding his arm in pain.)

ERNST. I thought we'd picked up all the young Polish pigs. Looks like we missed one.
PAWLINA. No! He didn't do anything!
ERNST. Ah, the boyfriend! *(BRUNO rises and gets his rifle. Looks at table.)* You see, Bruno, you never learn. You're not very observant. And you thought the party was for you. *(To TADEUSZ.)*

Put your hands up! *(TADEUSZ hesitates.)* Bruno! *(BRUNO kicks him. When TADEUSZ rises, he puts his hands over his head.)* That's better. When you get to Germany you'll learn how to do what you're told without even thinking.
TADEUSZ. But it takes two Germans to stop one Pole!
ERNST. Bruno! *(BRUNO kicks him again. TADEUSZ groans. He staggers, and they force him up. He is dazed. BRUNO and ERNST push TADEUSZ to the door, a gun at his ear and a gun at his back.)*
PAWLINA *(frantic)*. Where are you taking him?
ERNST *(turns and gives a mock bow)*. Don't worry, fräulein. We take good care of our Polish workers.
BRUNO *(a drunken grin)*. Because they're all volunteers. *(They exit. PAWLINA stands by the kitchen table for a second, stunned, then collapses.)*

SCENE EIGHT

SCENE: *The bunker at night, March 1944.*

AT RISE: *GOLDA, FRIEDZA, and MANIA sit in a row, all facing the same way. There is no room to stand. It is dark. MUNDEK is asleep beside GOLDA.*

FRIEDZA. Move over. I can't breathe.
MANIA. Friedza, there's no place to move. You're growing, that's all.
FRIEDZA. Mameh, look at all the room Mania has.
MANIA. Baby! Do you have to complain to your mother about every little thing?
FRIEDZA. My mother's still alive! *(MANIA grieves for her family.)* Made you cry! Made you cry!
GOLDA *(in Yiddish)*. Shah! Quiet! The two of you.
MANIA. A year and a half in a dirt hole. Like we've been buried. Buried alive.
GOLDA. It's the same for all of us.
MANIA. But you have each other! You have each other! *(Cries.)*
FRIEDZA. And she called me a baby.
GOLDA. Friedza, Mania is like a sister now. You must be nice to her.
FRIEDZA. No, she's not. I don't want a sister. And tell her to be nice to me.

GOLDA *(to MANIA)*. Try to set a good example.
MANIA. It's spring and I want to see the sunlight. I want to walk along the river. I want to smell fresh air. The air in here is putrid.
FRIEDZA. What's "putrid"?
MANIA. Go look it up.
FRIEDZA *(wistfully)*. I wish I had a book. Any book. *(Forgets argument and snuggles up.)* Tell me a story, Mania.
MANIA. About what?
FRIEDZA. Something happy.
MANIA *(quietly)*. I don't know about anything happy.
FRIEDZA. Make it up then.
MANIA. Once there was a place where you could eat all you wanted. The table was piled with...chicken...and wild strawberries...
GOLDA *(joining in)*. And loaves of fresh-baked *challah*.
FRIEDZA. And black currant jam. *(Pause.)* Mameh, I'm so hungry!
GOLDA. Every day we wait is another day we're alive. Praise God.
MANIA. I don't believe in God any longer.
GOLDA. You don't mean that.
MANIA. Where was God when they shot my brother? Where was God when they shot my sister? Where was God when they shot my mother and father? Where was He then? Where was He?
GOLDA. I'm not going to listen to this anymore. *(GOLDA rearranges them, and it is very difficult in the cramped quarters.)* Mania, sit there. Friedza sit there. Now, not another word until after dinner.
FRIEDZA. Dinner! How can you call a half a slice of bread dinner?
GOLDA *(slaps her hand)*. Be grateful for what you get.
MANIA. Mundek can have mine. I'm not hungry.
FRIEDZA. Can I have part?
GOLDA. No. Mania, you can't stop eating. You need your strength.
MANIA. For what? To die? *(SOUND: MUNDEK starts to scream. GOLDA tries to soothe him but can't. MANIA sobs.)* Shut him up! Shut him up! *(Strikes MUNDEK.)* Shut up!

(SOUND: MUNDEK wails at being hit. PAWLINA, entering with bucket and small kerosene lamp, has raised the straw on the above.)

PAWLINA. Give him to me. *(PAWLINA takes MUNDEK and rubs his mouth with a rag, tickles him, plays with him. MUNDEK is quiet.)*
GOLDA. What did you do?

74   Voices: Plays for Studying the Holocaust

PAWLINA. A little homemade vodka.
GOLDA. To a baby. You want to kill him?
PAWLINA. Just the pain. *(Examines MUNDEK's mouth.)* That's what I did when Jurek got his back molars. *(To MANIA.)* He's only crying because it hurts. *(She gives the baby back to GOLDA and helps them out of bunker.)* I've got some clean clothes here. I washed them last night.
GOLDA. Thank you, Pawlina. Thank you. *(They take clothes.)*
PAWLINA *(teasing)*. Friedza, you have to stop growing or your skirt will be way above your knees.
FRIEDZA *(looks at food bucket)*. What did you bring?
PAWLINA. Some boiled potatoes with milk. And a chunk of bread. It's all we had.
GOLDA. We'll divide. *(GOLDA and FRIEDZA eat.)* Bless you, Panna Pawlina.
MANIA. What's it like outside?
PAWLINA *(to MANIA)*. The snow's melting. And I saw a crocus in the meadow. *(To GOLDA.)* They say the Russians are beating the Germans. They'll be here by summer.
GOLDA. Did you hear that, Mania?
MANIA. I can't wait that long. I've got to get some fresh air, Panna Pawlina. Let me go to the meadow with you tomorrow.
PAWLINA. You know you can't.
MANIA. Just ten minutes. Before everyone's up. I just want to stand up straight and walk outside like a human being. I want to know I'm still a human being.
PAWLINA. Have some potatoes.
MANIA. I don't want any. I want to get out of here. I dream about the sun, sunlight on the mountain peaks, sunlight in our garden. *(Crying.)* Mama had roses.
FRIEDZA. They killed our garden.
MANIA. I want to see the sun again before I die.
GOLDA *(in a low voice to PAWLINA)*. I never thought we'd be here this long.
PAWLINA. Neither did I. It's too crowded, Golda. Friedza's growing. Mundek needs to walk. Mania's a young lady.
GOLDA. Children grow in spite of everything.
PAWLINA *(crosses to MANIA. Tries to feed her)*. Eat, Mania.
MANIA. Do you know what it's like to be in the dark all the time? So dark you can't even see your fingers? And when you bring the

kerosene lamp for ten minutes and leave, it's worse; because then it goes all dark again. It's always night. A night that never ends. I don't want to hide any longer. *(Sobs.)* Let them shoot me too.

PAWLINA. No! You've survived this long. Just a little longer. You have to be brave, Mania. Brave!

MANIA *(softly)*. Just to see the sun.

PAWLINA. I couldn't take you out, Mania, not even for a minute, unless you knew all the prayers.

MANIA *(eagerly)*. Which prayers?

PAWLINA. The Our Father, the Hail Mary, the Rosary of the Blessed Virgin, and the Apostles's Creed. Every Catholic girl knows those by heart. And any soldier could ask.

MANIA. I could learn them! I won a prize once at school for reciting poetry.

PAWLINA. These are much harder.

MANIA. Why?

PAWLINA. They're all in Latin. But I have an idea, Mania. A way to give you all more room, Golda. It'll take some time. Some planning. But by spring, Mania, if you can learn those prayers, you'll see the sun!

End of Act One

Act Two

SCENE: *The storage barn and bunker. May 1944. Two months later.*

AT RISE: *PAWLINA is outfitting MANIA to look like a Polish country girl (blouse, long skirt, apron, bare feet, hair in long braids wound around her head. PAWLINA places large cross around MANIA's neck. MANIA recites Pater Noster in Latin.*

MANIA	(Translation)
Panem nostrum quotidianum	Give us this day
da nobis hodie et	our daily bread.
dimette nobis debita	And forgive us our trespasses,
nostra, sicut et nos	As we forgive those who
dimittimus debitoribus nostris	trespass against us
Et ne non inducas in	And lead us not into
tentationem	temptation.
Amen.	

PAWLINA *(corrects her).* You forgot the last line. *"Sed libera nos a malo."* Then, Amen.
MANIA *(repeats correctly). Sed libera nos a malo.* What does that mean?
PAWLINA. Deliver us from evil. Remember to cross yourself a lot, too. Like this. *(Demonstrates touching with the three fingers of right hand, the forehead, heart, left shoulder, right shoulder. MANIA repeats.)* It's little things like that that could give you away. Now, here are your papers; put them in your pocket.
MANIA *(reads).* Cecylia Kozlowski.
PAWLINA. She died three months ago.
MANIA *(frightened).* What if they know that?
PAWLINA. The church records burned in a fire. They can't check. It wasn't easy to get.
MANIA *(whirls around).* OUTSIDE! I'm going outside. Thank you, Panna Pawlina. Thank you.
PAWLINA. You can thank me by not doing anything foolish.
MANIA. What do you mean?
PAWLINA. Don't look frightened. Walk with your head up, straight back, walk as if you worked in the fields. A country girl walks like this. *(There is a slight sway to her walk.)* Her feet are tough. Let's see

you. *(MANIA walks.)* Too much of the city in that. Swing your arms. And talk back to them.
MANIA. Talk back to them! Are you sure?
PAWLINA. Sure I'm sure. A farm girl would.
MANIA. You'll be with me, won't you?
PAWLINA. Yes. But you have to know what to do in case. I wish you weren't so pale.
MANIA. In case of what?
PAWLINA. Trouble. Any kind of trouble.
MANIA. Why do you have to work for the Germans?
PAWLINA. There's no choice. They took all the young Polish men to Germany. The women they've kept here. But it's still the same. Forced labor.
MANIA. Where are we going?
PAWLINA. Zoborow. A kommandant's home.
MANIA. You mean a home they took over?
PAWLINA. Probably.
MANIA. A Jewish home?
PAWLINA. I don't know. I haven't seen it. We'll go through the woods, so you can drink in the fresh air. Remember, you're a cousin on my mother's side. They haven't seen you before, because you just came. What's your new name?
MANIA. Panna Pawlina, couldn't I just go outside without all this fuss?
PAWLINA. Mania, if you want to go out, the safest place in the world is right under the enemy's nose. A Jewish girl would never be working for Nazis! But if the soldiers see a pretty face they haven't seen before, a girl who says she's just out for a walk, they'll be suspicious. Now do you want to go out or not?
MANIA. Yes! What are we going to do there? Cook?
PAWLINA. Clean. His wife is coming, and he wants it spotless by tonight, so I said I needed help and I'd bring my cousin.
MANIA. Did you say clean?
PAWLINA. Yes. Clean. Sweep, mop, dust, scrub the floors, wash the windows, beat the rugs. Whatever has to be done, we'll do.
MANIA *(as they exit)*. But Pawlina, I've never cleaned before!
PAWLINA. It's easy. I can't show you here; but when we get there, I'll explain everything. *(Reassuring her.)* Don't worry. If my little sister Bronia can clean, so can you. That part's simple!

Scene Two

SCENE: *The storage barn and bunker, late June 1944.*

AT RISE: *GOLDA is talking to MANIA in the bunker. FRIEDZA is listening.*

GOLDA *(in Yiddish)*. *Meshugenah!* Crazy! That's what you are. You had to have fresh air and sunshine! Now the whole German army is hunting for Cecylia Kozlowski.
FRIEDZA. I wouldn't try to go clean a house, if I didn't know how.
GOLDA. We're all in trouble because of you. You couldn't leave well enough alone.
MANIA. It was Panna Pawlina's idea too. She got the papers.
GOLDA. You can't stay here any longer. You're crazy. *(In Yiddish.) Meshugenah.* Get out!
MANIA. You can't throw me out. It's not your home.
FRIEDZA. We were here first. Me and Mameh and Mundek.
MANIA. And what about Mundek. All this time I was terrified someone would hear him scream. And I never complained, did I?
FRIEDZA. Not much. I don't want to die because of you. I'd like to see sunshine too. I'd like to run in the park and swim in the river. I'd like to go to school, I'd like to do a lot of things, if we ever get out. And now you've ruined it.
GOLDA. Go.
MANIA. Where? I don't know anyone. My family's gone. Where am I supposed to go?
GOLDA. Go wherever your eyes take you.
MANIA. I'll do what Panna Pawlina tells me to do.

(PAWLINA enters with food, clothes, lifts bunker cover and brings MANIA out.)

PAWLINA. Bruno was just here. They're suspicious. It's over, Mania. They're looking for *you*. But, if you can get to the Russians, you'll be safe.
GOLDA. How close are they?
PAWLINA. A few weeks, and this whole war will be over.
GOLDA. A few weeks. Praise God.
MANIA. Please let me stay! I won't go out again. I won't complain, I promise.

PAWLINA. It's for your own safety, Mania. If they find you here, you're dead. *(She helps her change clothes.)* They're hunting for you.
FRIEDZA. How could you scrub a chair with soap and water? Even Mundek wouldn't be so stupid.
MANIA. This is the only home I have. Please let me stay.
GOLDA. Do you want to kill all of us?
PAWLINA. You must go.
MANIA. Where? Where?
PAWLINA. Head for the Russian front. Head for Tarnopol. And stay off the road. *(Kisses MANIA on both cheeks.)* May the saints go with you. Here's bread. Hurry. Before they come back here. *(MANIA, now dressed in long skirt, shawl, flowered babushka and barefoot, exits. PAWLINA gives GOLDA and FRIEDZA food.)* There's no time for you to come out and stretch. I have to look for another hiding place for you. If I don't come back by tomorrow, run.
FRIEDZA. Why?
PAWLINA. Because it means we're all in danger. *(PAWLINA kisses each goodbye on both cheeks.)* Goodbye. Remember if anyone is caught, no one talks. *(PAWLINA covers bunker and exits.)*

SCENE THREE

SCENE: *The kitchen, Domicela's farmhouse and nearby countryside. Dawn. The next day.*

AT RISE: *PAWLINA hurriedly gathers a few belongings and some food. She stops briefly in front of the icon on the wall and prays.* SOUND: *A loud insistent knock at the door. PAWLINA crosses herself and opens door. ERNST enters.*

ERNST. You're up early, fräulein.
PAWLINA. The cow has to be milked.
ERNST *(examines the room)*. Is the cow far away?
PAWLINA. In the barn.
ERNST *(lifts package with PAWLINA's belongings)*. Are you going somewhere?
PAWLINA. What do you want?
ERNST. You know what I want. Where's the girl? The one you brought with you. Cecylia Kozlowski.

PAWLINA. She left.
ERNST. Then we'll have to find her.
PAWLINA. She's gone.
ERNST *(insists)*. Where?
PAWLINA. I don't know!
ERNST. You and I are going to take a ride, fräulein. If you don't point her out, we have a very nice German prison about seventy kilometers from here. It helps people remember. Once you get there, you Polish people never want to leave. *(ERNST throws her package on the floor and the contents spill out.)* You're under arrest.
PAWLINA. For what? I haven't done anything.
ERNST. You're a spy.
PAWLINA. No!
ERNST. Or she's a spy. Or a Jew. Either way, I'll find out, fräulein. I'll find out.
PAWLINA. I have nothing to tell you.
ERNST *(smiling)*. Ah, that's what they all say the first day. But by the third or fourth...*(PAWLINA tries to make a run for it. ERNST catches her at the doorway and throws her to the ground. He ties her wrists.)* Very foolish, fräulein. My soldiers are right outside. *(Opens door and calls.)* Tie her to the motorcycle. And search this house. *(Yanks her up.)*
PAWLINA. There's no one here. *(ERNST slaps her across the mouth.)*
ERNST. And gag her. *(Pushes her out the door, PAWLINA struggling.)*
PAWLINA *(offstage)*. JUREK!! JUR —

SCENE FOUR

SCENE: *A German prison, eight days later. There is a table in the room with food.*

AT RISE: *PAWLINA is being interrogated by ERNST. It is evident that she has been beaten by the bruises and swellings on her body. Her face is black and blue. ERNST goes to the table, puts food on a plate, crosses to PAWLINA whose hands are tied behind the chair.*

ERNST. Who did you spy for?
PAWLINA. I'm not a spy. I don't know anything.

ERNST. She was a Jew, wasn't she? You hid an enemy of the Third Reich!
PAWLINA. No.
ERNST. How many at your house?
PAWLINA. Four. *(ERNST slaps her battered face. PAWLINA winces.)*
ERNST. How many at your house?
PAWLINA *(breaking)*. Stop it! Stop it!
ERNST. Ah, we're getting somewhere. Finally. Look, Pawlina, there's a whole plate of food here. For every question you answer correctly, there's some food. For every question you don't answer, there's this. *(Fondles his whip. Unties her hands.)* I'll even let you hold the plate. Take some. After eight days, you must be hungry. *(The smell of the food is overwhelming. She is starving. She pushes food into her mouth. It is just enough to make her more hungry.)* That's enough. *(ERNST takes the plate away and puts it back on the table.)* You had your choice of jobs. Why did you choose the Kommandant's house?
PAWLINA. It was indoors. *(ERNST gets the plate of food but holds it just out of reach.)*
ERNST. What information did you hear?
PAWLINA. That his wife was coming at seven. *(ERNST strikes her shoulders with whip. PAWLINA winces.)*
ERNST. I'll break you yet. How many people at your house?
PAWLINA. Four! Four! I've told you four!
ERNST. And the girl who came to clean? Where did she live?
PAWLINA *(pauses)*. With us. *(ERNST strikes her legs hard with whip. PAWLINA cries out.)*
ERNST. Ah, then it was five! Say it.
PAWLINA. Five.
ERNST. That's right, Pawlina. You must try harder to remember things correctly. If you want to eat, you must try much harder. How many at your house last month?
PAWLINA. Five.
ERNST. That's right. And who was the extra person? *(ERNST gives her a small piece of potato on a fork.)*
PAWLINA. My cousin. *(The whip comes down across her face.)*
ERNST. That's not right! *(Calls.)* Guards!
PAWLINA. No! Not that again. No.
ERNST. Are you ready to talk? *(PAWLINA, with the strength of fury, leaps up, grabs fork from plate.)*

PAWLINA. Kill me. Go ahead. But first — *(Takes fork and jabs his eyes. A trace of blood comes.)*
ERNST *(bellows).* GUARDS!!!

(Two guards come running in, KURT and WALDO.)

ERNST *(wiping his face).* Take her to Cell D. *(KURT and WALDO surround a struggling PAWLINA.)*
KURT. Cell D!
WALDO *(to KURT).* Even the rats die in Cell D!
ERNST. Do as you're told!

SCENE FIVE

SCENE: *A German prison cell in Brzezany, Poland, and corridor outside.*

AT RISE: *KURT carries PAWLINA in and tosses her on the floor of the cell. She falls like a sack of potatoes. He looks at her, pokes her. She is motionless. KURT shakes his head, leaves cell and locks it. STANISLAUS enters. He is a temporary guard dressed in the clothes he was picked up in, another Polish "volunteer" for the German labor force (baggy trousers, old sweater, work boots, cap). They nod to each other. In the dim light, KURT opens the window grill of the cell and with a flashlight looks in. He hands STANISLAUS the flashlight to do the same.*

STANISLAUS. She looks half dead. Who is she? *(KURT gives STANISLAUS the key and lights a cigarette.)*
KURT. Just another Pole. Like you, Stanislaus. Like you. Only she wasn't a volunteer. *(Exits laughing.)*

(STANISLAUS walks down the corridor. LIGHTING: Comes up slowly. PAWLINA is now huddled on the floor against a wall, motionless. STANISLAUS enters with a container of soup under an old blanket. He unlocks the cell and enters.)

STANISLAUS. Hello. You sat up. *(PAWLINA doesn't move.)* I brought you some soup. *(There is no response.)* Tomato soup. I heard what you did. They said you were like a wild animal. *(STANISLAUS looks her*

over. She is shivering. Gently, he puts a blanket around her.) You don't look like a wild animal. You look more like my sister's child. May she rest in peace. *(Pause.)* Why are you here anyway?
PAWLINA. I don't know anything. Nothing. *(STANISLAUS lifts her face and looks at it.)*
STANISLAUS. Pigs! Treating our Polish women like that.
PAWLINA. Are you Polish?
STANISLAUS. From the Tatra Mountains. *(PAWLINA gives a little smile.)* That's better. *(Looks at her puffy eyes.)* Can you see all right?
PAWLINA. Yes.
STANISLAUS. Here. Try a little soup.
PAWLINA. I don't know if I can. They beat me...so hard...everywhere.
STANISLAUS. I'll feed you. *(He feeds her a few spoonfuls, which she manages to swallow.)* Can you walk? *(PAWLINA shrugs.)* I was watching you. They threw you in here earlier. You've been asleep for hours. I was afraid you were dead.
PAWLINA. I will be soon.
STANISLAUS. Are you a spy?
PAWLINA. What's a spy? What do they mean? I live on a farm in Halczyna near Zoborow.
STANISLAUS. Zoborow! You're only seventy kilometers away. *(PAWLINA shrugs indifferently. STANISLAUS whispers.)* The Russians will be here any day. They're only a few kilometers away. Are you Jewish?
PAWLINA. No.
STANISLAUS. Then why are you still in jail?
PAWLINA. They came and arrested me. They beat me for nothing. And they left me to die.
STANISLAUS *(thoughtfully)*. I like pigs. We have some on the farm. I keep them inside in the winter. They're friendly. It isn't really fair to call those soldiers "pigs," is it? *(PAWLINA stares at him.)* Bastards! That's what they are. *(Looks at her.)* Say it, and you'll feel better.
PAWLINA. What does it matter?
STANISLAUS. It matters to my pigs! *(Feeds her. PAWLINA tries to smile.)* Here. A little more soup. You've got a sweet smile. Well, it will be, when the swelling goes down. How do you feel?
PAWLINA. I wish I were dead.
STANISLAUS. You're young. You'll get better. *(Pats her shoulder gently.)*
PAWLINA *(groans)*. Ow!
STANISLAUS *(surprised)*. Did I hurt you?

84   *Voices: Plays for Studying the Holocaust*

PAWLINA. Look what those bastards did. Look. *(Shows him her shoulder. The wounds are raw.)* I'll never leave here alive.
STANISLAUS. Oh my God, they beat you that way!
PAWLINA. Tell me what they're going to do to me. Tell me.
STANISLAUS. I'm supposed to guard the prisoners at this end, that's all I know.
PAWLINA *(shrugs)*. I don't care anymore. Just make them do it quickly. Please.
STANISLAUS. Can you stand up? *(He helps PAWLINA up.)*
PAWLINA. Yes.
STANISLAUS. Walk around the cell.
PAWLINA. Why?
STANISLAUS. Do it! *(He walks with her.)*
PAWLINA. What are you going to do? *(Louder.)* What are you going to do to me now?
STANISLAUS. Sh-h. Help you get out of here. But we've got to be quiet. There's a big steel door. You saw it when you came in.
PAWLINA. I don't remember.
STANISLAUS. At the end of the hall. I'll get you there.
PAWLINA. Then what?
STANISLAUS. There's a dozen empty houses near here. Jewish homes once. Stay in one of them until morning. As soon as you hear people going to the fields, go home. Just start walking. Don't look back. *(PAWLINA sinks to the floor wearily.)*
PAWLINA. I can't. I can't even walk across this cell.
STANISLAUS. Yes, you can! You can! Go home, child.

Epilogue

SOUND: *Polish folk music. OTHER ACTORS replace suggestion of Prologue set.*

SCENE: *Mania's living room. The present. The dedication reception is over. The guests have gone. The pastries have been demolished.*

AT RISE: *MANIA, FRIEDZA and PAWLINA sit with their shoes off and their feet up.*

MANIA. Do you remember that first Christmas, when we were down in the bunker?
PAWLINA. How could I forget?
MANIA. There was a storm outside, and the wind was howling.
FRIEDZA. My mother said you couldn't possibly come out.
MANIA. And suddenly you were there with a kerosene lamp. When the light fell on your hair, you looked like an angel, an angel in the night. You pulled out a napkin full of Christmas cookies from your shawl. And for a minute I forgot the cold. I forgot the dark. I forgot to be frightened.
FRIEDZA. Pawlina, weren't you ever scared?
PAWLINA. Are you crazy? Of course I was scared, Friedza. But there was no point in telling you that. My God, when I saw what they'd done to our home...all that way...barefoot...my feet were covered with blisters...and all that was left of our farm was a chicken coop. You could still smell the smoke.
FRIEDZA. When we heard the Russian soldiers singing, Mameh crept out. They were giving all the children chunks of rye bread.
PAWLINA. But when I tried to find Mania, I nearly gave up. I almost walked right past you, Mania, huddled in that doorway.
MANIA. I thought you would never talk to me again. None of you. Pawlina, I didn't mean to get you in trouble. Friedza, I never meant that.
PAWLINA. Sh-h. Sh-h. Mania, tell me the name of my tree again.
MANIA. A flowering crab apple.
PAWLINA. We didn't have those in Zoborow.
FRIEDZA. There's a lot we didn't have in Zoborow.
PAWLINA. But when I was little, it was nice. I remember standing on a stool and helping my mother bake bread. We were so happy then, and we didn't even know it!
FRIEDZA. What would your mother say now if she knew that this afternoon you had a tree planted in your honor for saving Jews?
PAWLINA. She wouldn't believe it. But then she'd probably say, "A guest in the home —" *(MANIA and FRIEDZA join in.)*
ALL. "— is God in the home." *(They laugh, arms around each other and all together say it in Polish.)* Przyjaciel w domu yest bóg w domu.

The End

Synopsis of Scenes

Prologue: Mania's living room. A Chicago suburb. The present.

Act One
Scene One: A field in rural southeast Poland, late May 1942.
Scene Two: Outside Domicela's farmhouse that evening.
Scene Three: The interior of the storage barn that night.
Scene Four: The wooded area near Hanka's farm. Late that night.
Scene Five: Domicela's kitchen. The next day.
Scene Six: The storage barn and bunker late at night. Spring 1942.
Scene Seven: Domicela's kitchen. June 1943.
Scene Eight: The storage barn and bunker late at night. The end of March 1944.

Act Two
Scene One: The storage barn and bunker, May 1944.
Scene Two: The storage barn and bunker, June 1944.
Scene Three: Domicela's kitchen. Dawn. The next day.
Scene Four: An interrogation room in a German prison in Brzezany, July 1944.
Scene Five: A cell in the prison. July 1944.

Epilogue: Mania's living room. A Chicago suburb. The present.

Production Notes

Additional Character Notes

MANIA (in the present): Warm-hearted, gracious, attractively groomed.

MARYSIA PAWLINA (in the present): A determined, handsome woman with snow-white hair.

FRIEDZA (in the present): An elegant, sophisticated career woman.

MARYSIA PAWLINA (in the past): Compassionate, cheerful, resourceful.

DOMICELA: Hardworking, uneducated, proud.

GOLDA: Determined, pragmatic, generous, pretty, petite.

FRIEDZA (in the past): A bright, alert child, suddenly forced to be more adult than her years.

TADEUSZ: Member of the Underground.

MANIA (in the past): Warm, lively, emotional.

BRUNO: Tough, but fonder of beer and women. Homesick.

ERNST: Arrogant, efficient.

STANISLAUS: Fatherly.

Pronunciation Guide for Portion of Pater Noster in Latin

Panem nostrum quotidianum
da nobis hodie et
dimette nobis debita
nostra, sicut et nos
dimittimus debitoribus nostris
Et ne non inducas in

88   Voices: Plays for Studying the Holocaust

tentationem
Sed libera nos a malo.
         Amen.

PAHN-em NOHS-troom quo-ti-dee-AH-num
dah NOH-bis HO-dee-ey eht
dee-MET-tay NOH-bees DEB-ee-ta
NOHS-tra, SEE-koot eht nohs
dee-met-TEE-moos deb-ee-TORH-ee-boos NOHS-trees
eht nay nohn een-DOOK-as een
ten-tats-ee-OHN-em
said LEE-behr-a nohs ah MAHL-oh.
         Ah-MEN.

Pronunciation Guide (continued)

POLISH — Characters

MARYSIA PAWLINA	mah-REESH-a paav-LEEH-na
PANIUSIA SCHACHTEROVA	pan-USH-a shack-ter-OV-a
DOMICELA	dom-eh-TSEL-ah
KRASULA	krah-SU-la
JUREK	YUR-ek
BRONIA	BROHN-ya
HANKA	HAHN-ka
HENRYK	HEN-rick
TADEUSZ	tah-DE-oosh
MANIA	MAHN-ya
REGINA	ray-GHEE-nah
CECYLIA KOZLOWSKI	sa-SEEL-ya koz-LOUSE-ki
STANISLAUS	stahn-EE-swawf

Terms

MAMUSIA	ma-MOO-sha
PANNA	PAHNN-na
ZLOTYS	ZLOT-eez
HERBATNIKI	hehr-BAHT-nik-ee
BEZY	BEH-zay
PIERNIK WYBORNY	PYER-nik-vee-BOR-nee

Places

ZOBOROW	zuh-BORE-ov
HALCZYNA	hahl-ZEEN-ah
BRZEZANY	brehj-JA-nee
TATRA	TAT-ra
TARNOPOL	tar-NOPE-uhl

Expressions

PRZYJACIEL W DOMU	puh-shay-YA-shill ve DO-moo
YEST BÓG W DOMU	yest BOOHG ve DO-moo

YIDDISH — Characters

GOLDA	GOL-dah
FRIEDZA	FRIDJ-ah
MUNDEK	MOON-dek

Terms

MAMEH	MA-meh
TATEH	TA-teh
CHALLAH	KCHAHL-ah

Expressions

A GEZUNT AF DIR	ah-guh-ZUNT-af-deer
OY VAY	oee vaay
MESHUGENAH	muh-SHUG-uh-nah

GERMAN — Characters

BRUNO	BRUN-oh
ERNST	EHRNST
OTTO	OTT-toe
LUTHER	LUTH-er
KURT	COURT
WALDO	VALL-do

Expressions

FRÄULEIN	FROY-line
HEIL	HY-l
LIEBCHEN	LEEP-shin

Teaching Activities

- This activity requires students to couple characters from the play with legitimate reasons for their behavior. After researching conditions for Jews, non-Jews, and soldiers from the occupying armed forces in Poland, each student is to create a brief description that ends with a challenge to classmates to guess his or her identity. An example follows.

  > *Example:* Resistance against the Nazis took many forms. What my daughter did, hiding Jews, was one of them. I was afraid that her actions, however, would endanger our entire family because retaliation for such interventions were often taken against all relatives or even groups of people in a town or area. It wasn't just the perpetrator of the deed who was punished. Who am I? *(Answer)* Domicela, Pawlina's mother.

- In addition to the type of resistance found in this play, there were more than three hundred underground political and military groups in Poland who organized to defeat the German forces. Allocate class time for students, working in groups, to research resistance units in Poland and throughout Europe. Alert them to note how location (camps, ghettos, *etc.*) and political views impacted strategies adopted by these partisan organizations and distinguished them from each other. Findings may be reported orally or in writing.

- Group students in clusters of three, four, or five. Using the dialogue below, prompt each group to complete the story either orally, in writing, or by dramatizing their ideas. What else might they eat? What might they do to curb immediate hunger? Given this beginning dialogue, stories might develop in a number of different directions.

  > *Mania.* Once there was a place where you could eat all you wanted. The table was piled with...chicken...and wild strawberries...
  >
  > *Golda* (joining in). And loaves of fresh-baked *challah*.

Friedza. And black currant jam. (*Pause.*) Mameh, I'm so hungry! (p. 73)

- With pupils standing or sitting in a circle, review some of the things the characters who are in hiding say they miss (i.e., sunshine, fresh air, room to move). Then, play the following as a concentration game, with each student repeating what has come before and then adding what he or she would miss.

    Pupil #1: If I were in hiding, I'd miss playing with my friends.

    Pupil #2: If I were in hiding, I'd miss playing with my friends and sleeping in my own bed.

    Pupil #3: If I were in hiding, I'd miss playing with my friends, sleeping in my own bed, and having lots of pastries to eat.

- Carefully review the script with the class to insure understanding of character motivations. Then, with partners, ask classmates to improvise the following scenarios. Their responses should be firmly grounded in character and context.

    Scenario #1:
    Who: Golda and Pawlina
    What: Golda wants Pawlina to hide her and her children in the barn. Pawlina wants to help but her mother has forbidden it.
    Where: The storage barn

    Scenario #2:
    Who: Friedza, Hanka, and Henryk
    What: Friedza wants her mother's possessions returned to her. Hanka and Henryk want to capture Friedza and gain a reward for turning in a Jew.
    Where: Hanka's and Henryk's home.

    Next, using this same Who, What, and Where format, invite students to construct and dramatize improvisations based upon the events in this play.

- Assign students to research the life of Marysia Pawlina Szul. Next, pair them and cast one as a reporter and the other as Pawlina.

Engage them in creating an "on air" interview for a classroom radio or television program during which they reveal reasons why Pawlina acted as she did to save lives. Use audiotape or videotape and record the exchange. The interview can be set either at the end of World War II or immediately following the tree planting ceremony in which Righteous Persons were honored. Please note that this activity can be repeated for other Righteous Persons that the class might study.

- In Act II of the play, Mania is costumed as a Polish country girl, wearing a "blouse, long skirt, apron, bare feet, hair in long braids around her head" (p. 76). Stanislaus, a Pole doing forced labor, is costumed in "Baggy trousers, old sweater, work boots, cap" (p. 82). Designate one school day as costume day and invite students to construct similar outfits that, on the appointed day, they wear to school.

- Dr. Jan Karski, Wladyslaw Bartoszewski, and the Cardinal Archbishop of Lwów were Poles who have been honored as Righteous Persons. Study the deeds that have earned them this designation. Noting these activities as well as those of ordinary Poles like Marysia Pawlina Szul, identify strategies used by Christian Poles to save Jews.

- Read the interviews in *Rescuers: Portraits of Moral Courage in the Holocaust* by Gay Block and Malka Drucker. As a class, discuss how these rescuers exemplify the concept that one person can make a difference, even when the odds seem insurmountable.

- Compile an annotated bibliography of books about rescuers. Give students opportunities to examine and to report on the books in this collection. Which do they find most interesting and why? This project can be repeated for other topics, such as the Holocaust in Poland.

- In class, view the film *The Other Side of Faith* and compare this story to *Angel in the Night*.

- In this play, Mania describes how she escaped from the Nazis. Invite students to imagine that they are this character and to pantomime the following actions.

    You wake up early and, sensing something is wrong, look out your window and see many, many soldiers.

    You crawl through a secret hole in your attic.

    You lay flat and crawl along the roof gutters.

    You reach the ground, master your fear, look all around you for soldiers and seeing none, run away into the country.

After students have participated in this pantomime, ask them how they felt as Mania. Encourage them to change other episodes in the play into pantomime sentences and to dramatize them.

Chapter 3

Plays and Activities: Intermediate Study

Kindertransport

The Playwright: Diane Samuels

Diane Samuels has authored a number of plays for young audiences. *Frankie's Monster* and *Chalk Circle*, both staged at the Unicorn Theatre, were named as best plays by *Time Out* magazine in 1991. *The Bonekeeper*, produced at the Tricycle Youth Theatre, was short-listed for the W.H. Smith Awards for Children in 1992. Written with Sara Milne and associates of the Homerton Youth Theatre for the Lloydes Bank Young Theatre Challenge, *The Life and Death of Bessie Smith* was performed at the Royal National Theatre. The one-act play, *Watch Out For Mister Stork*, has been staged by or associated with the Soho Theatre Company Writers' Festival, the Finborough Theatre, and the Regents Park Open Air Theatre. National touring productions of Samuels' plays include the Theatre Center's staging of *Turncoat* and the Quicksilver Theatre Company's performances of *One Hundred Million Footsteps*. In

1995, SNAP People's Trust produced her script, *How to Beat a Giant*. Appealing specifically to eight- to thirteen-year-old audience members, Samuels also has written *Forever and Ever*, a piece about divorce. BBC radio has aired the playwright's works, *Frankie's Monster*, *two together*, *Watch Out For Mister Stork*, *Swine*, *Hardly Cinderella*, and *Doctor Y*. She also develops material for the Aroyal National Theatre.

Prior to devoting her full attention to her writing career, Diane Samuels taught in London's inner city secondary schools for five years. Her education included studies in history at Cambridge and training as a drama teacher at Goldsmiths' College in London. She has written for the stage and for BBC radio and now maintains an active schedule as a dramatist. Born in Liverpool, England, in 1960, Samuels currently resides in London with her husband Simon Garfield and their two sons, BJ and Jake.

The Play

Through the protagonist, Eva the child and later Evelyn the adult, past and present come together. This play places family dynamics, personal history and identity, and Holocaust survival within the context of a life saved through the Kindertransport program. The central character, Eva Schlesinger, was nine years old when she was put aboard one of these trains in 1938 carrying only a few valuable possessions. So that she might escape the horrors of Nazi Germany, she was sent away from her own family to live among strangers in a new country. As an adult, her own daughter's questions force her past and the life she has forged in England to collide.

Three specific incidences inspired playwright Samuels to write *Kindertransport*: (1) in talking with a friend whose father had been on a Kindertransport, she was struck by how strongly the guilt of survival had passed from parent to child; (2) another friend's ignorance that her mother had been at Auschwitz until, at her father's funeral, the friend overheard her mother's revelation; and (3) the televised admission by an adult who had been rescued through the Kindertransport program that, although she had survived and her parents had died, she harbored strong feelings of rage toward them for sending her away. Samuels interviewed those who had been Kinderchildren and incorporated their personal experiences into this script.

Kindertransport opened at the Cockpit Theatre in London on April 13, 1993, when it was performed by the Soho Theatre Company. The play first was staged in the United States by the Manhattan Theatre Club at City Center, Stage 1. This New York production opened in May 1994. The play, winner of the 1993 Meyer-Whitworth Award and Co-Winner of the Verity Bargate Award For New Plays, has been performed regularly at a number of theatres, including the Vaudeville Theatre in London and The Market Theatre in Johannesburg. Such diverse venues as the Apple Tree Theatre in Chicago, the University of Wisconsin-Parkside, Appalachian State University, AXIS Theatre in Baltimore, and The New Gate Theatre in Providence have been sites of American performances.

Information about the Play and the Holocaust

Children, because they were seen as capable of producing future generations, were a threat to the Third Reich. As tentacles of Nazi destruction spread throughout Europe, children were ensnared and imprisoned or killed. Within hours of arriving at Auschwitz, for example, children were gassed. Mothers with their small offspring and pregnant women met the same fate. In all, some 1.5 million children died during the Holocaust. The Kindertransport endeavor saved nearly 10,000 youngsters from being added to this number.

Started by Dutch social worker Gertrude Wijsmuller-Meyer, The World Movement for the Care of Children from Germany arranged for the placement of German-Jewish children in British homes. Using names sent by local Jewish refugee committees throughout Germany, this organization maintained a list, bearing descriptions and photographs, of Jewish children in need of safe havens abroad. Only England had responded to a worldwide appeal in 1938 to save endangered children from the horrors of the Holocaust and the British people, rather than their government, had collected funds necessary for the rescue. Travel permits for the children were arranged through the British Home Office and negotiated with German police. Passports were altered so that males bore the name Jacob and females bore the name Sarah. All of these passports were stamped with the letter J for Jew. Although some of the Kinderchildren were placed with relatives or friends, most were "non-guaranteed" and required direct sponsorship from the relief organization.

Special Kindertransport trains took girls and boys ranging in age from four to sixteen across the continent where they then were boarded onto boats for Britain, America, or Paraguay. The first such transport for Britain arrived in Harwich on December 2, 1938. The rescue program ended on September 2, 1939, with the outbreak of war between Britain and Germany. Some 700 children, at one period of time, were making their way into Britain each week through this operation. Of the 9,254 children entering the country in this way, 7,482 were Jewish.

Personal accounts by Holocaust survivors rescued through this endeavor reveal that the conditions the children encountered on their journey affected them physically and emotionally. They were leaving a terrifying situation at home, but also leaving the security of parents and other loved ones. These little refugees brought few belongings with them, often carrying possessions in paper bags or a small suitcase. To insure that they were physically ready to pass the medical inspection given upon arrival in England, they were first sent to an internment camp for delousing. They were taught happy songs that often hid their true feelings.

After crossing the sea, the children encountered still more new and varied experiences. Some, upon arrival, were issued gas masks to wear or given hard-boiled eggs and sandwiches to eat. Some recall being taken to an elegant hotel for housing and engaging in seemingly normal activities while others remember being sent to a camp and receiving two blankets, a wash bowl, and sleeping in a cold hut. Some children became ill. Some were examined by adults for possible adoption, even if their own parents were still living. Some would find that, after having lived abroad, they could not communicate with their parents if they were reunited because they no longer shared a common language. Over 80 percent of these Kinderchildren, however, never saw their parents again.

Assistance given to the children by adults, themselves concerned with the war effort, was uneven. Kindertransport children have memories of conflicting personal realities such as being given birthday presents but not having a sense of belonging. Some tell of being sent to school but left to learn English on their own. In addition to being forced to move residencies several times, Kinderchildren found that schools were equally temporary. Because of the war, classrooms were set up in improvised locations. Retired teachers returned as instructors because younger ones were in the service. For these youngsters, adjusting to families and to school in their strange new country was sometimes fraught with difficulties.

Both scholarly evidence and individual accounts confirm that some of the children who were rescued in this way were able to overcome their fears and feelings of confusion and to adapt wholeheartedly to their new lives. For others, the negative psychological effects of their relocation resulted in distrust, a preference for self-reliance, and a habit of limiting self-disclosure that lasted a lifetime. Approximately 2,500 of those rescued and brought to Great Britain left there for North American destinations after World War II.

As a group, Kinderchildren share a special bond that, for some, has lasted beyond childhood and the war years. There are those, for example, who as adults remain in communication with each other through a newsletter and reunions designed to bring them information and fellowship. In Israel, there is a special Kinderforest. Still, by necessity, the journeys of those youngsters transported from Germany by train and boat to survival and freedom in England were uniquely personal.

Synopsis of Act One, scene one

The opening scene of the play faithfully chronicles the journey taken by those youngsters who left Germany aboard a Kindertransport. Using juxtaposition, the scene introduces Eva, the child, as she prepares to leave her mother and Germany and the adult Eva, now Evelyn, as her own daughter prepares to leave home. Eva is seen boarding the Kindertransport and riding the train to freedom outside of Germany, at sea, and arriving at Harwich where her new life will begin. Years later, Evelyn and her daughter, Faith, sort through boxes stored in an attic. Faith's discovery of the book and mouth organ so important to her mother as a child sets in motion the unleashing of tangled feelings and an exhumation of the past.

Kindertransport

TIME AND PLACE: The play takes place in a spare storage room in Evelyn's house in an outer London suburb in recent times.

LIST OF CHARACTERS:
EVELYN: An English middle-class woman. In her fifties.
FAITH: Evelyn's only child. In her early twenties.
EVA: Evelyn's younger self. She starts the play at nine years old and finishes it at seventeen years old. A Jewish German becoming increasingly English.
HELGA: A German-Jewish woman of the late 1930s. In her early thirties. Eva/Evelyn's mother.
LIL: Eva/Evelyn's English foster mother. In her eighties.
THE RATCATCHER: A mythical character who also plays the Nazi Border Official, the English Organizer, the Postman, the Station Guard.

Act One
scene one

(*Pipe music.*

Dusty storage room filled with crates, bags, boxes and some old furniture.

EVA, *dressed in clothes of the late thirties, is sitting on the floor, reading. The book is a large, hard-backed children's storybook entitled* Der Rattenfänger.
HELGA *enters. She is well turned out in clothes of the late thirties. She is holding a coat, a button, a needle and some thread.*)

EVA. What's an abyss, Mutti?
HELGA (*sitting down and ushering* EVA *to sit next to her*). An abyss is a deep and terrible chasm.
EVA. What's a chasm?

HELGA. A huge gash in the rocks.
EVA. What's a ...

(EVA *puts down the book. Pipe music stops.*)

HELGA. Eva, sew on your buttons now. Show me that you can do it.
EVA. I can't get the thread through the needle. It's too thick. You do it.
HELGA. Lick the thread...
EVA. Do I have to?
HELGA. Yes. Lick the thread.
EVA. I don't want to sew.
HELGA. How else will the button get onto the coat?
EVA. The coat's too big for me.
HELGA. It's to last next winter, too.
EVA. Please.
HELGA. No.
EVA. Why won't you help me?
HELGA. You have to be able to manage on your own.
EVA. Why?
HELGA. Because you do. Now, lick the thread.

(EVA *licks the thread.*)

That should flatten it...and hold the needle firmly and place the end of the thread between your fingers...not too near...that's it...now try to push it through.

(EVA *concentrates on the needle and thread.* HELGA *watches closely.*)

See. You don't need me. It's good.
EVA. I don't mind having my coat open a bit. Really. I've got enough buttons.
HELGA. You'll miss it when the wind blows.
EVA. Can't I do it later?
HELGA. There's no "later" left, Eva.
EVA. After the packing, after my story...
HELGA. Now.

(EVA *gives in and sews.*

Footsteps. The key jangles in the door lock. It unlocks. The door opens. EVELYN *and* FAITH *enter.* EVELYN *is carrying a tea towel. They are not aware of* EVA *and* HELGA*'s presence.* EVA *and* HELGA *are not aware of theirs.* EVELYN *looks through the boxes.)*

EVELYN. Most of it's junk.
FAITH. You don't keep junk.
EVELYN. Do you want anything in particular?
FAITH. Not really.
EVELYN *(opening a box)*. Pans?
FAITH. All those?
EVELYN. Are you intending to cook or eat raw?
FAITH. I was thinking of take-out...
EVELYN. Have them.

(EVELYN *hands the box over to* FAITH *who receives it.)*

EVELYN. What else? Pans, lights, crockery, cutlery? I've got a television somewhere...
FAITH. You sound like a shop assistant trying to make a sale.
EVELYN. Just don't be a difficult customer.
FAITH. I wasn't going to be.
EVELYN. Good. I told Mum we wouldn't be long.

(EVELYN *opens a box and takes out a teacup.)*

EVELYN. Would cups and saucers be of any use?
FAITH. I prefer mugs.
EVELYN. What about for visitors?
FAITH. They can have mugs, too.
EVELYN. I'll give you this set of cups and saucers just in case.
FAITH. Mum, I...
EVELYN. Here's a spare teapot, too.
FAITH. I don't really want two teapots.
EVELYN. One might break.
FAITH *(handing the spare one back)*. Just keep it.
EVELYN. Must you be so ungrateful?
FAITH. You don't have to do this.
EVELYN. Who else is going to?

FAITH. Dad sent me another check.
EVELYN. Would you use a strainer?
FAITH. Not really.
EVELYN. I'm sure his money will come in very useful if you save it.
FAITH. I really wouldn't mind buying my own stuff.
EVELYN. You usually approve of my taste.
FAITH. It's not that.
EVELYN. I'm glad to hear it.
FAITH (*inspecting the crockery*). You should keep your things.
EVELYN. I don't think I need them as much as you do, darling.
FAITH. You might one day.
EVELYN. They shouldn't be left to molder in a box when they can be used.

(EVELYN *opens a box and takes out a glass. She polishes it.*)

Glasses?
FAITH. Those must be worth a fortune.
EVELYN. Nothing is too good for my daughter.
FAITH. Might be too good for the flat.
EVELYN. You said you were very pleased with this one.
FAITH. The rent's so high for what it is.
EVELYN (*polishing*). You said it was worth it.
FAITH. Maybe you should have come to see it.
EVELYN. You're quite capable of choosing a flat without my help. You have your friends to advise you.
FAITH. I think they want different things from me.
EVELYN. Isn't it a little late to realize that?
FAITH. Maybe it's not such a good idea to move.

(EVELYN *concentrates on polishing and replacing glasses.*)

I don't feel right about it.

(EVELYN *continues to polish. Pause.*)

EVELYN (*scrutinizing a glass*). This is chipped.
FAITH. What do you think about waiting till I can afford to buy somewhere?
EVELYN. I think that if you say you're going, you should go.

FAITH. I can get the deposit back.
EVELYN. Like you got the deposit back last time?
FAITH. That was different.
EVELYN. It sounds remarkably similar to me.
FAITH. I'm not sure I like it at all, really.
EVELYN. Oh Faith, for heavens' sake. You're impossible.
FAITH. I wish you'd come and see it.
EVELYN (*polishing madly*). How on earth did that glass get damaged? I put in enough paper.
FAITH. Are you angry with me?
EVELYN. Absolutely not.
FAITH. Are we still friends?
EVELYN. Of course. (*She polishes.*)
FAITH. I don't want to go.
EVELYN (*still polishing*). Will eleven glasses be enough?
FAITH. You can forget about the glasses.
EVELYN. You'll need something to drink from in your new home.

(EVELYN *continues to polish.* FAITH, *helpless, watches.*)

EVA (*sewing*). Why aren't Carla and Heinrich going on one of the trains?
HELGA. Their parents couldn't get them places.
EVA. Carla said it's because they didn't want to send them away.
HELGA. Carla says a lot of silly things.
EVA. Why's that silly?
HELGA. Of course they would send them away if they had places. Any good parent would do that.
EVA. Why?
HELGA. Because any good parent would want to protect their child.
EVA. Can't you and Vati protect me?
HELGA. Only by sending you away.
EVA. Why will I be safer with strangers?
HELGA. Your English family will be kind.
EVA. But they don't know me.
HELGA. Eva. This is for the best.
EVA. Will you miss me?
HELGA. Of course, I will.
EVA. Will you write to me?
HELGA. I've told you. I will do more than miss you and write to you. Vati and I will come. We will not let you leave us behind for very

long. Do you think we would really let you go if we thought that we would never see you again?
EVA. How long will it be before you come?
HELGA. Only a month or two. When the silly permits are ready.
EVA. Silly permits.
HELGA. Silly, silly permits.
EVA. The needle's stuck.

(HELGA, *with difficulty, pulls the needle through.*)

Finish it off for me.
HELGA (*handing the sewing back to* EVA). No.

(EVA *takes it and carries on sewing.*
EVELYN *is still polishing glasses.* FAITH *is still watching her.*)

FAITH. Mum, please stop doing that.
EVELYN (*holding up the glass*). They really need washing.
FAITH. I'm not doing this to muck you around.
EVELYN. You can't stay here forever.
FAITH. Do you really want me to go?
EVELYN. What I want is irrelevant. It is your life, Faith.
FAITH. It affects you, too.
EVELYN. You've made a commitment to moving into that place. Stick by it.
FAITH. It feels all wrong.
EVELYN. It seems perfectly straightforward to me.
FAITH. What do you want?
EVELYN. I want you to make a mature and reliable decision. An adult decision. This continual vacillation is not helpful to either of us.
FAITH. I don't want to move out yet.

(EVELYN *stops polishing.*)

EVELYN. Yet?
FAITH. For a while.
EVELYN. What does that mean?
FAITH. Until after I've finished college.
EVELYN. Are you absolutely sure about this?
FAITH. Yes. I definitely won't move out.

EVELYN. So, I don't need to sell the house.
FAITH. No.
EVELYN. I can phone the estate agent?
FAITH. Yes.
EVELYN. And say no?
FAITH. Yes.
EVELYN. You won't change your mind again?
FAITH. I don't understand why you have to sell the house if I leave...
EVELYN. Will you or will you not change your mind?
FAITH. No.
EVELYN. Song and dance finally over?
FAITH. Yes.

(EVELYN *puts back the glass and closes the box.*)

EVELYN. I expect you to keep to your word. (*She picks up the chipped glass.*)
FAITH. Why are you taking that?
EVELYN. A chipped glass is ruined forever.

(EVELYN *exits.* FAITH *retreats back into the attic.*)

HELGA. Try to meet other Jews in England.
EVA. I will.
HELGA. They don't mind Jews there. It's like it was here when I was younger. It'll be good.
EVA. When you come, will Vati get his proper job back like he used to have?
HELGA. I'm sure he will.
EVA (*finishes sewing*). Finished.
HELGA. Now, let me check the case.
EVA. I packed what you said. It's very full.

(HELGA *picks up a case hidden among the boxes and opens and checks through it.* EVA *watches her.*
FAITH *finds a trunk. She is tempted to look inside. She hesitates. She takes courage and tentatively opens it.*)

HELGA (*pulling out a dress*). This suits you so well.
EVA. I'll only wear it for best. Promise.

HELGA (*refolding the dress*). Someone will have to press out the creases when you get there.
FAITH (*pulling out a toy train*). Runaway train?
EVA. Did I fold it wrongly?
HELGA. No. The case is far too small.

> (FAITH *makes the sound of a train whistle as she pulls pieces of train track out of the box. She starts to lay them out on the floor.*)

FAITH. Runaway train went down the track
And she blew, she blew
Runaway train went down the track
And she blew, she blew
Runaway train went down the track
And blah de blah, she won't come back
and she blew, blew, blew, blew
Blew!

> (FAITH *continues to lay the track.*
> HELGA *pulls a mouth organ out of the case.*)

HELGA. What is this doing in here?
EVA. That's my mouth organ.
HELGA. You're not allowed to take anything other than clothes.
EVA. But it was my last birthday present and I'm just beginning to get the tunes right.
HELGA. The border guards will send you back to us if they find you with this. Then where will you be?
EVA. I'm sorry.

> (HELGA *gives the mouth organ to* EVA *and sets to reorganizing the case contents.*
> FAITH *looks into another box. She turns it upside down. A load of dolls falls onto the floor. None of them has any clothes on.* FAITH *picks up a doll.*)

FAITH. Lucy? (*She gently sits Lucy by the train set. She picks out another doll.*) Gloria. (*She gently sits Gloria next to Lucy and then does the same with each of the other dolls.*)

HELGA. There's no room for anything else. Where are your shoes?

(EVA *reaches over to right by* FAITH's *feet and gets a pair of shoes.*)

FAITH (*laying out another doll*). Barbara. (*She continues to lay out the dolls.*)
EVA. Here.
HELGA. Put the heel of the right shoe to your ear.
EVA. Why?
HELGA. Do it.

(EVA *puts the heel to her ear.*)

What can you hear?
EVA. It sounds like...
HELGA. Yes?
EVA. Ticking.
HELGA. My gold watch is in there.
EVA. How?
HELGA. The cobbler did it.
EVA. I'll look after it for you.
HELGA. And in the other heel are two rings, a chain with a Star of David and a charm bracelet for you. All made of gold.
EVA. For me?
HELGA. From my jewelry box. A traveling gift.
EVA. Thank you.
HELGA. My grandfather used to wear a black hat and coat. "You are my children. You are my jewels," he told me. "We old ones invest our future in you."

(EVA *hugs* HELGA.
LIL *enters.*)

LIL. You two have the quietest arguments.
FAITH. Is she not pleased?
LIL. So so.
FAITH. You think it's better if I stay, don't you?
LIL. I'm keeping out of it.
FAITH. Sorry, Gran.

LIL. What for?
FAITH. Spoiling the start of your visit.
LIL. I've seen worse.
FAITH. Where is she now?
LIL. Cleaning the windows.
FAITH. I said I'd definitely stay.
LIL. She's begun in the sitting room.
FAITH. The cleaner came in yesterday.
LIL. She's even got the stepladder out.
FAITH. What about the pink overall?
LIL. Oh, yes.
FAITH. Oh God.
LIL. She'll sparkle the glass and then it'll be done.
FAITH. It wasn't that bad.
LIL. Leave her to it.
FAITH. She's not talking either, is she?
LIL. Lock jaw's set in.
FAITH. Don't you just love it?
LIL. Coming down?
FAITH (*looking at the toys*). I found some of my old things. I'd no idea she'd kept them.
LIL. You've made a mess, haven't you?
FAITH. Just laying them out.
LIL. You'll make your mum even worse.
FAITH. What's wrong with looking at my old toys?
LIL. Is she cleaning her guts out downstairs for you to wreak havoc in her precious attic?
FAITH. Gran, there's no harm meant.
LIL. There's harm caused.
FAITH. I'll pack them up before she comes in here again.
LIL. You're trying to set her off on purpose, aren't you?
FAITH. No.
LIL. Well, stop being soft and put them away now.
FAITH. Why is it that I can't do a simple, ordinary thing without getting it in the neck?
LIL. Since when have you done things simply where she's concerned?
FAITH. Believe me, I hate it when she gets like this.
LIL. You could do a much better job of keeping her sweet then.
FAITH. Story of my life.
LIL. Just get this lot boxed and neaten up the room. I'll do tea.

(LIL *exits.* FAITH *reluctantly starts to put the dolls back into the box.*
HELGA *and* EVA *break their embrace.*)

EVA. Listen.
HELGA. What?
EVA. I've nearly got it right.

(EVA *starts to play a tune on the mouth organ. She plays well.* EVA *finishes playing.* HELGA *applauds.* FAITH *pulls out a small box. She opens it and looks inside.*)

HELGA. Now it's time for bed.
EVA. Not yet. Let me stay up. It's my last night.
HELGA. We will carry on as we always do. Bedtime is bedtime.
EVA (*moaning*). Mutti.
HELGA. Which story do you want?

(HELGA *turns and picks up* EVA's Rattenfänger *book.* EVA *quickly sneaks her mouth organ into the case and closes it.*)

EVA. *The Ratcatcher.*

(FAITH *pulls out a hard-backed children's storybook identical to the one* HELGA *is holding. Pipe music.*)

FAITH. *Der Rattenfänger.*
HELGA. Not that one, Eva.
EVA. You said I could choose.
HELGA. Choose something else.
EVA. I don't want anything else.

(HELGA *opens the book and turns its pages.* EVA *draws away from her, puts on her coat and hat and picks up the case.*)

FAITH. *The Ratcatcher?*
EVA. What did you say an abyss was, Mutti?
HELGA. I hope you won't ask questions like this when you're in England.
EVA. Why not?

HELGA. Listen.

(FAITH *opens the book and flicks through it. She finds an inscription in the front of the book.*
EVA *sits close to* HELGA.)

"Beware little children. Take heed and learn the lesson of Hamlyn where one bad soul brought tragedy upon the whole town."
FAITH. "Hamburg. 1939."
HELGA. "Happy Hamlyn after the rats had been led away...

(FAITH *carefully looks at the first page.*)

...A town teeming with life. Full to overflowing. And every day, the good people counted their blessings. Every single one."...Eva?
EVA. I'm listening.
FAITH (*looking at a picture*). Counting their blessings for being so lucky...
HELGA. "They all knew how fortunate they were. All except for one very wicked soul who was ungrateful and did not count."
FAITH (*looking at another picture*). Mr. Ingratitude. Jesus.
HELGA. "We are forgotten. We are lost..."
EVA. "...We are destroyed..."
HELGA. "...cried out all the uncounted blessings."
FAITH. The cloud...
HELGA. "Then a cloud appeared in the clear, blue sky casting a shadow down below."
EVA. "Who is not counting?"
HELGA. "Whispered the shadow."
EVA. "Who has forgotten their blessings?"
HELGA. "It hissed."
EVA. "I will find you."
HELGA. "It spat."
EVA. "I will search you out whoever, wherever you are."
FAITH (*turning onto another page*). My God, and the shadow growing legs...
HELGA. ...and strong arms and spiky nails...
EVA. And eyes sharp as razors.
FAITH. The Ratcatcher.

(*The shadow of the* RATCATCHER *hovers.*
A train whistle blows. Sounds of a busy railway station.
HELGA *remains stuck in bedtime story mode.* EVA *puts on her coat and hat and label with her number on it — 3362.*)

HELGA. The Ratcatcher searched for the ungrateful one. He searched and searched but all in vain.
RATCATCHER. Who is to pay for the lost blessings?
HELGA. He raged.
RATCATCHER. If not the one guilty soul, then all.
HELGA. And he raised an enchanted pipe to his snarling lip, making a cruel promise to all the people of Hamlyn.
RATCATCHER. I will take the heart of your happiness away.

(*The* RATCATCHER *plays his music.*
The sounds of the railway station become louder and louder.
Another train whistle.)

EVA. Mutti! Vati! Hello! Hello! See. I did get into the carriage. I said I would. See, I'm not crying. I said I wouldn't. I can't open the window! It's sealed tight! Why've you taken your gloves off? You're knocking too hard. Your knuckles are going red! What? I can't hear you!

(*Sound of long, shrill train whistle.*)

Louder! Louder! What? I can't hear! I can't...See you in England.

(*Sounds of train starting to move.* EVA *sits.*)

I mustn't stare at that cross-eyed boy.

(*Train whistle blows.*)

What if he talks to me?

(*Sounds of children chattering. Suddenly a young child cries and cries.*)

You mustn't cry. There's no point.

(*The crying continues.*)

Stop it.

(*The crying continues.*)

We'll all see our muttis and vatis soon enough.

(*The crying calms slightly.*)

And don't look at that cross-eyed boy.

(*The crying continues.*)

Hoppe, hoppe reiter
Wenn er fellt dann schreit er
Fellt er in den graben
Fressen ihn die raben
Fellt er in den sumpf
Macht der reiter plumpf.

(Hop hop hop hop rider
Do not fall beside her
If into the ditch you fall
The Ratman gets you all
And don't have the desire
To fall into the mire.)

(*The crying calms. Sounds of children laughing.*)

(*Announcing to all around her.*) Did any of you know? In England, all the men have pipes and look like Sherlock Holmes and everyone has a dog.

(*Enter a Nazi border* OFFICER. *He approaches* EVA. FAITH *watches.*)

OFFICER. No councillor in here?
EVA. She's in the next carriage.
OFFICER (*picking up* EVA*'s case*). Whose case is this?

EVA. Mine.
OFFICER. Stand up straight.

(EVA *stands.*)

Turn your label around then. It's gone the wrong way. Can't see your number.
EVA (*turning the label round. Quietly*). Sorry.
OFFICER. Speak up.
EVA. Sorry.
OFFICER. Sir! Sorry, Sir.
EVA. Sorry, Sir.
OFFICER. No one will know what to do with you if they can't see your number.

(*Silence.*)

Will they?
EVA. No, Sir.
OFFICER. Might have to remove you from the train.

(*Silence.*)

Mightn't we?
EVA. Yes, Sir.
OFFICER. D'you know it at least?
EVA. Pardon, Sir?
OFFICER. Know your number. If you don't know it, you might forget who you are.
EVA. 3362, Sir.
OFFICER (*taking out a pen*). Don't want you to forget who you are now, do we?
EVA. No, Sir.
OFFICER. Let me remind you.

(*He draws a huge Star of David on the label.*)

There. That should tell 'em wherever it is you're going. Best to keep them informed, eh?
EVA (*terrified*). Yes, Sir.

(OFFICER *opens and searches the case, throwing everything onto the floor. He finds the mouth organ.*)

OFFICER. You can't take valuables out of the country. Can't take anything for gain.
EVA. I wouldn't sell it, Sir.
OFFICER. What's it for then?
EVA. For music, Sir. I play it, Sir.
OFFICER. You any good?
EVA. I suppose so...
OFFICER. Go on then. Prove it's not just to make money.

(EVA *takes it and plays nervously, badly.*)

You need more practice. Better keep it. (*He body-searches* EVA.) What money have you got? (*He digs into* EVA*'s pockets and takes out a few coins, which he takes and pockets.*)

Better clean up the mess.

(EVA *starts to clean up.* OFFICER *feels in a pocket and produces a toffee.*)

OFFICER (*giving the toffee to* EVA). Here kiddie. A sweetie for you.

(OFFICER *ruffles* EVA*'s hair and exits.* EVA *grips the toffee tightly and tidies up the clothes into the case.*)
(*Sounds of a train speeding along. Children's excited chatter. In German,* "The border, the border, the border.")

EVA. It is the border! The border! Can't get us now! We're out! Out! Stuff your stupid Hitler. Stuff your stupid toffees! (*She throws down the toffee.*) Keep them! Hope your eyes fall out and you die the worst death on earth! Hope you all rot in hell forever and ever! Hope no one buries you! Hope the rats come and eat up all your remains until there's nothing left!

(*Sounds of a train stopping. Sounds of a buzzing, busy, happy crowd at a railway station. A voice saying in Dutch,* "Have as many sweets and as much lemonade as you want.")

(*greedily eating and drinking*) You know what? That Dutch lady said we can have as many cakes as we want. And sweets. And lemonade. I'm going to stuff my pockets for later. Who says it's naughty? They all want us to be happy, don't they? Well, that's what I'm doing. Making myself happy.

(*Sounds of a ship's horn and the lapping of waves. Tired, muted children's chatter.*)

You know what? If you lick your lips you'll taste the salt. Sea salt. What d'you mean, Hook of Holland? It can't be. It's nothing like one. It isn't. Look at it. How's that a hook? (*Coughing.*) Excuse me...(*About to vomit.*)...it won't come...No, I'm fine...Really...It's just nothing...Nothing will come out of me.

(*Sounds of a ship's horn.*)

This is Harwich, you know. It really is England.

(*Sounds of disembarkation. Children's chatter and adult English voices,* "Come along now," "Keep moving," "Move to the right, please.")

Can you just go through like that? Don't they search you?

(EVA *stops and bends down suddenly.*)

(*picking up one penny*) A penny. They have big money here. It must be a sign of good luck.

(EVA *pockets the penny.*
RATCATCHER's *music.*)

HELGA. In the piper's wake they skipped. All the children up the mountain, on and on till...crash. With a roar the rock opened, the music stopped, and the children disappeared into the abyss.
FAITH (*reading in German*). "Drumless Street."
HELGA. And the weeping people renamed the street where the children had last been seen, "Drumless Street." A hollow highway where music was forbidden. Then chisel and hammer battered into the

walls of Hamlyn the tragic tale of the lost kinder who left in the summer of 1284 and were never seen thereafter.

(FAITH *starts to play a discordant tune on the mouth organ.*)

(*Blackout.*)

Teaching Activities

- Acquaint students with *Kristallnacht*, a pogrom resulting in thirty thousand Jews being sent to concentration camps, countless others slain or beaten, and Jewish property destroyed. Also share information about the Movement for the Care of Children from Germany, an organization formed as a result of *Kristallnacht* that brought children to safer locations outside of Germany. Ask the students to imagine that each is a Jewish child in Germany and to describe his or her life experiences from November 9 and 10, 1938 (*Kristallnacht*), to December 10, 1938, when children were put on the first Kindertransport. For this assignment, students should research Jewish life in Germany in 1938, keep a diary for the child he or she is to portray and, as the character, write a personal narrative and orally share it with the class.

- For a nine-month period during 1938-39, Kindertransports brought children to safety. Often those put on the trains were separated from parents and other family forever, left with few if any possessions, or found themselves unable to rebuild relationships with family once reunited. Ask the students to respond to the following questions:

    If you were aboard a Kindertransport, what would be your thoughts and feelings as the train left Germany?

    Knowing that you could only take one suitcase with you, what possessions would you take? Why would you select these? What is their significance?

    In this play, Eva takes a mouth organ, two gold rings, a charm bracelet, and a Star of David with her as reminders of her life in Germany. If you had to select one object to take to a new home in a foreign land, what would it be and what would it signify for you?

- Some survivors lost the kind of family history that photographs or similar possessions record. Ask pupils to imagine that they have no photographs or similar family records. How would they describe the significant people in their lives to others? Ask each person to make an audiotape as a segment for an imaginary radio program.

Title the segment, "Descriptions of My Family." Descriptions should not be limited to physical characteristics but should include memories of special events and other personal recollections.

- Before students arrive for class, restrict certain areas of the classroom and display appropriate signage. Some seats, for example, may bear signs restricting any student wearing blue clothing from sitting there. A pencil sharpener may be designated for use only by students with brown eyes. Enforce these restrictions for a portion of the class period. A few students may be assigned to serve as monitors. Other students may be offered rewards for reporting violations. In the remaining class time, hold an open forum in which all students have an opportunity to share feelings and to question reasons for certain behaviors and attitudes evidenced during the activity. Guide the discussion toward recognition of parallel discriminatory experiences for European Jews. Next, ask students to imagine that they are Jewish parents living in Germany in 1938 and to weigh the feelings such discriminatory practices might engender against the emotional bonds linking parents and children. How might conflicting emotions influence decision-making for or against putting children on a Kindertransport?

- An open-ended story is one in which a beginning is provided but students then must complete the story. Common practice is to complete the story either in writing, orally with three to five contributors, or through dramatization. A properly written open-ended story beginning can be shared many times and completed with always differing results. Use the following open-ended story starter with students. Any of the three techniques described above can be used to complete it.

    > I am Eva. Because of the political situation in Germany, I am on a Kindertransport bound for England. Although I am only nine years old, I am traveling without any other family members. As the train carries me toward my new life, I...

- As a class, coordinate the reading of this play with the study of German efforts to isolate and ultimately eliminate the Jewish population. Identify political, cultural, and social measures, including laws and propaganda, designed to adversely impact Jewish life. Whenever possible, include visual and auditory examples from sources such as songs, films, posters, newspapers, legal documents, and radio broadcasts. Next, have students form teams charged with investigating options available to German Jewish parents for securing safety for their children both within and outside of Germany. Findings can be reported orally. After each team has shared its information, students can create a chart for classroom display. Political, cultural, and social measures can be listed on this chart, as can parental options such as the Kindertransport program.

Measures	Parental Options
(Place content here.)	(Place content here.)

- Compare the story of what happened to the children in *The Pied Piper of Hamlin* to what happened to the children transported from Germany on the Kindertransport. Ask students to validate this analogy.

- Students will need to locate and read personal accounts of Holocaust survivors who were saved through the Kindertransport effort. Using either a traditional theatrical one-act structure or working with the narratives solely as monologues and using a readers' theatre format, they next should develop these into a play. If others in the school or the community are invited to a performance, the hosting class may wish to compile a program for the event. In addition to the cast, it would be interesting to include a brief biography of each survivor and a bibliography of narrative sources.

- Challenge students to locate and listen to the song, *Lift Up the Flag*, as originally written in German by Horst Wessel. Then, either with students in the class who are studying that language or as a joint project with a school's German class, translate the song into English and analyze the words used. Ask class members to delve into the background of the composer and to postulate why this song became the Nazi anthem. Next, look at the lyrics that appear below and ask students why they think that these are sometimes omitted from translations.

    Wenn das Judenblut vom Messer spritzt, dann geht's nochmal so gut — When Jewish blood runs from the knife, things will go twice as well.

    Paula J. Draper, *Holocaust Resource* (Willowdale, Ontario: Holocaust Education and Memorial Centre of Toronto, 1985), 7.

    Solicit opinions as to how students think Jewish children in Germany might have felt when they heard this anthem. Finally, suggest researching both happy children's songs that young people journeying to England on Kindertransports might have learned and patriotic songs popular in the British Isles in 1938 and then invite comparisons to *Lift Up the Flag*, noting differences in subject, mood, lyrics, and music.

- *Goodbye Marianne*, a play by Irene Watts, addresses the same subject as *Kindertransport*. Provide an opportunity for students to learn more about this rescue program by reading both plays and comparing their content.

- The Kindertransport Association, founded in 1989, and its counterparts in England and Israel engage in charitable work for needy children in homage to the lifesaving efforts of its namesake. Suggest that students use personal computers to contact the organization (http://home.att.net/edsdanzig/index2.html) or its founder, Ed Behrendt (e-mail edsdanzig@worldnet.att.net), to learn more about the charitable and educational work done by this group.

T-Money & Wolf

The Playwrights: Kevin Willmott and Ric Averill

Raised in Junction City, Kansas, Kevin Willmott received a B.A. in drama from Marymount College and an M.F.A. from New York University, Tisch School of the Arts. He has received several awards for his writing and has gained recognition as both a screenwriter and a playwright. *Shields Green and the Gospel of John Brown*, a screenplay co-written with Mitch Brian, was purchased by Chris Columbus' 1492 Productions for 20th Century Fox. *Captive*, another co-written screenplay, has gone to producer Robert Lawrence, also at 20th Century Fox. Acclaimed producer and director Oliver Stone has hired Willmott to co-write *Little Brown Brothers*. The writer has scripted, produced, and directed the film *Ninth Street*, starring Martin Sheen and Isaac Hayes. Willmott also has worked as a civil rights and peace activist.

Ric Averill, artistic director and principal playwright for the Seem-To-Be Players, holds both a B.F.A. in music composition and an M.A. in children's theatre from the University of Kansas. He co-founded the Seem-To-Be Players with his wife, Jeanne. The company, comprised of professional actors and musicians, develops original plays in Lawrence, Kansas, and tours them throughout the Midwest. The troupe is affiliated with the Mid-America Arts Alliance Regional Touring Program and the Kansas Touring Program. In addition to his work with this theatre group, Averill has held the presidency of the Association of Kansas Theatre and is an artist-in-education in his home state. He directs Lawrence's Summer Youth Theatre Program and is a guest director for Lawrence High School's Experimental Theatre series.

Averill's work as a playwright has earned positive recognition. His adaptation of *Alice in Wonderland* was commissioned by the Kennedy Center and his play, *The Bremen Town Musicians*, was performed at the International Showcase '95 in Philadelphia. Both of these shows, as well as *Trickster Tales from the Melting Pot*, *The Seem-To-Be Just So Stories*, and *The Seven Voyages of Sinbad the Sailor* have been seen on tour. Averill has won the American Alliance for Theatre and Education Unpublished Play Reading competition and the Kansas Playwriting Fellowship for *Reliable Junk*, which also was selected for the 1997 Bonderman Youth Theatre Playwriting Symposium (now called the

Waldo M. and Grace C. Bonderman IUPUI National Youth Theatre Playwriting Symposium).

The Play

This one-act play, winner of the American Alliance for Theatre and Education Distinguished Play Award, brings together an old man imprisoned for being a Nazi war criminal and a young black youth incarcerated for murdering a nun. It draws a thought-provoking parallel between the murder of Jews during the Holocaust and the slayings caused by drug trafficking in the minority ghettos of America.

The play was originally developed at Lawrence High School in Kansas and was produced by the Black Student Union and the Experimental Theatre series. It received additional support from the Seem-To-Be Players. The play traveled to the Association of Kansas Theatre Convention in Topeka and the Mid-America Theatre Conference in Kansas City before being further refined through a professional staged reading in May of 1993 at the John F. Kennedy Center in Washington, D.C. This presentation was a part of the New Visions/New Voices symposium, a program under the auspices of the Kennedy Center's Performances for Youth and Families Education Department. *T-Money & Wolf* was subsequently showcased in Boston at the American Alliance for Theatre and Education national conference.

Information about the Play and the Holocaust

"How could this happen? How could ordinary German citizens let this occur?" These are perplexing questions young people ask about the Holocaust. In *T-Money & Wolf*, they see how divergent elements could come together to change a typical German youth into an executioner and, subsequently, a war criminal imprisoned for life. The play then challenges students to reflect upon how genocidal events are set in motion and to apply this to the drug trade in the ghettos of contemporary America. Although separated geographically and in time by more than half a century, in both countries social pressures, relationships, and economics can be found at the core of the bloodshed.

Conformity was a goal that the Third Reich embraced for German youth. As early as 1924, Adolf Hitler was espousing the virtues of character, willpower, decision-making skills, and responsibility to the state for the young. He touted these assets, along with physical fitness, as being more desirable than intellectual acumen. In truth, the Third Reich had no need for youngsters who were independent thinkers.

It was the purpose of organizations such as Hitler Youth and the League of German Girls to mold young people to the Reich's ideal. These organizations initiated a process of indoctrination into the Nazi way of life that led to young people accepting without question the rewards of loyal comradery and the social, cultural, and political gains associated with service to the state. This total allegiance ultimately produced German males who served the Nazi Party faithfully throughout their compulsory duty in the Reich Labor Services and in the army, and females who felt it their mission to produce pure Aryan children. As a further result, citizens willingly delivered friends, family, and neighbors to certain death, and youth even reported their parents to the Gestapo.

In 1938, seven of the ten million children in Germany belonged to Hitler Youth organizations. These groups were organized in a military manner, undergoing weekly meetings in clubhouses during winter months and engaging in hikes and other outside activities during summer. Officers came from the members themselves and the leader of Hitler Youth served in the cabinet and reported directly to the *Führer*.

Training, linked to leadership roles and social acculturation, began at age ten when a young person, if selected for the program, had formal schooling brought together with National Socialist education. From ten to fourteen, attention was directed toward building character and physical prowess. At fifteen, holding dear the visions and opinions of the National Socialists became paramount. By eighteen, some could be admitted to the Nazi Party. After completing labor and military duty, one thousand elite young people between the ages of twenty-three and thirty could apply for admission to the Order, a four-year Reich leadership training endeavor. During this formative twenty-year period, from ages ten to thirty, it became increasingly clear that young people could attain prestige and acceptance only if they belonged to the elite Nazi coterie.

Hitler believed that Aryans were superior and he instilled this belief in his nation's youth. Features such as blue eyes, blond hair, and fair skin identified them as members of the "master race" and united them both physically and psychologically. Others, they grew to believe, were inferior and that made it permissible first to exclude them from social activities and school and later to commit acts of violence and humiliation against them. As the war effort made life more difficult for both Aryan and Jewish children, the former group banded even more tightly together. When Aryan children suffered hardships because there was not enough food or family members had been lost to the war, they blamed Jews, even those who formerly had been their friends. Subsequently, when Jews were no longer recognized as individual human beings but rather were viewed as a group responsible for deprivation and despair, executing them became an honorable task.

That indoctrination of young Germans into this way of thinking and behaving was largely successful is evidenced by victim casualty figures and accounts of liquidations by zealous perpetrators. As described by one prison psychologist at the Nuremberg Trials, the archetypal member of the Gestapo was, "An inhuman, murderous robot, quiet and correct in military bearing, functioning intellectually on a high level of mechanical efficiency, utterly devoid of human empathy" (Holocaust Education and Memorial Centre, 27). This definition could well be more inclusive. If killing at first gave Germans pause, it was expected that this would soon fade and be replaced by, if not enthusiasm, certainly acceptance, for that was the ethical price exacted by Nazi stalwarts. Those who could not kill easily or who struggled with the morality of their actions were branded as soft outsiders.

Conformity, however, and the actions mandated by it, were not without consequences. When the Nazis were defeated, certain nefarious wrongdoers were brought to trial. The most famous of these trials was held at Nuremberg, Germany, from November 1945 through October 1946. There were other trials held in Nuremberg that lasted through April 1949, as well as legal proceedings at Wiesbaden, Ludwigshafen, and Dachau. Those who were most responsible for the atrocities but who managed to escape the Allied victors were pursued by Nazi hunters and, when captured, extradited from the countries in which they were hiding and put on trial.

T-Money & Wolf

A Play in One Act
For 11 Men and 9–11 Women, extras possible

TIME AND PLACE: A contemporary prison cell, in the streets and homes of contemporary Newark, New Jersey, and in the streets and homes of Munich, Germany, early 1930s.

LIST OF CHARACTERS:
T-Money's Story
   Terry/T-Money — lean, handsome Black youth, 16–18
   Butterfinger — his Homey, tall, lean Black, 16–18
   Pop 'N' Fresh — another Homey, heavy-set, Black, 16–18
   Double-J — Terry's brother, a Black youth, 10–12
   Daddy Mack — a slick drug dealer, Black, 25–30
   Latasha — Terry's lean girlfriend, Black, 16–18
   Sister Salimu — a Black activist Catholic nun, 30–35
   Lisa — Latasha's crew, a petite, pretty, White youth, 16–18
   Barbara Jean — Latasha's crew, Black, tall, tough, 16–18
   Gloria* — another friend, Hispanic, 16–18
   Tawana** — a pregnant, crackhead friend, 16–18
   Party People — various friends in the Party scene (optional)

   *These lines could be given to Lisa
   **These lines could be given to Barbara Jean

Wolf's Story
   Wolf — charming, energetic, White, German youth, 13–15
   Old Wolf — White man, 70–75
   Stefan — Wolf's very Aryan older brother, White, 16–18
   Stefan and Wolf's Mother — war widow, White, 30–40
   Heidi — Stefan's pretty, neatly-dressed girlfriend, White, 16–18
   Sarah — Wolf's childhood friend, Jewish, 13–15
   Ann — Sarah's mother, Jewish, 35–45
   Tim — Wolf's German childhood schoolmate, lean, red-headed, 14–16
   Ruth — the witness, Sarah and Ann's Jewish neighbor, 25–35

Kurt — a Brownshirted SA storm trooper, White, 25–30
Carl — slimy, potential Gestapo-type, White man, 20–30

DIRECTOR'S NOTE: African-American slang and the code language of the street changes frequently. *T-Money & Wolf* was written using the slang popular at the time. When appropriate, slang should be updated to keep the dialogue fresh.

SCENE ONE
A collage; Streets of Newark and Munich.

(Sounds of a riot, voices of actors mix with sirens — both contemporary and European — mixed with shouts and the sounds of breaking glass. From one side of the stage, TERRY (T-MONEY), POP 'N' FRESH and BUTTERFINGER enter and dash across the stage. They are looting. YOUNG WOLF, STEFAN, and CARL enter from the other side. They are breaking windows.)

T-MONEY. Man, ain't nothin in here worth takin'!
BUTTERFINGER. All the liquor is gone!!
POP 'N' FRESH. Man, they just broke in Wilson's Department Store! They got TV's, VCR's...come on!!! *(They run off, passing CARL, STEFAN and WOLF who cross and begin to talk.)*
STEFAN. Carl! Pull up some more bricks! Not that store! Just the Jewish shops!
CARL. No one's been down this block!!
STEFAN. Come on!!!
CARL. Wait for me!!!

(KURT, a storm trooper, enters. They stop, look at him. He smiles and gives tacit permission to go on.)

KURT. You boys be careful, now!
STEFAN. Let's go!
WOLF. This is crazy!!

(Sirens resume. Then as ALL run off, OLD WOLF and T-MONEY move into two of the pools of light that will be used for monologues.)

T-MONEY. It was an accident. I didn't mean for it to happen. Man, things got all whacked!
OLD WOLF. My appearance here is a result of a long and unplanned odyssey. *(Jail music comes up. OLD WOLF takes his place on "jail cot." T-MONEY begins to pace in semi-darkness.)*

SCENE TWO
A contemporary prison cell.

OLD WOLF. Will you sit? *(T-MONEY grunts, paces.)* You are driving me crazy.
T-MONEY. You already crazy, man! All the people in the world, I gotta be slammed up with and they put me in with some shriveled up skinhead. *(No response.)* Hey, now, I shouldn't be complainin'. You a star. I seen you on the tube. What was that place you kill all those people at? Where you did all them Jews? Anyway, you the man...you the star, man. *(Still no answer.)* Understand this. You in with Money, now. Money don't play that. *(Gets right in OLD WOLF's face.)* And don't be gettin' in my face, 'cause I will back you up. You hear? You hear? *(OLD WOLF stretches and turns to look at T-MONEY.)*
OLD WOLF. I'm going to be here the rest of my life. They wanted to deport me to Israel, to execute me. My attorney tells me he will fight to keep me here. He is very good, and he has connections. I don't like it here. You don't like being here with me, but here we are. And I think I can help you.
T-MONEY. Yeah, you gonna help me.
OLD WOLF. I CAN help you. We have more in common than you like to believe. We're known killers, you and I. If we keep the others afraid of us, they won't bother us.
T-MONEY. Man, ain't nobody gonna bother me.
OLD WOLF. There are no loners in here.
T-MONEY. Hey, I ain't losin' respect hangin' with some Nazi.
OLD WOLF. There are more Nazis here than you can imagine. It's not just Nazis though; there's people here who want you dead. You need protection.
T-MONEY. You crazy, man. Only thing we got in common is we in this damn cell together. That your side and this is mine, so keep *you* out my face.

OLD WOLF. You seem smart. You think about it.
T-MONEY. You must be out your damn mind! Why didn't they put Butterfinger in here with me...

(BUTTERFINGER *enters, lights shift, rap music booms up and* T-MONEY *stands and joins* BUTTERFINGER *for the next scene.* OLD WOLF *exits.*)

SCENE THREE
A street in contemporary Newark, New Jersey.

BUTTERFINGER. Man, what it is? *(They are wasting time, talking "trash," listening to music, waiting for something — anything.)*
T-MONEY. Man, it was wild. People was goin' off! Bustin' out windows!! Takin' everythin'! But, hey, they shoulda known people was gonna act all whacked when they killed that old lady.
BUTTERFINGER. The police just shot her dead off in the back. Boom!!
T-MONEY. And then, AND THEN, they gonna let them police off from killing this old Grandmama, please. PEOPLE WENT OFF!
BUTTERFINGER. You get anything good?
T-MONEY. I got me a nice color TV. Got me a clock radio for my mama. I was lookin' for a juicer but they didn't have none.

(POP 'N' FRESH *enters singing, à la Ren and Stimpy.*)

POP 'N' FRESH. Happy, happy, joy, joy, happy, happy, joy, joy...
BUTTERFINGER. Man, shut up wit' dat whacked up...
POP 'N' FRESH. Yo, man, you feel bad at all about what we did last night?
T-MONEY. Yeah, I feel bad. I don't feel so bad as to take that garbage back. We went on a shoppin' spree, BOY-E! Come on down, the price is right!!! *(Gives* BUTTERFINGER *five.)*

(SISTER SALIMU *enters and looks at the* MEN. *She is dressed in a mixture of African designs and street clothes.*)

SISTER SALIMU. Hi, fellas. Well, they certainly destroyed the neighborhood last night.

T-MONEY. Sister, they got to understand — we ain't gonna take the police killing people like that no more.
SISTER SALIMU. The police are wrong! They've been wrong a long time! Now your mama ain't got no place to buy groceries in her own neighborhood.
POP 'N' FRESH. Yo, man, here comes your brother.

(DOUBLE-J, a smaller version of Terry, comes running in. He is carrying a super-blaster water gun.)

T-MONEY. Man, you squirt me, I'm kickin' yo' ass.
DOUBLE-J. Ah, shut up, you think you so bad.
T-MONEY. Squirt me and you'll see how bad I am. You know it ain't summer, nigga, find something else to play with, big Chicken McNugget head! *(DOUBLE-J squirts imaginary enemies.)*
DOUBLE-J. I put some gas in here — shot Jimmie Bivens in the eye. It swoll all up. *(They grunt at him.)*
SISTER SALIMU. Jimmy Bivens is doin' real good. He comes down to the Rec Center. He's on the ball team. Why don't you come down? *(DOUBLE-J just brushes her off.)* Well, be careful. God bless. *(She exits.)*
DOUBLE-J *(imitates her)*. "Jimmy Bivens is doin' real good." Jimmy Bivens is a big water head boy.
T-MONEY *(changing the subject, moving attention from DOUBLE-J)*. Man, I saw these new jumpers over at Foot Locker. Man, they was dope. They was white; had a "pump," right? And this thing called a "lifter"? I saw Daddy Mack coming out of the liquor store. He had a pair — $225.
DOUBLE-J. I guess your size 12's won't be seeing a one of them, HA, HA! *(T-MONEY hits DOUBLE-J in the chest. POP 'N' FRESH notices Crazy Larry off across the street.)*
POP 'N' FRESH. Check out Crazy Larry! *(ALL look across the street.)*
BUTTERFINGER. Yo! Yo! Larry! You crazy, man!
VOICE *(from offstage)*. YEAH, I KNOW!
BUTTERFINGER. Well, at least he *know*.
POP 'N' FRESH. How'd he go off? I remember playing ball with him. He was cool.
T-MONEY. Ah, he went to that Desert Storm. Peep this; like the word I got was they ran over a bunch of them rag-head-Iraqs in tanks and whatnot — buried 'em alive. Now he be hearing them screaming,

dying, carrying on in his head. Homey gets a check now from the government for losing his mind for the country, U.S. and all. You think about it, that's a GOOD gig!
BUTTERFINGER. I know I'd lose my mind for some money, ENOUGH money.
T-MONEY. Same thing as going some rounds with Mike Tyson. For that BIG money — I'm a live large. For him kickin' my ass — KICK my ass!

(LATASHA and her partners, LISA and BARBARA JEAN, walk up to the fellas. With them are TAWANA and GLORIA, her sidekick.)

LATASHA. What up?
GANG *(all together, various greetings)*. You...you...what up, what up...
T-MONEY *(kissing LATASHA)*. Miss Thang...*(POP 'N' FRESH moves up to BARBARA JEAN.)*
POP 'N' FRESH. Yo, yo, Barbara Jean, when you gonna give me some?
BARBARA JEAN. Give you some what? Only way you getting some is some woman die and will it to you. *(ALL break out laughing.)*
POP 'N' FRESH. You always dissin' me.
BARBARA JEAN. You needs to be dissed! You ain't about nothing. Big pork-rind-eating-lard-behind ain't going no place but these projects.
POP 'N' FRESH. And you is, huh? You going somewhere? Where you going? You so smart, intelligent. If you was all THAT, you wouldn't be on that PIPE.
GANG *(laughing as TAWANA and GLORIA exit)*. Hoooo! Dissed! Dissed! *(Girls comment as TAWANA leaves.)*
LATASHA. Ummm. Look at Tawana. Belly all stuck out.
BARBARA JEAN. Home girl should have kept them legs crossed.
LATASHA. Who she havin' that baby by?
LISA. Chris.
BARBARA JEAN. Chris in jail. Man, that's sorry.
LATASHA. I ain't havin' no baby unless my man got a job and can take care of me. You know?
LISA. I know that's right.
BARBARA JEAN. My man got to have plenty of money...period!
POP 'N' FRESH. Your man may have some money, but he ain't gonna give yo' ass none.

T-MONEY. Yo, yo, chill. Daddy Mack! *(They all stare as the sound of a car is heard. DADDY MACK is driving by offstage.)* Daddy Mack got it going on! *(Sound of car stopping and door slamming.)*
DOUBLE-J. He's coming over here!
LISA. Mack is *fine*.
BARBARA JEAN. Umhum...
BUTTERFINGER. See how he got his Mercedes sitting low? See, that's how I want mine.
LATASHA. I didn't know you had one.
T-MONEY. Yo, yo, chill.

(DADDY MACK enters. He dresses real slick, hip-hop.)

DADDY MACK. What's happening?
T-MONEY. You. *(DADDY MACK gives T-MONEY a look, knowing he's admired.)*
DADDY MACK. Look here, I need somebody to watch my ride, while I take care of some business...*(ALL volunteer, DADDY MACK looks at T-MONEY.)* What's your name?
T-MONEY. Terry...
DADDY MACK *(renaming him)*. T-Money. T-Money. Look here. *(DADDY MACK gives T-MONEY a twenty.)* I don't want nobody leaning on it, touching it — I don't even want nobody staring at it hard. Know what I'm saying?
T-MONEY. Yeah, I got your meaning.
DADDY MACK. Some miscellaneous punk scratched my ride with a key one time...That ride cost 100 grand. Far more than his life value...*(He laughs, ALL laugh, mesmerized by DADDY MACK.)* A man ain't worth but two hundred — in the open market. *(Smiles.)* You got my back, Money?
T-MONEY. Mack, whatever happens, I'll put a "S" on my chest and handle it.
DADDY MACK. Money...*(As he walks off, shakes hands, nods, flashes a smile and the peace sign.)* Later...peace. *(He exits.)*
BARBARA JEAN. Mack act like he like you.
T-MONEY. Mack know the deal.

(Lights fade and music starts up again moving from heavy Black sampler rhythm to chaotic European contemporary jazz, rising in a climax of shattering glass. T-MONEY and gang,

LATASHA and gang all exit as WOLF enters and lights shift to indicate bedroom with two "beds.")

SCENE FOUR
Stefan and Wolf's bedroom, Munich, early 1930s.

(WOLF is half asleep in one of the beds. There is the sound of breaking glass and a flash of light. STEFAN is seen running through the light. One more crash and then silence. A "window" creaks as STEFAN sneaks into the bedroom.)

WOLF. Stefan? Stefan, is that you?
STEFAN. Shhhhh! Go back to sleep, Wolf.
WOLF. What's going on out there? Are you all right?
STEFAN. Everyone was there — burning and smashing. We threw rocks — it was a like a carnival or a crazy cinema scene. You've never seen so much shattered glass.
WOLF. Did you get anything? The last riots people were bringing stuff home!
STEFAN. You think I'm going to steal from a bunch of damn Jews?
WOLF. You're crazy, Stefan. What if the police had come by?
STEFAN. They watched us. They probably figured we were making their job easier. Cleaning up the neighborhood.

(STEFAN and WOLF's MOTHER enters the room.)

MOTHER. Are you boys all right? I thought I heard something up here!
WOLF *(looks at STEFAN who motions him to silence)*. Stefan just opened the window, so we could hear. They're smashing glass all over the place.
MOTHER *(as she closes the "window")*. The police just stand around and watch. No one stops this insanity any longer.
STEFAN. Why should they? It's just Jew shops. Maybe they'll catch on and move to Poland, where they belong.
MOTHER. Stefan, you have friends in that neighborhood. Sarah, and...
STEFAN. *Wolf* has friends in that neighborhood.
WOLF *(to STEFAN)*. You didn't see if they...
STEFAN. From the window? *(MOTHER notices exchange, looks at STEFAN and realizes he is still partly dressed.)*

MOTHER. What are you doing, Stefan? Sleeping in your shoes? You're not to be going out at night!
STEFAN. I'll go where I want, when I want...
MOTHER. I don't want any son of mine running with a gang of thugs, looting and burning! That's ugly...
STEFAN. What's so ugly about a fire?
MOTHER. Stefan, you're out of control. Go to sleep. We'll talk more in the morning. *(She exits.)*
STEFAN. It was beautiful, Wolf. At one store, Carl and I ran up to the glass and made faces, like the carnival. And the glass was kind of warped so our faces leered and the fire from the shop across the street looked like it was coming from our heads. Then I stood back and smashed his reflection and he smashed mine.
WOLF. Did Sarah's place get hit?
STEFAN. How should I know? Don't worry, she'll probably move anyway. A lot of them are. That's what Tim told me.
WOLF. When? Was he with you?
STEFAN. Hell no, of course not. He's a rabbit. I talked to him after school. He said he saw Sarah's father talking to old man Mosher the night before last — about where they might go to set up shop. Look, kid, I know you like Sarah, but it's just not the right time to be seen with a Jew girl — Makes *me* look bad.
WOLF. Ahh, you've got Heidi.
STEFAN. Maybe. You never know with Heidi. Sometimes she fails to see the wisdom of being who I want her to be! But come with me tomorrow. We're having a meeting. There'll be some girls your age there, and Carl and some of my friends. You're a little young, but if you want to join, I'll get you in.
WOLF. They wouldn't want me.
STEFAN. They won't care if you're with me. But listen, Wolf, it isn't just a club — once you're in, you're in. You don't just change your mind. Are you ready to be a part of something bigger than you can even imagine?
WOLF *(hesitant)*. Yes — I mean, I want to be with you.
STEFAN. Smartest thing you've said all night.

(Sound of shattering glass again. Military-like jazz music is heard. This fades into street rap again as T-MONEY and DADDY MACK enter to complete a deal. Lights shift to night on the streets.)

Scene Five
A street in Newark.

(T-Money saunters across the set, stops and "knocks" on the door. Daddy Mack steps "out." T-Money gives him a wad of bills. Daddy Mack peels a couple off and smiles at him.)

Daddy Mack. Money! Mo — ney. *(T-Money and Daddy Mack exit as Stefan and Wolf get "out of bed" and grab school bags. Music shifts to pastoral European.)*

Scene Six
A street in Munich.

(Stefan and Wolf move into the daylit street. Stefan sees Heidi, his pretty, blond girlfriend entering. He runs to center and jumps out, ambushing her and blocking her path.)

Stefan. Wolf, this poor child needs protection on the long path to education.
Heidi. From you, maybe.
Stefan. It's dangerous in these streets, Heidi. Didn't you hear about last night?
Heidi. How could I help it? My father was out all night.
Stefan. I saw him.
Heidi. You weren't out there.
Wolf *(with pride)*. He didn't come back until three in the morning. Mother was about to go crazy.
Heidi. Who did you sneak out with?
Stefan. Friends. I'm not giving you any names.
Heidi. Right. This is just another one of your stories.
Stefan. Oh, really? Carl came over at two o'clock. We smudged charcoal on our faces and went straight for Mosher's shop. You go down there and look at his sign. It doesn't say exactly what it used to.
Heidi. What did you write?

STEFAN *(grabs WOLF, covers his ears roughly)*. Can't say. Someone has to shelter the youth from the decadent realities of the new Germany.
HEIDI. Tell me.
STEFAN. Someone has to shelter the women, too.
HEIDI *(grabs WOLF and pulls him to her, cuddling him. He is embarrassed)*. Maybe the women ought to shelter the youth?
STEFAN *(pulls WOLF roughly away from her)*. Maybe this punk little brother better watch how close he gets to someone else's territory.
WOLF. It was her. It wasn't me!
HEIDI. It was. It was me. Wolf has this animal attraction for me.
STEFAN. You want to hear animal. I'll make him squeal. *(Grabs WOLF, shoves him down by pinching his neck.)*
WOLF. Stefan!!
STEFAN. Can you get away from home tonight, Heidi?
HEIDI. It depends. Why would I want to?
STEFAN. I'm taking the little one to the youth meeting — try to make something useful out of him.
HEIDI. I don't want to sit around some sweaty beer hall and sing songs.
STEFAN. There are girls there. Girls you like. People you already know are in and you don't even know it.
WOLF. People you don't know are in and you don't even care...
STEFAN *(to WOLF)*. You'll care! When you get your pin and armband. Women can't resist a man in uniform. Right, Heidi?
HEIDI. Especially a modest one.
STEFAN. Ten o'clock. I'll come get you. Wolf and I. *(Hands them each a piece of candy.)* You get rations. Extra rations. Bread, coffee, candy — We'll fatten you up, Heidi.
HEIDI. What's wrong with the way I look now?
WOLF. I think Stefan is trying to tell you he likes *big* German women.
STEFAN *(hitting him)*. Shut up! You're lucky I even let you tag along.

(They start off when SARAH enters. She sees them and warily crosses to the "other side of the street.")

WOLF. Sarah. *(SARAH ducks away. STEFAN and HEIDI shun her and STEFAN pulls WOLF back from her.)*
STEFAN. Wolf!
WOLF *(looking back after SARAH)*. What's wrong with saying hello to Sarah?

STEFAN. You'll find yourself a real woman at the meeting tonight.
HEIDI. I'm going to find a real man at the meeting! *(WOLF shakes off his discomfort over SARAH and takes HEIDI's arm. STEFAN grabs her other arm. They start off.)*
WOLF. You're greedy, Heidi. You've already got two real men!
STEFAN. One and a half!

(WOLF reaches over and thwacks STEFAN who thwacks him back. They begin a playful tussle that suddenly turns serious when STEFAN hits WOLF hard in the stomach. WOLF doubles over, HEIDI takes STEFAN's hand and leads him off as T-MONEY enters jail scene doubled over from a blow he's received in prison. Prison blues theme starts up. WOLF staggers off as T-MONEY staggers on.)

SCENE SEVEN
A contemporary prison cell.

OLD WOLF. I told you the boys play rough.
T-MONEY. Man, just shut up.
OLD WOLF. You don't have to be afraid. This does not have to happen to you again.
T-MONEY. I know it's not — 'cause I'm gonna kill whoever messes with me!
OLD WOLF. Then you can hang your "Home, Sweet, Home" sign right here beside mine. Put up your girlie calendar. You're here forever.
T-MONEY. Shut up. I'm here forever anyway. *(OLD WOLF just lays back on his cot.)*
OLD WOLF. You're young, T-Money. For the young ones, this place is very dangerous. Don't get me wrong — I don't want from you what the others want.
T-MONEY. Hell, you ain't gettin' it either.
OLD WOLF. It's very difficult to stand alone in here.
T-MONEY *(pause)*. What's really in it for me?
OLD WOLF. Do you have an attorney?
T-MONEY. This dude the Court appointed.
OLD WOLF. I help you with the law. My attorney, my connections, maybe you *won't* have to be here the rest of your life.
T-MONEY. You can do all that?

OLD WOLF. You assist me. Everyone's afraid of me. I can protect you.
T-MONEY. All right, bet, bet.

(T-MONEY walks from the jail scene to hip-hop music into the street as DADDY MACK approaches. They do handshake. DADDY MACK pulls a gun.)

SCENE EIGHT
An alleyway in Newark.

DADDY MACK. All right, bet! Bet! See, see, a Nine is nice. The grip on 'em is sweet. You want it to fit in yo' hand. You don't wanna be grabbin' it — it should be an extension of you, know what I'm sayin'?
T-MONEY. Yo, Mack, look, I don't know if I wanna be packin'.
DADDY MACK. You ain't punkin' out on me, is ya?
T-MONEY. Naw, man, I'm down. Just...I ain't never been 'round no "smoker" before.
DADDY MACK. Then you lookin' to get smoked. You be runnin' what's MINE, understand. Somebody up and abscond on what's MINE, you gonna have to put a hole in his body. You makin' much bank now. You ain't some nappy-head runner makin' change. With advancement comes responsibility, my brother. *(Shakes his head, thinking of what he's done to stay on top.)* Man, I have...for the business...Phhhhh! You got to be willing to off a whole household full of roaches. If you ain't and I lost what's MINE? I'm a have to kill you real good.
T-MONEY *(laughing).* Man, you crazy, Mack!
DADDY MACK. Boy, you mean nothin' to me! You just a roll a money. You just make sure you be havin' my bank...you be one of these dead black water bugs on the evening news. *(Hands T-MONEY the pistol.)* Squeeze it.
T-MONEY *(takes it, holds it up, then puts it back down).* Man, I ain't a good shot. What if I hit somebody I ain't shootin' at?
DADDY MACK. Mushrooms. Shoulda known better than be on the damn streets; *streets* ain't SAFE.

(WOLF enters. T-MONEY aims, fires. WOLF crosses to SARAH's door and whispers.)

Scene Nine
An alleyway in Munich.

WOLF *(stage whisper)*. Sarah! Sarah!!!

(T-MONEY and DADDY MACK exit as SARAH enters as though from her house.)

SARAH. Wolf?
WOLF. Why weren't you in school? I missed you!
SARAH *(comes out to join him on door stoop)*. I didn't feel like going. People are acting stranger at school every day.
WOLF. It's just a strange time, Sarah, it'll pass.
SARAH. Like you passed me in the street this morning.
WOLF. I'm sorry. It's Stefan. I...don't think he likes you.
SARAH. So what your brother says dictates what you do?
WOLF. You know that's not true. Come on, go for a walk with me?
SARAH. I can't. I'm not leaving here at night, Wolf. It's not safe for me. Our shop was hit last night.
WOLF. How badly?
SARAH. The storefront window was smashed and someone painted a swastika on the door.
WOLF. It wasn't Stefan, was it? I don't think he would...
SARAH. It might as well have been. Father made us hide and tried to talk to the Brownshirts but they just laughed — then knocked him down. He's talking about moving.
WOLF. You can't move. It's just a game, Sarah. If they knew who you were...
SARAH. I guess it's enough that they know *what* we are, Wolf.

(As she is talking she sees KURT enter and approach. She ducks back "inside.")

WOLF. What are you saying? Sarah, come out and talk... *(KURT walks up to WOLF.)*
KURT. What are you doing here, young man? *(WOLF looks up, then at KURT.)* Who are you?
WOLF. I'm Wolf, I, uh...
KURT. Wolf? Where's your identification?

WOLF *(shuffling through wallet for identification)*. I was just on my way to...
KURT. Where? This neighborhood's off limits now. You get lost?
WOLF *(as he shows identification)*. My brother was going to take me to a meeting. I just fell behind.
KURT *(looks at identification, recognizes the name and smiles)*. You're Stefan's brother?
WOLF *(relieved)*. You know him?
KURT. I'm going to the same meeting. You can come with me.

(WOLF exits, led by KURT. SARAH comes out and watches them leave. Her eyes linger as OLD WOLF enters. Jail music. OLD WOLF and T-MONEY enter and cross to their cots. T-MONEY paces. OLD WOLF watches him.)

SCENE TEN
A contemporary prison cell.

OLD WOLF *(to T-MONEY)*. You have a woman, Terry? *(SARAH exits.)*
T-MONEY *(pause, he sits on his cot)*. Yeah, I got me a woman. I got me a son, too. Bet you got nothin'.
OLD WOLF. Nothin'? For forty years I've been a successful American businessman. A landscaping service.
T-MONEY. Yeah?
OLD WOLF. I made a good living and now they come along and strip forty years of my life from me! They come like storm troopers and take my picture and these Jews come out of nowhere!! Saying "he did this" and "he did that"! My God, it was over forty years ago! Forty years of being an American. Forty years of paying taxes. Every American has secrets. You think this country is perfect?
T-MONEY. You right there! Ain't nothin' but brothers in this mother jumper!!
OLD WOLF. This country is filled with prejudice and now they try to deport me because I obeyed orders and killed some Jews! What was I supposed to do — die? You had to kill Jews. That was the law. Hell, my first woman was a Jew!
T-MONEY. You did her? *(OLD WOLF looks at T-MONEY. This question/realization puts him in a strange frame of mind.)*

OLD WOLF *(eyes growing distant and glazed).* Yeah, I killed her. My best friend, too. It gets in you. It's like a lawn. These weeds keep coming up — things get in your way. You can't stand to walk in the depths so you mow it down, blade after blade. And then everything's clean. *(He leans back and looks up.)* Sometime try lining people up — and drop them one after the other. Watching them crumble like blades of grass. You're a baby. You're a baby.

(T-MONEY looks at him a little taken aback. There is European "night" music as they exit and STEFAN and WOLF take their places in their respective beds. MOTHER enters.)

SCENE ELEVEN
Wolf and Stefan's bedroom, Munich.

MOTHER. Wolf, Stefan? Are you up yet? Wake up. There were sirens in the night and Mrs. Schmidt told me Sarah's shop was half burned out. Where did you boys go last night?
STEFAN. Go away.
WOLF. Let us sleep.
MOTHER. Somebody threw a torch through Sarah's shop window.
WOLF. Is she all right? Are her folks all right?
MOTHER. No one knows for sure where she is. You boys don't know anything, do you?
STEFAN. No. We just went to the youth meeting. Look, we brought home some bread and sugar...*(Gets rations from under the "bed," hands them to her.)*
MOTHER. Stefan, we don't need this! How much trouble are you in?
WOLF. You should have heard what they said at the meeting last night. Germany's changing and we're going to be a part of it.
MOTHER. You sound like your brother and he sounds like the...
STEFAN. Like what? Like I'm starting to think for myself?
MOTHER. Just the opposite! No son of mine comes up with the idea that Jewish shops should be destroyed.
STEFAN *(climbing half out of bed).* There's not room for everybody in this country, Mother.
MOTHER. So let's get rid of...Sarah? She's a pretty bad person!
STEFAN. She's a Jew. Are you a Jew-lover? You want me to start telling people my mother's a Jew-lover?

MOTHER. Stefan! You forget who you're talking to!
STEFAN. I'm talking to you! *(Grabs her and turns her toward him.)* That's who I'm talking to!
MOTHER *(taken aback)*. My God, what would your father say?
STEFAN. My father? My father? My father was shot in a stupid war. A war we're going to finish! What would Father say? He'd say for his sons to follow a strong leader — to form a strong Germany — to achieve a greatness he was never allowed. Don't ask me what Father would say, 'cause you might not want to hear the answer. *(He storms out.)*
WOLF. Mother, I'll check on Sarah. But Stefan's right. You have to let us take care of things.

(He exits into street. MOTHER stays behind, slumps down on the bed. HEIDI enters behind her and moves into one of the monologue spotlights. She is older than before.)

HEIDI. They both joined the army, Stefan and Wolf. Stefan was killed — maybe three months into the war.
MOTHER. He was killed not more than five miles from where his father had died.
HEIDI. His mother told me that at least a hundred times. At the end of her life, it was all she would say, other than asking me if I knew where Wolf was.

SCENE TWELVE
A street in Munich.

(Military music is heard as scene shifts into the street. WOLF re-enters and TIM approaches.)

TIM. Wolf! I've got to talk to you.
WOLF. We need to talk.
TIM. What are you doing going to those meetings? Your brother's acting like a crazy man.
WOLF. The whole country's crazy. I haven't seen you for a couple of weeks.
TIM. Can I still trust you?
WOLF. Can I still trust *you?*

TIM. Look, Wolf, Sarah and her younger brothers are at my house.
WOLF. That's dangerous, Tim.
TIM. They're hiding. Their father is off trying to find a way out of the country and their mother won't leave the shop. You've got to help me. We can't support so many people. Can you get me some extra rations?
WOLF. What are you talking about? Tell Sarah to go home to her mother.
TIM. She can't. The Brownshirts are looking for her. They've got to get out!
WOLF. Nobody's going to do them any harm.
TIM *(points to the pin on WOLF's lapel)*. Wolf, you've been going to those meetings with Stefan — don't you listen? They *hate* Jews. They intend to drive them *all* out of the country.
WOLF. Just the new ones, Tim. Just to make jobs for *our* people. You should come to a meeting. Come tonight — we sing, we drink beer. They pass out rations...
TIM. Damn it, Wolf. Look at me! I'm asking you for help. You can get extra rations.
WOLF. You want me to steal?
TIM. Look, it's just for a while. Until Sarah's father can arrange to get them out of the country.
WOLF. This could be trouble.
TIM. Look — get some rations, come by tonight. Please, we need your help. Please.
WOLF. All right. I'll do it if I can. But, Tim, you need to join us. You don't understand what's happening to this country.
TIM. That's the truth.

(STEFAN enters, with CARL, a youthful Brownshirt, in a hurry. They are carrying rocks.)

STEFAN. Wolf, come on — we're breaking up windows at the shirt factory!
WOLF. What about the meeting?
STEFAN. It's not until later. Come on! Tim can come along — if he's with us. *(Looks at TIM, with some resentment.)*
TIM. I don't think so.
WOLF. I think I ought to...

STEFAN *(handing WOLF rock)*. Here! Time for thinking's over. Let's have some action! One...two...three...

(TIM walks off. STEFAN, CARL and WOLF each cock their arms back to throw the rocks. T-MONEY enters, followed by LATASHA, BUTTERFINGER and BARBARA JEAN. As rocks smash, T-MONEY knocks on the "door" to DADDY MACK's high rise apartment. Rap music booms up.)

SCENE THIRTEEN
Daddy Mack's Crib, Newark.

(DADDY MACK enters, crosses to answer "door.")

DADDY MACK. Yo!
T-MONEY. It's me, Money! *(DADDY MACK opens the "door" and greets them.)*
DADDY MACK. What it look like?
T-MONEY. You, man.
DADDY MACK *(showing off his room)*. You likes?
LATASHA *(ALL comment at the same time as they look around.)* This is nice.
BARBARA JEAN. This is sweet.
BUTTERFINGER. Too cold!
T-MONEY. This is nice!
BUTTERFINGER. I want to live here!
T-MONEY. Damn, Mack, damn. Damn, damn, damn. You got the fly crib! Mack, this is dope.
DADDY MACK. You know, I'm trying to get into this taste thing. I got this woman comes in, tells me what to buy.
T-MONEY. Ah, it's bad.
DADDY MACK. That's what I'm tellin' you. Set you some goals; put your mind, you know, together. You can get anything they got out there.
BUTTERFINGER. I seen on TV late one night. This dude was talking about buyin' houses — with no money down? Then you sell these houses and get rich. Man, he had houses, boats, cars...
T-MONEY. Yeah, had him all these fine women, too!
LATASHA. You need to chill on that.

DADDY MACK. Mack will hook you up, understand. Mack will Hook-You-Up!
BARBARA JEAN. Mack, you got some?
DADDY MACK. Do I got some? Do I got some? What you got for me? *(Moves on her, suggestively.)*
BARBARA JEAN. Depends on what you got for me.
DADDY MACK. I got what you need, girl. That's what I got. *(T-MONEY and BUTTERFINGER smile, looking at each other knowingly.)*
BARBARA JEAN. Come on, Mack. I don't wanna...
DADDY MACK. Come here.

(They go in the "bedroom" offstage as DOUBLE-J enters and knocks at the "door.")

T-MONEY. Yeah?
DOUBLE-J. Come on. Let me in!
T-MONEY. I told you, boy, not to follow me here. Now, take your behind home!
DOUBLE-J. Come on, man, let me in, man. I wanna see Mack's crib!
T-MONEY *(opens "door," grabs him)*. Man, look, this is business here. Understand? I'm at work.
DOUBLE-J *(looking around at apartment)*. Damn, this is nice!
BUTTERFINGER *(knocks on "bedroom" door)*. Yo, let me hit that pipe!
DADDY MACK *(from offstage)*. Get away from that door!!
T-MONEY *(to DOUBLE-J)*. All right, you done seen it. Now, take your narrow ass home.
DOUBLE-J. Man, I'm a tell Mama what you doin'.
T-MONEY. *Tell* Mama. You know why? 'Cause I be taking care of them bills for Mama. She know the deal. Now, get your little pooh butt ass out my face.
DOUBLE-J *(a little sad)*. Man, you jive to me.
T MONEY. Go downstairs and wait for me in the street!! Now! Now! NOW!!!

(DOUBLE-J exits. BARBARA JEAN and DADDY MACK re-enter from other room. She is a little strung out.)

DADDY MACK *(to BUTTERFINGER)*. Now you can go in there. Go on and get some of that pipe...y'all family. Know what I'm saying?

(BUTTERFINGER *goes back in with* DADDY MACK *and* BARBARA JEAN.)

T-MONEY *(to* LATASHA*).* You see what I'm sayin', now? This could be us livin' like this. Livin' large. We could be down. Me and you, all this. I want you to have this with me. I want you to come with me. I need you. *(Kisses her gently.)*

LATASHA. I wanna be with you.

(Gunshots outside, from street. DADDY MACK, BUTTERFINGER *and* BARBARA JEAN *re-enter. All go to "window," looking down on street.)*

DADDY MACK. The fellas is gettin' busy. Look at 'em run. That's how they run when someone gets popped.

T-MONEY *(recognizing* DOUBLE-J*'s body).* Oh, God! That's Double-J! That's Double-J! Oh, God!

*(*T-MONEY *runs off. Others exit as* ANN *and* SARAH *enter. Pastoral music comes up, soothing as lights shift.)*

SCENE FOURTEEN
Sarah's house, the Jewish Quarter, Munich.

*(*ANN *is seated,* SARAH *is pacing. They are arguing.)*

SARAH. Oh, God, Mother, you're not listening.

ANN. It's not my job to listen. You're the daughter; you do the listening. I'm the mother; I'll do the talking.

SARAH. Don't do this. Come with me. It's safer at Tim's than it is here.

ANN. This is a little problem. Little problems become big problems then they become little problems again. This is as big as the problem is going to get.

SARAH. How can you say that? Every day there are signs, posters, meetings — condemning and blaming us. The Nazis are getting more votes than we have people in the entire country.

ANN. We've always been a minority.

SARAH. When Father gets back, I want you to come to Tim's with us. Pack the things you want to take and we'll move.

ANN. You can say move. This is easy for you to say. You're young. But this is our country. We were born here. I tell you they will not drive us from our own country.

(RUTH, their neighbor, enters.)

RUTH. Ann, Sarah, I've come to say goodbye. We are moving.
ANN. How can you move?
RUTH. We take our bags, we get on a boat and we go to live with relatives in America.
SARAH. You see how easy it is?
ANN. She has relatives. That is why it is easy for her. We have no relatives in another country. Right here are our uncles and aunts and cousins.

(There is a knock at the "door." TIM enters, looks around.)

TIM. Sarah, I think Wolf's going to help. He'll bring some extra food for your brothers and mother.
SARAH. Why even ask him for help? He's changed, Tim.
ANN. I don't like this talk. Wolf is a good boy. I would stand up in court and tell the world — forgive him whatever he does — he is like a son to me. I won't hear this talk.
SARAH. I'll be there, Tim. Mother, I'm going. When I come back, you're going to pack and you're going to go with me! I don't want to hear any more argument! *(She exits.)*
ANN. She doesn't want argument. She forgets who is the mother.
RUTH. You go with her now, Ann, it's not safe for you here.
ANN. This is a little problem. When it becomes a big problem — then we'll see — but I know these things — it will become a little problem again and then you will all say, "Why did we move?"

(DOUBLE-J enters into a monologue spot. Soft bluesy jazz slides under his first few lines. RUTH and ANN exit.)

DOUBLE-J. I kinda liked dying. In a strange sick kinda way. I liked playing with guns and everything so when they shot me for real — it hurt. Hurt real bad. I was screaming and bleeding and what not, but it was cool at the same time. Like it wasn't really me, like it was a movie. I remember Mama crying and screaming, holding me and everything. I felt sorry for her — being sad and all — but dying was cool. I had known other dudes that had died; D. Walker, Bobby Simms, Donnie Lamont. We talked about them like war heroes; John Wayne, Desert Storm, Purple Hearters. I knew I'd be one of them now — and being the youngest...eleven. They'd REALLY talk about me. Yah, dying...dying was cool.

(RUTH enters into another pool of soft light. She is older, wearing a shawl. DOUBLE-J's spot dims but doesn't go out. He stays frozen.)

RUTH. I know it was him. I can tell in part because of his eyes. There was a gentleness there — not like in some of the other guards. But then he would move from friendly to teary-eyed and his eyes would glaze over and he'd suddenly shout, "Damn you!" "Damn you, all!" And he would shoot someone. He just went crazy. They warned the newcomers to the camp not to talk to him. Not to look at him. Because once he befriended you, it wouldn't be long till he would kill you. Then when they brought Ann in, he went berserk. He lined up twenty of us, all ages, all women — and he yelled the orders. I was shot in the arm. I was so small. I burrowed deep into the pile of bodies and slipped off in the twilight. There is a part of me that can still see the gentleness in him — but I also remember his eyes. He is crazy and he is a killer. I know of at least thirty people he killed in cold blood. I can remember most of their names. Moshe Shellenberger, Ann Stroble, Naomi Kravits, D. Walker, Bobby Simms...

(POP 'N' FRESH enters and joins her speaking the names, taking her place in the spotlight as she exits. DOUBLE-J exits during reading and his light goes out.)

POP 'N' FRESH. Ann Stroble, Naomi Kravitz, D. Walker, Bobby Simms, Donnie Lamont. I understood Terry better than anyone. People say a lot of different things about him not having a father and all that kinda stuff. Like that's what did it. But, hey, we all knew dudes that did what Terry did — dudes with fathers, mothers, grandmothers — it didn't matter. The thing that had Terry was stronger than all that. It was like a god — a religion or something. He tried to get me in the business but I couldn't hang. I didn't need it like he did. I knew I could get out of the project on my own if I had to. Fortunately, I listened to Sister and them. At the time I didn't realize I was, but I was. It's funny knowing Terry like I did — knowing he was headed for something bad. I was still shocked when it happened. I guess I thought he'd never do something like that. I thought he would chill after his brother Double-J got killed. *(He exits.)*

(As lights shift and music comes up, we hear the Turkish March from Beethoven's 9th. The setting is now a "meetinghouse." Extra rations are set out. KURT *moves into place behind the table. Also in attendance are* STEFAN, CARL, WOLF *and* HEIDI. KURT *is delivering a passionate speech. ALL are responding with cheers and applause.* STEFAN *and* HEIDI *encourage* WOLF.*)*

SCENE FIFTEEN
A meetinghouse, Munich.

KURT. Tomorrow night we will induct new youth into this program.
STEFAN. That's you, Wolf!
KURT. Wear your pin, wear the swastika, the symbol of our faith, outwardly, so that the entire country will know what you stand for.
HEIDI. This is it, Wolf! I'm so proud of you.
KURT. All of us united can rebuild Germany and give it back the values that made us great once and can make us great again! *(ALL cheer. Cheering gets rhythmic and frenetic.)* Please line up and receive your extra rations, then we'll go down to the ale house and drink to our new youth! *(They receive rations,* WOLF *takes as much as he can and pockets a little extra.* CARL *notices him.)*
CARL. Need a little extra, young man?
WOLF. Excuse me?
CARL. It looked to me like you took a little extra ration.
WOLF. My mother — she's in ill health.
CARL. Or perhaps you have a sweetheart on the side?
WOLF. I don't know what you're talking about.
CARL. I am Carl. I am a friend of Tim's.
WOLF. I've seen you around. I didn't know you knew Tim.

150 *Voices: Plays for Studying the Holocaust*

CARL. Yes, in fact, we've been worried about Tim. He has missed a lot of school. And now, your mutual friend has disappeared — this Sarah.
WOLF. I don't know where she is.
CARL. Oh, don't be ashamed. Sarah is such a pretty one. So you will take her this extra ration?
WOLF. No.
CARL. I won't tell. I'm just surprised at Tim. But perhaps he will join us soon?
WOLF. I think he's going to, actually. Tomorrow. I'll take him some literature.
CARL. Excellent. When will you see him?
WOLF. Tonight — I don't know.
CARL. Here, then, have some of mine. *(Gives him more rations.)* Perhaps the girl will smile on me as well.
WOLF. Thank you.
KURT *(getting everyone's attention)*. Let's raise a toast to the Führer!

(They give the Nazi salute and yell "Sieg, Heil!" "Sieg, Heil!" All the T-MONEY and LATASHA GANG enter their party — hands flying into the air in time with the salute — singing and dancing. GERMANS exit as NEWARK YOUTH enter, filtering through each other.)

SCENE SIXTEEN
Terry's house, Newark.

ALL. Hip-hop hooray!! Ho! Hey! Ho!
Hip-hop hooray!! Ho! Hey! Ho!

(They break up into "party groups." SISTER SALIMU enters and moves from one to the other, offering help and advice.)

SISTER SALIMU. Tawana?
TAWANA. Hey, Sister.
GLORIA. What are you doing here, Sister?
SISTER SALIMU. Tawana, are you getting enough rest? You look tired.
GLORIA. She's up all the time.
TAWANA. I'm all right.

GLORIA. Why are you at the party, Sister? Shouldn't you be at mass or something? *(They laugh.)*
TAWANA. Sister, you be havin' nose problems. You be all in other people's business.
SISTER SALIMU. If you stay on that crack, it'll kill you and the baby. Let me help you.
TAWANA. You ain't my mama.
GLORIA. Yeah, her mama don't even tell her what to do.
TAWANA. You look here. You go tell those kids what to do. You don't tell me what to do. Come all in this party — talkin' all this garbage. Look, you need some damn kids of your own.
GLORIA. Yeah, Sister, you need a man.
TAWANA. Yeah, get a life and quit dippin' in my business. *(SISTER SALIMU crosses to another part of the party. Focus shifts to LATASHA and her GIRLS.)*
LATASHA. You see what Terry bought me? *(Shows off a new diamond ring. The GIRLS "oooh" and "ahhh" over the ring.)*
LISA. Girl, that is nice!
BARBARA JEAN. Terry bought you that?
LATASHA. He sure did!
LISA *(sings Prince song)*. Diamonds and pearls...*(She laughs.)*
LATASHA. Ladies, you are looking at a D-flawless three karat ring.
LISA. DAMN! Tell Terry to get me one. *(LATASHA gives her a shove.)*
BARBARA JEAN. Where Terry get some money for all that?
LATASHA. Where you think he got it? He got it working for Daddy Mack. You know. You got a problem with that?
BARBARA JEAN *(she does)*. No.
LATASHA. I ain't having all that. Ever since me and Terry hooked up and he started doing nice things for me, you be looking all nasty 'round the mouth. You jealous?
BARBARA JEAN. Jealous?! Please. Girl, you better not be so concerned about the way I be looking as you are with what TERRY be looking AT. If you get my meaning.
LATASHA. You trying to say he's "clocking" you?
BARBARA JEAN. It ain't just about me, homegirl. It's everybody. Just like he bought you that ring — he thinks he can buy anything and anybody now.
LATASHA. You buggin'. Get out my face!
BARBARA JEAN *(walking off)*. All right, cool. But these ain't nothing but the facts, *ma'am*. *(She exits.)*

LISA. She be trippin'.
LATASHA. I know. *(Half to LISA, half to herself.)* I should kick her big-buffalo-behind. *(LISA and LATASHA go off to a corner of the party. The MEN move down, T-MONEY showing them a car dealer advertisement for a sports car.)*
T-MONEY. Yeah, and they got this option package where you can get a spoiler and them nice rims, with the tinted windows, no extra cost.
BUTTERFINGER. You really gonna get this?
T-MONEY. Am I gonna get it?
BUTTERFINGER. That car cost a lotta money. I know you be makin' bank, but $30,000? Where you gonna get them kinda greenbacks? Ain't no bank gonna loan you no money. You gonna get a part-time job at Mickey-D's flippin' them McNuggets? That's a whole *hella* lotta McNuggets!
POP 'N' FRESH. Maybe he gonna be working that shake machine, too. *(They laugh as SISTER SALIMU approaches. She addresses them by their given names; T-MONEY is Terry, BUTTERFINGER is Robert, POP 'N' FRESH is Clarence.)*
SISTER SALIMU. Terry, Robert...Clarence. *(ALL laugh and tease.)*
BUTTERFINGER. Clarence...AHHHHH!
SISTER SALIMU. What are you reading, Terry?
TERRY. Ah, you know...
SISTER SALIMU *(takes the booklet and looks at it)*. Thinking about a new car? That's a nice one. Getting that car — how is that gonna make you feel?
T-MONEY. Make me feel? How you think it's gonna make me feel! Good!
SISTER SALIMU. What happened to the Malcolm X book I gave you?
T-MONEY. Sh...I read it.
SISTER SALIMU. And?
T-MONEY. He was a great man and all that, but that was then!
SISTER SALIMU. That was then! You sound just like him — Detroit Red.
T-MONEY. Look, Sister, you been real nice to my mama and all that, but, hey, you don't always know the deal.
SISTER SALIMU. What's the deal, Terry?
T-MONEY. What's the deal?
SISTER SALIMU. Yea, Terry, what's the deal, Terry? WHAT'S THE DEAL? *(He pulls out a wad of bills from his pocket. ALL back up a little, surprised by amount.)*
POP 'N' FRESH. T-Money!

T-MONEY *(slaps the wad, showing off and showing her what he thinks)*. This is the deal. It ain't about Malcolm X, Martin Luther King — none of them niggas. It's about this! *(Holds up the money.)* ...DEAD Presidents! It's about haves and haves not. Those that got some and those that ain't. It's about power; Bank power. Ain't no such thing as Black power when you ain't got no money. If that had been some niggas robbing that S&L...they would have been all up on the news covering up they face. It's about Cold Hard Cash. Sister, you know the problem with all that talk? You believe I'm gonna *be* somebody. You think we *all* gonna be somebody and I know, I KNOW I ain't never gonna be nobody — and you know I'm tellin' the truth! *(Looks at others. They mumble agreement.)*

GANG. I hear that. Know that's right. Yeah!

T-MONEY *(directly to SISTER SALIMU)*. See, you don't know nothing about this 'cause you ain't never had no money. You can't be a man with no money and you damn sho' can't be free! I'm a be a man and I'm gonna be free!

SISTER SALIMU. You been listening to that Daddy Mack. Everything you said is true. EVERYTHING. Yeah, we're nobody. We're morally bankrupt. So you've decided to be one of the takers, one of the HAVES. Well, take — Take his, and his, and hers, take mine. That won't make you a man and it won't set you free.

T-MONEY. See, you be in that church. You don't know what's happening out here!

SISTER SALIMU. Don't lay that mess on me. I know more than you will ever know about it. Everyday I see people like you, young Black men, fine men, good men, shot down DEAD by other Black men. I presume so they can have their share of the American Dream. You're not talking about a dream; you're talking about a nightmare.

T MONEY. Sister, don't nobody wanna hear all that.

SISTER SALIMU. Just shut up and listen! You're smart; you've got a future. You can get out of this place, YOU ALL CAN. You've got to believe. You've got to see beyond this, to better things.

T-MONEY *(pointing to car booklet)*. This is better things, Sister! This is looking beyond all this. For the first time in my life I believe I have this!

LATASHA *(entering argument)*. Terry, what's wrong?

T-MONEY. She be coming up here talking all this smack. Yo boom. We don't wanna hear it.

LATASHA. You shouldn't be talking this way to Sister.

T-MONEY. Shut up! I'll talk any way I want to. She ain't nobody. *(To SISTER SALIMU.)* I know you a nun and all that, but people don't care about that no more — not when it comes to this. *This* is business!
SISTER SALIMU. There's a war going on out there, Terry. People dying, mothers losing their children, babies shot down dead in the street, nobody cares; the government, the politicians, it's genocide.
T-MONEY *(sarcastic).* Please.
SISTER SALIMU. There's two kinds of genocide — a truck can come and pick you up and take you off to a death camp, or a truck doesn't come, in fact, no one comes because you've been left in a bad situation so you can die. You wanna be a part of killing off a race of people?
T-MONEY. I ain't killed nobody!!!
SISTER SALIMU. The truth hurts, doesn't it? I'm tellin' ya now, Terry. I see ya selling that poison — I'm gonna take it and I'm gonna take your money. *(There is silence. We know that this is serious.)*
T-MONEY. This ain't none of your business, Sister. Understand? Now, go back to that convent...
SISTER SALIMU. No, Terry!
T-MONEY. This is bigger than you!
SISTER SALIMU. No, Terry. I swear if I see you, I will take your drugs and your money and destroy them, you hear me? You hear me?!
T-MONEY. I don't know about all that. I know this; you mess with my money, you gonna get hurt.
LATASHA. Terry! *(He slaps her.)*
SISTER SALIMU. Don't lay your hand on her again.
T-MONEY. Stay out of my business!

(There is a beat, silence. BARBARA JEAN enters, out of breath, from outside.)

BARBARA JEAN. Did y'all hear? They found Daddy Mack, dead in his car. He was full of holes. Daddy Mack is dead! *(There is a brief pause as they absorb the information.)*
SISTER SALIMU. Yeah, I can see being a taker is really gonna make you a man. *(ALL look at each other. Then they exit slowly as ANN moves into monologue spot. Soft jazz music comes up and plays during first part of monologue, then fades.)*

ANN. I didn't think he'd kill me. I knew the problem was big, but I didn't think it would get as big as it did. I saw Wolf when I got to the camp. I asked him what he was doing there and he told me they sent him there to learn how to kill. I asked if he had learned how and his eyes grew distant. He began to yell. I knew I was going to die and I knew that was a big problem. But then he would have to hide what he did and that was his problem, and I hoped that at last it would be his turn to suffer and not mine. *(BARBARA JEAN enters a pool of light. As she starts her monologue, ANN exits and her light fades.)*

BARBARA JEAN. We were all surprised when Terry went off on Sister. It was funny because we all knew then that Terry had changed, that he had crossed the line. Everyone knew. We all knew Terry was different now that he wasn't Terry anymore, he was T-Money. Terry was *possessed!* All he ever talked about was money and what he was gonna get. He had all these gold chains, he got him a gold tooth. Some people dug it — really looked up to him, for having money and all. But mainly people thought it was sad — not out loud but to themselves. Terry thought everybody believed he was IT. You know, I just wished we would have said something, snapped our fingers and pulled him from this trance. I feel guilty for that. Like it was partly my fault. I was too busy with my own problems. Most people feel like there was no stopping him. Myself, I don't know. I know this. There are no innocent bystanders. *(Exits.)*

SCENE SEVENTEEN
Tim's house, Munich.

(Military music picks up as lights change for Tim's "living room." WOLF enters.)

TIM. Wolf, did you bring the food?
WOLF. Yes. Who is Carl?
TIM. Carl? I don't know. Who do you mean?
WOLF. Some man named Carl. He seemed to know all about you — and about Sarah.
TIM. Wolf, this is trouble. I'll get Sarah — but you can't stay long. If anyone asks you about these rations, tell them you got them for me. Only me, you understand?

WOLF. I'll say what I want to. *(Pause, while TIM tries to think of what to say to him.)*
TIM. Thank you, Wolf.

(SARAH enters and sits, not looking directly at WOLF who stays standing, aloof. TIM exits.)

SARAH. Tim talked you into bringing us the food?
WOLF. I would have anyway, if I'd known where you were. Why are you hiding?
SARAH. They burnt out half the shop, Wolf. They'll burn out the rest eventually and I don't want my brothers in it when they do. I can't get my mother to leave.
WOLF. Maybe I could talk to her.
SARAH. Would you? She's always liked you. Wolf, what's happening?
WOLF. What do you mean?
SARAH. To you, to us, to the country. You once asked me to marry you, on the playground. Do you remember? It's not a trick question, I won't hold you to it. We were only seven. But I remember — and now I know that if you were even seen with me, your friends would...
WOLF. That's ridiculous. I do what I want.
SARAH *(turns and looks directly at him. He turns away)*. Even while you wear that? *(She points to the pin.)*
WOLF. I don't believe everything they teach us. We have to wear this. It doesn't hurt to say a few things you don't believe in to get what you need. *(Indicates rations.)*
SARAH. It doesn't?

(There is a bustle and in walk KURT and CARL — they are pushing TIM between them.)

KURT. Wolf? What are you doing — talking with this Jew?!!
WOLF. What?
SARAH. Let him go!!!
TIM. I can explain.
CARL. You certainly have some explaining to do. These people are in possession of an excessive amount of rations.
WOLF. But you gave me these!
CARL *(to WOLF)*. Stay quiet!

WOLF. I took those rations. I took them from the meeting and gave them to...
KURT. Careful what you say, Wolf. You could be drummed out of the Party. It is against our rules to support a Jew. Do you wish to give up your chance to be one of us?
WOLF. But I did. I took the rations and...
TIM. He gave them to me. I don't have enough for my family. Wolf and I have been friends for a long time and...
KURT. And he knew you were hiding this Jew?
WOLF *(unsure of himself)*. Yes?
TIM *(on top of WOLF's answer)*. No!
KURT. Wolf! Did you or didn't you?
CARL. Careful how you answer, Wolf. Not only your party affiliation, but your life may be on the line.
SARAH. It doesn't matter, Wolf, protect yourself.
TIM. He didn't know anything about this. I did this on my own.
KURT *(waiting for WOLF's answer)*. Wolf?

(STEFAN enters.)

STEFAN. Wolf. Mother needs us at home. Did you get the extra rations? I heard there was some confusion. *(ALL look at WOLF. This is his moment of truth.)*
WOLF. I got extra rations for my mother. I just stopped by to see Tim. I didn't know he would take them and give them to her.
KURT. Good. *(Pause. He looks at CARL and smirks.)* Let's kill this Jew...*(He shoves SARAH down.)*
CARL *(shoving TIM down)*. And the Jew-lover.
WOLF. Here?
KURT. Why not?
STEFAN. We'll say they were looting.
CARL *(laughing)*. They've got the rations.
WOLF. Aren't we supposed to take them in?
KURT. And let someone else do it?
CARL. Are you afraid, Wolfgang?
WOLF. No.
STEFAN *(gives WOLF a gun)*. Here, you do it, Wolf.
WOLF. I...I can't.
KURT. Are you with us or not!
STEFAN. Do it, Wolf!

WOLF. But, Stefan...
STEFAN. All right...*(Indicates TIM.)* Then him!

(T-MONEY enters from the other side of stage and starts across. SISTER SALIMU runs up, grabs him and spins him around, takes his drugs and throws them down. He pulls his gun.)

T-MONEY. Sister, don't do that!
WOLF. Tim? *(TIM keeps his head down. T-MONEY shoves SISTER SALIMU, but she comes back at him, struggles.)*
STEFAN. Do it!
T-MONEY. Don't make me do it! *(WOLF squeezes the trigger as T-MONEY pulls on the gun. A shot rings out. TIM and SISTER SALIMU slump to the ground. SARAH jumps up and starts off. KURT grabs her.)*
STEFAN. Now, her!

(WOLF hesitates, STEFAN grabs the gun from him and fires. SARAH slumps down and lands on top of SISTER SALIMU. WOLF, CARL and STEFAN walk off. OLD WOLF moves to "prison cot." YOUNG WOLF stands beside him. T-MONEY moves to "prison cot." LATASHA stands beside him. KURT moves to center spot. SISTER SALIMU and BUTTERFINGER move to outside spots for monologue scene.)

SCENE EIGHTEEN
Monologues.

KURT. We only did what we were told.
CARL and STEFAN *(exiting)*. We only did what we were told.
BUTTERFINGER. When Daddy Mack got offed, we shoulda chilled, right THEN, we shoulda cooled out. But naw, the BANK had our minds. We wasn't thinking about nothing but them digits. Here I am, doin' time.
WOLF. When I came to America, one of the questions they asked was, "What was your occupation?" I answered gardener.
OLD WOLF. Gardener.
WOLF. Gardener.

OLD WOLF. They didn't ask me what I *planted*. *(OLD WOLF, WOLF and T-MONEY exit slowly.)*
LATASHA. Terry...Terry...I love you. I do...I've got something to tell you...I'm going to have a baby.
KURT. But that one, Wolf — he was reluctant to kill. Eventually I sent him to Buchenwald. He did well. He became a most accomplished killer.
SISTER SALIMU. When I became a nun, I knew I wanted to serve my people. This was my neighborhood. I grew up here. I knew the risk, but when Terry killed me...I still couldn't believe it.
BUTTERFINGER. When I think back on what we did it was like somebody put some voodoo on us, a spell, a curse! I wish my mind had been right. I swear I wouldn't be here now.
LATASHA. We're going to get married and we'll have a nice house and a big yard where our kids can play. It's going to be good, real good, you'll see...
BUTTERFINGER. At least Pop 'n' Fresh got out. At least he listened — Clarence — and we always said he was stupid.
KURT. He got out — after the war. I'm sure his charm got him safe passage. He probably married and lived a good life.
LATASHA. I love you, baby, I love you.
KURT. Some got out — some got caught. He could be living a free and happy life in a country with no problems, like America.
LATASHA. We'll have a nice house and a big yard where our kids can play, you'll see...
SISTER SALIMU. My God...I don't want them to destroy Terry because of me. In the end, they always want to destroy but they never want to save in the beginning.
KURT. We only did what we were told.
BUTTERFINGER. That Bank had our minds.
SISTER SALIMU. It wasn't Terry that fired that gun; it was T-Money. That thing is what brought this sorrow upon us.

(Lights dim as they exit. Jail music. OLD WOLF and T-MONEY re-enter.)

SCENE NINETEEN
A contemporary prison cell.

(T-MONEY *is messed up, his shirt ruffled.* OLD WOLF *shuffles into scene behind him.*)

T-MONEY. Man, where was you?
OLD WOLF. You're all right, now.
T-MONEY. No, man, where was you? You supposed to be my protection.
OLD WOLF. They would have killed us both. I got help.
T-MONEY. Damn. I got no respect now. I'm done with you. That's out! That's over. You ain't done nothin' but mess me up! I ain't gonna be your Maytag no more!
OLD WOLF. You're a fool, T-Money. You're making a mistake, a stupid mistake. Don't do this!
T-MONEY. You know what your problem is? You afraid to die. You should have died with the Jew girl you killed and that other boy!
OLD WOLF. I am *not* afraid to die! I lived six years with a gun pointed at my head! You know nothing about death!
T-MONEY. Yo, peep this. I ain't afraid to die. I'd trade places with my brother in a heartbeat. But you — you want me with you 'cause you afraid of the Homies in the yard. You afraid of everybody. Everybody's afraid of you, and you still afraid! You a stone trip.
OLD WOLF. But you're nothing, ghetto-nigger-Jew. Just a black nothing...Schwartza.
T-MONEY. Man, I'm gonna mess you up!
OLD WOLF. You've got your own concentration camp down there, Money — but you don't need us guards — you people just kill yourselves off. America has the Nazi system beat and you're doing the exact same thing I did and if you hadn't been stupid enough to get caught you'd be out there killin' more niggers right now! (T-MONEY *grabs a sharpened kitchen knife from his bunk and backs* OLD WOLF *up to his cot.*)
T-MONEY. Yeah, well, you in the death camp now. You chained to the wall, you gonna die here, old man. (T-MONEY *jumps* OLD WOLF *and puts knife to his throat, a pause.*)
OLD WOLF. Do it...Do it!!
T-MONEY (*looks at him, slowly removes the knife and backs off*). No, man. It ain't gonna be me. You deserve to suffer. You deserve to

listen to me the rest of yo' sorry life. *(Pause.* OLD WOLF *pulls himself up.)* Maybe if I don't kill you, I'll get out here one day.
OLD WOLF. You *can't* kill, can you, T-MONEY? Takes a man to kill — to follow through. That is what is necessary to survive.
T-MONEY *(backing away)*. Man, GET AWAY from me!! Keep that madness to yourself.
OLD WOLF. I am as normal as you are.
T-MONEY. No, man, you a cannibal.
OLD WOLF *(laughs, steps away from him)*. You're a very funny child.
T-MONEY. Man, just stay away from me! That's yo' side! You stay there! Don't come near me! Don't say nothing, you hear? Don't ask me nothing. Don't call my name. Don't call me Money! My name's Terry, you hear? You hear? Terry! *(Lights go down.)*

End of Play

Production Notes

Set Concept:
Onstage there are four "columns" of stone or concrete block topped with barbed wire. The columns are covered with graffiti appropriate to both time periods. Between each column there is a curtain of slit black fabric. The curtains are the entrances and exits for the actors. In front of the columns is a unit set which consists of platforms and levels. Two of these thrust forward and represent the prison cots, beds, doorstoops, and furniture. The units are lit to indicate the playing areas of the separate scenes. Five special areas are lit with spots for monologues. Music appropriate to the upcoming setting and mood is played during light shifts. Lighting and music are very important to establish mood.

Teaching Activities

- As a class, watch the Spike Lee film *Four Little Girls* about the September 15, 1963, bombing of a black church in Birmingham, Alabama. Next, ask students to discuss how the burning of American black churches in the summer of 1996 is reminiscent of persecution of minorities in Germany as Hitler rose to power. Compare these 1963 and 1996 acts of violence against blacks in the United States with the destruction of synagogues during *Kristallnacht* and other acts of persecution against Jews in Germany.

- Discuss peer pressure with pupils. Query them as to some of the things they might be convinced to do at the urging of friends. What are the perceived consequences of not going along with the crowd? Challenge the students to draw a relationship between peer pressure they might experience and the peer pressure faced by German youngsters and adolescents being urged to become members of Hitler's youth movement.

- Invite classmates to role play a scene in which a group of friends tries to convince a reluctant friend to join Hitler's youth movement. What are some of the arguments that might be presented by both sides? Follow this by asking students to identify scenes from the play that deal with pressure to conform and to stage these in the classroom.

- Compare the actions taken against Jews in Nazi Germany to the violent situations associated with drugs and gangs in America today. Ask students to debate the question, "Are drugs causing genocide among America's minorities?" and to support their respective positions.

- Discuss similarities in the situations that resulted in T-Money and Old Wolf being imprisoned. Provide an opportunity for students to make collages or posters that give visual form to these correlations.

- Provide opportunities for students to experiment with unifying the monologues in this play into a single performance. Readers theatre or choral readings are two suggested approaches. Then, ask them to describe the emergent messages when monologues are juxtaposed like this. Which voiced messages make the strongest impression and why? How does this type of staging differ from reading or seeing the entire play?

- Students may wish to cast, rehearse, and stage this play or, using the adaptation method described above, perform monologues from it. They then may invite other classes to see their show. Holding a talkback session between audience and cast afterward allows audience members to ask questions and share their responses to the work.

- Hitler stressed the importance of youth to the Third Reich. Special organizations such as Hitler Youth and the League of German Girls catered to this population. Query students with the following: (1) What was expected of a member of Hitler Youth? (2) Why might young people join? (3) Are there comparable organizations in America today and, if your answer is affirmative, who do you think joins them and why? Request oral or written answers.

- Ask students to select one of the following quotes and one of the characters from this play. Require that, in role, each class member refutes or agrees with the quoted point of view. Stipulate that answers must be firmly grounded in the prevailing norms of life for the character. When this part of the exercise has concluded, encourage each pupil to explain why he or she selected that particular character and quote. Ask, too, that each describe the process used for gathering needed information and formulating his or her response.

    The following quotes appeared in the November 1995 newsletter of the MENSA chapter in Los Angeles. MENSA is the organization whose membership is regarded as highly intellectual. This newsletter "circulates to a readership that claims IQs in the top 2 percent of the public."

    1. "Those people who are so mentally defective that they cannot live in society should, as soon as they are identified as defective, be humanely dispatched."

2. Or that Adolf Hitler's greatest offense was not the killing of 6 million Jews in the holocaust [sic] but "the fact that his actions prevent a rational discussion of the creation of the master race."

In defending her decision to publish the articles — which appeared to propose extermination of the homeless, the mentally retarded, the old, and the infirm — newsletter editor and MENSA member Nikki Frey was unapologetic and surprised that anybody would be offended.

3. "I would not print anything I thought was truly harmful or offensive," she said. "I didn't think it was harmful; I don't think it's even that offensive — nobody wants a deformed child."

In another issue of that same publication, Jon Evans wrote,

4. "It is not clear to me just exactly why anyone would expend time and effort and money on the homeless.... Granted, there are a few people who have fallen beneath the blows of circumstances and are unable to afford any place to live, but they are few and far between. The rest of the homeless should be humanely done away with, like abandoned kittens."
   Nora Zamichow, 11 January 1995, "'Nazi ideas' quoted in MENSA bulletin outrages member," *The Saginaw News*, A4.

5. Thomas Robb, leader of the Ku Klux Klan, "said that his group's main goal is to end federal government actions that have attempted to integrate the races and protect the civil rights of minorities."

6. "All people are entitled to their own homeland and self-determination," Robb said. "The Founding Fathers intended to maintain a white culture."

7. "(Different races) coexisting at the same time and place, that's against the laws of physics. I didn't make it that way. One (race) has to be dominant. The government can't serve two cultures."
   Steven Verberg, 5 July 1996, "Klan leader softens message of hate for broader appeal," *The Saginaw News*, A1.

- Use either or both of these mapping exercises with the class. For the first activity, display a map of the world. Using push pins of the same color, mark the known routes by which drugs enter the United States today. Using pins of another color, mark the routes of European trains carrying victims to Auschwitz during the Holocaust. Ask students to respond to these visual images of fatal transport. In the second activity, again display a map of the world. Identify and mark those regions where genocidal activities now are occurring. Use this as the backdrop for a television show staged in the classroom. Using a news show format, have students research the nature of these conflicts and then, assuming roles as broadcasters, deliver reports to the classroom audience.

- As a class project, create an annotated videography. Entries should include videos and recent films about the drug trade in American minority ghettos and stories about German youth in the Third Reich. Be certain to include popular films, television shows, and documentaries.

- Pose the following question to the class, "What arguments do you think lawyers defending Old Wolf and those prosecuting him would use relative to his deportation to Israel? Both sides know that he could be tried there for war crimes." Following this, ask students to form four teams and to engage in the following written task. Imagining that the case is to be presented to a jury, Team #1 is to develop Old Wolf's attorney's opening statement while Team #2 is responsible for the prosecution's opening arguments. Team #3 is to create an editorial arguing for his extradition while Team #4 is to create one favoring incarceration in a United States penitentiary. All four teams should nominate a spokesperson to read these position statements aloud. If desired, assume T-Money is charged with murdering Sister Salimu and adapt this activity with Teams #1 and #2, respectively, presenting defense and prosecution arguments against and for prosecution. Teams #3 and #4 should editorialize, respectively, for dropping the charges or for appropriate punishment.

At Nuremberg, both Nazi Party and German government officials faced charges of conspiracy to wage a war of aggression, war crimes, and crimes against humanity. Challenge the class to conceptualize a criminal proceeding against Old Wolf and to decide which of these charges would be leveled against him were he to be extradited and tried for his actions. Require that students support their choice(s).

Chapter 4

Plays and Activities: Advanced Study

The Man in the Glass Booth

The Playwright: Robert Shaw

Robert Shaw earned his artistic reputation both as an actor and as a writer. His stage, screen, and television performance credits are numerous and his literary accomplishments substantial. As a writer, Shaw is responsible for five novels, four screenplays and scripts, and four play and poetry titles. In 1962, he received the Hawthornden Prize for his novel, *The Sun Doctor*. *The Man in the Glass Booth* marked his debut as a playwright and earned him a 1969 Antoinette Perry (Tony) nomination.

Trained at the Royal Academy of Dramatic Arts in London, Robert Shaw first appeared professionally on stage as Angus in the Shakespeare Memorial Theatre's production of *Macbeth*. His stage credits include many Shakespearean roles as well as a variety of other parts. He appeared in thirty plays from 1949 through 1974, including *The*

Caretaker and *The Dance of Death*. In *Luther* and in *Gantry*, he was cast in the title roles. Shaw worked as a film actor from 1951 through 1978 and gained international recognition. He is best remembered for the characters he created in *From Russia With Love*, *A Man for All Seasons*, *The Sting*, *Jaws*, and *The Deep*. He received an Academy Award nomination for his work in *A Man for All Seasons*.

The son of Dr. Thomas Shaw and his wife, Doreen, Shaw was born on August 9, 1927, in Westhoughton, Lancashire, England. He was twelve years old when his father committed suicide. The actor and writer married three times, first to actress Jennifer Bourke, then to actress Mary Ure, and, in 1976, to Virginia Jansen. These unions produced ten children. Shaw made his home in Ireland until his death from a heart attack in 1978. During his life, he deeply wished to be recognized as a serious writer. Shaw was working on *The Ice Floe*, a novel he expected would cement his literary reputation, at the time of his death.

The Play

Flanked by *The Flag,* written in 1965, and *A Card from Morocco*, written in 1969, *The Man in the Glass Booth* was the second in a trilogy of novels by Shaw. Authored in 1967, it was his best-known literary work. The story of Nazi impersonator Arthur Goldman was adapted for the stage and premiered in London, also in 1967. A successful Broadway run followed and resulted in a Best Play of the 1968–1969 theatre season designation in the Best Plays yearbook. The play was directed both in London and New York by Harold Pinter and starred Donald Pleasance as Goldman. Respected actors F. Murray Abraham and Abe Vigoda were also in the Broadway cast. *The Man in the Glass Booth*, produced by Glasshouse Productions and Peter Bridge, Ivor David Balding & Associates, Ltd., and Edward M. Meyers with Leslie Ogden played in New York at the Royale Theatre. It was a nominee for an Antoinette Perry (Tony) Award in the Best Dramatic Play category but lost to *The Great White Hope*. The story was later made into a movie with Maximilian Schell.

That the play often drew mixed reactions is, perhaps, as much a result of the subject matter and enigmatic protagonist as it is the dramatist's delivery of content. Controversy enveloped the script on both sides of the Atlantic. Still, its merits as a thought-provoking piece of theatre can hardly be denied. With the trial of Adolf Eichmann serving both as a model and as a factual basis for comparison, Shaw shaped a fictional work that is both complex and perplexing in its imaginative combination of history, philosophy, and human psychology.

Information about the Play and the Holocaust

In the Nazi quest for world domination, there were those who ordered heinous and barbaric acts and those who executed the orders. At war's end, some of the most ruthless of these individuals were caught and brought to trial, others committed suicide to avoid judicial examination, and still others scattered to various parts of the world seeking refuge. *The Man in the Glass Booth*, with its clearly broad connection to war crimes and criminals, invites a more focused look at the post-war Nuremberg Trials, Nazi war criminals in America, and the trial of Adolf Eichmann in Israel.

Twenty-one of twenty-four indicted Nazi leaders stood trial in the first of a series of judicial proceedings known as The Nuremberg Trials. This International Military Tribunal presided over by eight judges (two each from the United States, Great Britain, France, and the Soviet Union) lasted from November 20, 1945, to October 1, 1946. Conspiracy, war crimes, crimes against peace, and crimes against humanity were the charges leveled and the brutality of the evidence was unrelenting. Prosecutors from the allied countries above presented exhibits such as filmed footage of the horrible sights that met British and American troops entering the Dachau, Buchenwald, and Bergen-Belsen Concentration Camps and documented torture, murder, forced labor, disregard for civilians' basic human needs, death by starvation and freezing, and medical experiments with prisoners as subjects. Annihilation further was evidenced by visual records of piles of clothing and human hair and, of course, the infamous gas chambers. A seventeen-thousand page trial transcript resulted from the testimony of nearly one hundred witnesses, official documents and photographs, affidavits, and films being entered into the court's record. After deliberating for a month, it took judges a day and a half to announce verdicts. Of eleven defendants sentenced to death, ten were hanged on October 16, 1946. The eleventh, Hermann Goering, took cyanide the night before his scheduled execution. Seven were fated for long prison stays that commenced in July 1947 at Spandau Prison in the British sector of Berlin. Three were found not guilty.

Other trials followed. Nuremberg was again the site when American judges held trials for 177 top-level German officials. Others charged with more conventional wrongdoings faced American military commissions. European nations and the occupying powers likewise held legal proceedings and meted out justice. Culpability was examined for perpetrators and collaborators such as SS officials, doctors, lawyers, government and military officials, and industrial leaders.

Americans held about five hundred trials, involving about seventeen hundred defendants, at Dachau. These dealt largely with conventional charges of criminality. More than one thousand defendants, for example, were tried for acts committed at concentration camps in the American-occupied zone. Often, those accused faced survivors who had intimate knowledge of the heinous deeds.

Punishment, however, was not always complete or long-lasting. Only about twenty percent of Nazi war criminals were ultimately tried and, for some who were imprisoned, new political priorities in the 1950s resulted in reduced sentences or parole. Americans, for example, found conducting war crimes trials an arduous task. As the Cold War began to dominate American thought, moving toward improving relationships with Germany seemed a more desirable course.

Thousands of Nazi war criminals evaded capture and trial and made their way directly to the United States where, like other immigrants, they started new lives. They needed to do little more than lie in order to gain legal entry to this country, largely because the Displaced Persons Act based admission to the United States largely upon nationality, stated occupation, and ancestry. This, combined with indiscriminate background checks, often made it easier for perpetrators of Nazi crimes to enter this country than it was for surviving victims to do so. America brought 400,000 displaced persons to her shores from 1948-1952, looking more to what they could do for the country than to what they had done in the war. Stewards of Nazi policy able to lie about their backgrounds and professions easily entered the country and then lived quietly so as not to draw attention to themselves. When the Displaced Persons Act expired in 1952, the Immigration and Nationality Act made it even easier for Nazi offenders to come here.

An absence of American government policy to the contrary made the presence of war criminals in this country allowable. If, however, the true identities of these individuals were later revealed, they faced legal action. Denaturalization and then deportation were favored ways to deprive them of their rights as citizens and to send them packing. Faced with these consequences, the accused often denied their Nazi past in spite of hard evidence to the contrary.

One of the most famous war criminals was Adolf Eichmann, who was found living in Argentina. Eichmann had been in charge of deportation units responsible for slaughtering millions. Tracked down by Simon Wiesenthal, he was brought to Israel for trial.

Unable to bring Nazi criminals to justice until the establishment of the Jewish state, Israelis vowed to neither forgive nor forget once this was possible. The groundwork for Eichmann's trial was laid when, on March 27, 1950, the Nazi and Nazi Collaborators (Punishment) Law was introduced in the Israeli legislative body, the Knesset. Important features of this bill were that (1) it allowed trial in Israel for acts committed outside of that country's borders; (2) it provided for punishment of actions that were not defined as crimes when they were committed; and, (3) it was retroactive. Already under consideration was the Prevention and Punishment of Genocide Law. Together, these bills were designed to avenge past inhuman treatments and to insure that such barbarities would not occur again.

Eichmann's trial began April 11 and concluded on August 14, 1961. The first count against him read as follows:

> (a) The accused, together with others, during the period 1939 to 1945, caused the killing of millions of Jews, in his capacity as the person responsible for the execution of the Nazi plan for the physical extermination of the Jews, known as "the final solution of the Jewish problem."
>
> Paula J. Draper. *Holocaust Resource* (Willowdale, Ontario: Holocaust Education and Memorial Centre of Toronto, 1985), 51.

Israel was determined to accord Eichmann a fair trial, something he had never given those whose deaths he orchestrated. Victims who had survived faced him in court. In addition to hundreds of these witnesses, 1600 documents were entered into evidence. Although Eichmann claimed that he was merely carrying out orders, he was found guilty and hanged on May 31, 1962. So as not to defile Israeli land, after cremation his ashes were scattered at sea.

Synopsis

Arthur Goldman, the central character in *The Man in the Glass Booth*, has established a reputation as a wealthy German-American businessman and is living comfortably in the United States until he is kidnapped and arrested as an ex-Nazi war criminal and returned to Israel for trial. Rather than deny the charges, the brusk and often offensive Goldman seems to relish the opportunity to use the judicial proceeding as a forum for his philosophical diatribes. He willingly assumes the identity of a vitriolic and unremorseful Nazi butcher, offering himself as a target for the hatred of concentration camp survivors. As a sacrificial villain, Goldman is willing to take upon himself the emotional weights carried by Jewish survivors. He is, however, unmasked as a former prisoner in a Nazi concentration camp before he can complete his ruse. Goldman, in point of fact, was not the captor but the captive.

The scene that follows shows Arthur Goldman's explosive war crimes trial and the unmasking of his true identity. The courtroom drama unfolding here is both repelling and compelling, grim and gripping, and, undoubtedly, emotionally riveting.

The Man in the Glass Booth

(The PROSECUTOR's *voice on microphone speaks in the blackout.*)

PROSECUTOR'S VOICE. How could it happen? Why did it happen? What of the Allies? Why the Germans? And why the Jews? I tell you only a Jewish court will render justice to Jews; I tell you it is our duty to sit in judgment on our enemies, I tell you it is our right. But I make no ethnic distinctions — I would indict this man for crimes against other peoples if crimes there were — but this man...this monster...has concerned himself with Jews, is only concerned with Jews. This monster has only murdered Jews! And when I look at this monster *I* am only concerned with Jews. *(The* LIGHTS *come on.)* You will hear Jewish witness after Jewish witness, Jewish suffering after Jewish suffering. Yes, I will show you the calamity of the Jewish people in this generation; yes, I will show you the calamity of Jewry; yes, I will show you what we suffered, and I will show you why. Because...because the whole tragedy of Jewry is to be my central concern. *(The PROSECUTOR sits down.)*

(During the blackout, the cell has changed into a court. GOLDMAN enters with a GUARD, sits in a bullet-proof glass booth; The PRESIDING JUDGE at a table; The PROSECUTOR at another; MRS. ROSEN, STEIGER and DURER at another.)

GOLDMAN. Excuse me.
JUDGE. Yes.
GOLDMAN. Having heard with admiration for many days the magniloquence of the Prosecutor...having listened to his many points...his many intentions...may I make a personal observation? I mean...not knowing your Israeli legal procedure precisely, not wishing to disturb it — I just ask. What I mean *is*, Your Honor — it's obvious you got to be Orthodox around here.
JUDGE. What kind of personal observations?
GOLDMAN. Eh?
JUDGE. What kind of personal observations?
GOLDMAN. Been put off my stroke. *(He points to the audience.)* Just seen Mrs. Dorff out there. Jesus. She's blond. And they told me she was dead. My German wife, you understand, Marlene. Excuse me, Your Honor. Call me a bigamist. Bit of a shock. Changed her name, I shouldn't wonder. Wearing a wig, I don't doubt. *(He grins at MRS. ROSEN.)* Don't get jealous, Rosy — that's all over and done with.
JUDGE. Adolf Karl Dorff —
GOLDMAN. Rosy's a jealous woman! "That's one thing I'll never forgive," she said. That's what you said, didn't you, Rosy? Hi, Mrs. Dorff. Hi, Marlene.
JUDGE. Adolf Karl Dorff, what kind of personal observation?
GOLDMAN. Please don't shout, Your Honor. It echoes in here. If I get frightened I might revert. All the time I've got to watch that. It's about the indictment.
JUDGE. Specific to the indictment?
GOLDMAN. No, very general.
JUDGE. Then your turn will come in its proper time.
GOLDMAN. Who's gonna decide that?
JUDGE. The Court will decide that. Don't provoke me.

GOLDMAN. I'm sorry, Your Honor. I'm sorry, I didn't mean to do that. That's not my intention, but the point is, Your Honor, you know your local rules and I don't. Except on times when I'm directly answering Jewish questions, I think I should be able to put up my Gentile hand and ask you if I can make a Gentile observation. I mean what are we interested in here, Your Honor, justice or the suffering of the Jewish people?

JUDGE. I shall decide that. Very well. I shall rule on each observation.

GOLDMAN. Thank you, Your Honor. *(To* MRS. ROSEN.*)* Rosy, you might tell Marlene, I saw her friend in Manhattan and he was looking just great.

JUDGE. Keep to the indictment, Dorff.

GOLDMAN. Excuse me...the mind wanders...Your Honor, when your prosecutor comes in, comes in from her press conferences, and getting on the T.V. — which I didn't — and makes her very magniloquent jerk-you-in-the-tear-ball speeches — and has been raising questions of suffering and how could all this have happened, and why did it happen to the Jews, and what was everybody else doin', and why did we Germans do it so bad and so on and so forth? Now these are very great questions: but if I understand justice, Your Honor, it's nobody's suffering that should be on trial here, it's what I done. It's what I did. It's what I did that's the point. Did I not hear, Your Honor, the prosecutor conclude her opening speech by "the whole tragedy of Jewry is to be our central concern"?

JUDGE. You did hear that.

GOLDMAN. But I, I, Your Honor, *I* am your central concern.

JUDGE. Yes, yes. I shall make you my concern.

GOLDMAN. Thank you, Your Honor. May I point out somethin' else?

JUDGE. Yes.

GOLDMAN. I saved your two young Jewish guys and Mrs. Rosen, my interrogator, murder; Charlie Cohn invites them into my Manhattan apartment and what would they have done if I'd refused to accompany them out? Is that not such a crime as you would call my own? Would not the pistol have been at the back of my head?

JUDGE. Irrelevant.

GOLDMAN. But I mean what's got to be proved, Your Honor — that I'm not fit to live?

JUDGE. From now on when you digress, I shall switch your microphone off.

GOLDMAN. Judge, you're honest! I appreciate ya!

(MRS. LEVI *enters the stand.*)

MRS. LEVI. Levi. Forty-seven people were led barefoot to the quarry. Dorff stood at the bottom of the steps watching his men load jagged boulders on their backs, then these people had to carry them to the top of the cliff. Each journey the boulders grew heavier. In the evening, forty bodies were lying along the road.

GOLDMAN. Yes, I remember that, but *you* did great — remarkable constitution. Course, some of you might be wonderin' why Mrs. Levi and her head friends got on the train in the first place — got on the train to the quarry. There was only three guards, as I recall — Kirlewanger's got a villa in Cairo, I'm here, and Pohse's drawing a pension in Hamburg — anyway, why did all these people keep gettin' on cattle trains and goin' to quarries and suchlike? Might I enlighten you on that, Your Honor?

JUDGE. No, I know why. Their fate was beyond their knowledge. Every conjecture was arbitrary. They had no foundation.

GOLDMAN. Yes, that's it. I always confused 'em. Everything was done so simple. Ask for your suitcase, I said: "Sure, later!" Ask for your baby, I said: "Sure, stick with the kid." All very peaceful, all very calm. Of course if I had to make an example I'd use my imagination — stuff your genitals in your mouth, burn your feet off...somethin' like that. Couldn't follow any precedents. Couldn't allow any heroes...you follow? *(Silence.* MRS. LEVI *leaves the stand. An* OLD MAN *enters.)* What I don't get, Your Honor, is why the prosecutor does not demand the exposure of all the German authorities who permitted me to get on with my German work, and all those Jews who helped me? I got West German names here of civil servants, businessmen, ministers, priests, doctors, lawyers, generals, whores and housefraus...Here we are in alphabetical order: Mr. I. G. Braun, former ministerialat...

PROSECUTOR. I object — Not admissible evidence.

JUDGE. Sustained.

OLD MAN. Marowski. The Star of Bethlehem reached down and radiated life into my inert body. I opened my eyes and gazed...

(*But* GOLDMAN *flings open the door of the glass booth.*)

GOLDMAN. This man is a nut.
OLD MAN. *(Shouts.)* The Star of Bethlehem, a power above nature, reached down into my inert body and radiated...
GOLDMAN. *(Crosses to stand. Shouts.)* Shut your mouth or I'll have you shot!
JUDGE. Take the prisoner back! *(GOLDMAN turns.)* I will not have you intimidating the witnesses. *(GOLDMAN starts back, then halts and stamps his feet.)* Colonel Dorff! Lock the prisoner in the booth.

(The GUARDS do so. The OLD MAN bursts into tears and is helped from the stand.)

GOLDMAN. *(He goes back toward the booth, but stops and looks at the audience.)* What's happened to Marlene? You done away with her, Rosy?
MRS. ROSEN. May I answer this?
JUDGE. Yes.
MRS. ROSEN. Mrs. Dorff does not wish to give evidence. She is returning to her...family and children in Bonn.
GOLDMAN. *(Clapping his hands.)* Very wise. Faithful wife, you see. Like a Hebrew wife. Like Brooklyn Rosy would be.

(GOLDMAN goes back into the booth. A YOUNG MAN enters the stand. GOLDMAN reappears out of the booth.)

YOUNG MAN. Tzelniker.
GOLDMAN. *(Shouts.)* You South African Jewish?
YOUNG MAN. Yes.
GOLDMAN. You live in Johannesburg?
YOUNG MAN. Yes.
GOLDMAN. Doin' well?
YOUNG MAN. Yes. I am doing very well.
GOLDMAN. No further questions.
JUDGE. *(To witness.)* Continue.
YOUNG MAN. Adolf Dorff is a murderer. On May 7th, 1942, he shot my mother and father before my eyes. That is all I have to say.

(Within the booth, GOLDMAN is seen to clap. The YOUNG MAN leaves the witness stand. Another witness, MR. LANDAU, enters.)

LANDAU. Landau. To be truthful, on the journey when Dorff and his men transferred us from Dachau to Buchenwald, although the journey lasted just as long as the one when I went to Dachau — a journey on which very many were murdered — on this journey under Dorff no one actually was murdered.
GOLDMAN. This man is an idiot!
JUDGE. Dorff, I will only allow you to speak as long as you are respectful. *(He switches on* GOLDMAN'*s microphone.)*
GOLDMAN. Excuse me, Your Honor. 'Course, nobody was murdered on that second journey. No need for it. The method! Can't you follow the method? That first journey was an initiation and an initiation's a project. An initiation's a defilement. Make 'em kick each other, make 'em accuse each other, make 'em curse their God, make 'em speak of their wives' intercourse and their own. Make 'em do it with their wives, make 'em do it with other wives, make 'em do it with children. After that they'll do anythin' — no need to waste your energy twice. And I always swore in the anal sphere. They always had to get permission to defecate. "Jewish prisoner number six million and a half most obediently prays to be permitted to defecate." What I was always looking out for, what I was always looking for when I was in the camps...were the survivors. What I sought was those not walking dead, those degraded and defiled but still human. I sought 'em with my pistol. And they were always different. They was cunning and tenacious. But I had an eye for 'em. I could smell 'em. They smelled of freedom. And I sought 'em out and I shot them because I could not let them live.
JUDGE. Thank you, Colonel Dorff.
GOLDMAN. One moment, Judge. One moment. I'm just warmin' up. You switch me off if I'm not respectful. Okay. So I've no need to mention names. Names! You can always get names. So we're all Jews. All Germans. And we all got names. *Too many names!* In the camps, fellas...you all got to be members of the Party. You follow? You got to be Nazis. All of you. You follow? Very few exceptions. You gotten to believe in our German superiority, you tortured your own traitors, you took our old uniforms, you fixed 'em up, and you give us a snappy salute. You got to love us. You follow? And as for the Pope. Don't think he won't go back on all this dispensin'. Don't think he's not got doctrinal and political considerations. Wait for the usual pall of silence, fellas. They'll reread the Gospels and make another statement about the Pill. One of

those four-men commissions. And I am delighted, truly delighted that the prosecutress does not hold the German people responsible for the Fuehrer. The Prosecutor is a realist and great for trade. The prosecutor drives a Volkswagen. But why would we dwell on the past? What are these anti-semitic daubings in London and Chicago? These desecrations in Cologne? Deprivations in Russia? These publications in Stockholm? And speaking of love, let me speak to you of our beloved Fuehrer. Let me pay him tribute. People of Israel. (GOLDMAN *looks at the* JUDGE *as if expecting to be denied: calmly the* JUDGE *gazes at him. The* JUDGE *considers* MRS. ROSEN, *then nods to* GOLDMAN, *who rises with microphone.*) People of Jewry, let me speak to you of my Fuehrer with love. (GOLDMAN *pauses. Very quietly.*) He who answered our German need. He who rescued us from the depths. His family background was not distinguished, his education negligible. At the end of the First World War not even a German citizen. To whom did he appeal? To the people. His power lay in the love he won from the people. When he spoke, at first he was shy, he would hesitate, he would stammer, his body stiff, he felt for his love like a blind man, the voice hushed, the voice was flat, then the words came stronger, came steadier, his body grew free, he would bang out his right arm like a hammer, louder and louder he spoke, a torrent, a waterfall, the climax was shouted and shouted, out and up and beyond, and the end was absolute. Silence. Utter silence. A great wide sweep of the right arm and so to the tremendous cry, the vast overwhelming cry, the call of love from the people. Deutschlanderwache. Heil Hitler. Sieg Heil. Sieg Heil. Sieg Heil. Do I see you begin to raise your hands? Do I hear you stamp your feet? He gave us our history. He gave us our news, he gave us our art. He gave us our holidays, he gave us our leisure, and he gave our newly marrieds a copy of *Mein Kampf.* At the end we loved him. In Gotterdammerung we loved him. With the killers of the world at our throats, the hordes from the east and west, the capitalists and the communists, the bombers of cities, the murderers of our children, with bullets in our guts we loved him. Starving we loved him. With his head wobbling, his left arm slack, his hands a-tremble, we loved him. His generals lost him the war. His subordinates were unworthy. There was no successor. There was only him. Hess was mad, Goering reviled, Himmler rejected. He? He was loved. "Great King. Brave King. Wait yet a little while and the days of your suffering will be over. Already the sun of your good fortune stands behind the clouds and soon, beloved Fuehrer, soon this sun will rise upon you." He never deserted us. All but he! He, only, loved to the end. While he lived, Germany lived. And the people demanded it. We never denied him. People of Israel, we never denied him. And those who tell you different...lie. Those who tell you anything else, lie in their hearts. And if, if he were able to rise from the dead, he would prove it to you now. All over again. If only...if only we had someone to rise to...throw out our arms to...love...and stamp our feet for. Someone...someone to lead. *(Pause. Then calculatedly.)* People of Israel...people of Israel, if he had chosen you...if he had chosen *you...you* also would have followed where he led.

(Pause. An OLD WOMAN *rises in the front of the audience and says quietly:)*

OLD WOMAN. This man is not Dorff.
JUDGE. What's that?
OLD WOMAN. This man is not Dorff.
JUDGE. Not Dorff?
OLD WOMAN. This man is not Dorff. I must interrupt now because he is enjoying himself too much.

(Silence. A GUARD *moves towards the* OLD WOMAN.*)*

JUDGE. Wait! Wait a moment. I know this woman. Yes,...Come into the court. *(*PEOPLE *help the* OLD WOMAN *to the stand [Stage].* GOLDMAN *sits motionless.)* Enter the stand, Mrs. Lehman.

(The WOMAN *enters the witness stand.)*

OLD WOMAN. I have sat and sat. Mr. Goldman was enlightening me. He made many points. Many, many points. But in the end I could not understand him. *(*GOLDMAN *puts down the mike.)* I knew him. I knew his cousin...Dorff. And I knew his wife and children. Mr. Goldman had three children. Teresa died on the train. Arthur and Jacob in the first year. Mrs. Goldman in the second. Christine. *(Pause.* GOLDMAN *sits.)* When Dorff came to our camp he would talk to this man and call him, "Cousin...," "Cousin Arthur." Dorff would smile at this man, pat this man, give him food...so all could see. There was a likeness. A family likeness. I think Dorff must have been part Jewish or all Jewish. Dorff would come on Holy Days, give Mr. Goldman food and laugh. Mr. Goldman would wait till Dorff had gone, then give away the food. People followed Mr. Goldman. He never had enough food to give them. People lay on the ground for him. The food was too rich. Bars of chocolate. People cursed Mr. Goldman. People died because of the food. People died because they wanted it too much. And Dorff could come back and sit watching, and laugh and tell the German band to play "Rosamunda." Dorff would sit there sniffing in the sweet brown smoke from the chimneys, and laughing at Mr. Goldman, and calling him Cousin Arthur. It was a game. *(Pause.)* And sometimes he would speak in memory of Mr. Goldman's children. *(Pause.)* So when we were abandoned...at the end of the war...the Germans left us in a great hurry and someone led us to the German barracks outside the electric wire. On the tables were plates of frozen soup. The wine was yellow ice. There was frozen Schnapps. And we warmed and drank it all. Mr. Goldman was there. I remember him. We huddled together. They lit a fire from the benches, and sang. And Mr. Goldman told jokes. *(Long pause.)* But Dorff came back. He was shooting us all methodically, he would shoot in the nape of the neck, then throw the twisted body into the snow. We sat and waited for our turn. "Cousin," Dorff shouted, "Cousin Arthur, watch me for I shall never leave you." And then four boys, young boys on big horses, rode into the hut. They had fur hats. When he saw them, Dorff dropped his gun and fell on his knees. At first they did not fire at Dorff — the Russian boys. Then one of them got down from his great horse, and picked Dorff up, and carried Dorff out of the hut, and threw him onto the wire. Dorff screamed and pulled off the wire, and they threw him back onto it again. He stuck on the wire. And we all ran and tore at Dorff. We tore him to pieces. But I remember thinking: Mr. Goldman has stayed in the hut.

(Silence. MRS. ROSEN *enters the booth, undoes* GOLDMAN'S *tunic, looks at* GOLDMAN'S *left armpit.* GOLDMAN *is silent.* MRS. ROSEN *comes out of the booth.)*

MRS. ROSEN. Must have burned himself...no S.S. insignia there in the first place. Just burned a hole...the man just burned a hole in his armpit.
JUDGE. And his forearm — the Jewish number?

(MRS. ROSEN *looks at* GOLDMAN'S *forearm.*)

MRS. ROSEN. Grafted over. The skin grafted over. He must have grafted his number over. I was always looking for a lie. Once I told him that. I said to him, "Something about you makes me look for lies." But not this kind of lie, you understand.
JUDGE. You did not look hard enough, Mrs. Rosen.
MRS. ROSEN. *(Crosses back and sits.)* He sickened me and that is why I must have lost my judgment. He will have got to our agents. Bribed some of our agents. The photographs were his photographs — the X-rays, his X-rays.

(Silence.)

OLD WOMAN. I do not think we would have followed where the Fuehrer led.

(GOLDMAN *raises his head, smiles at her.*)

JUDGE. What was the point of all this, Goldman?
MRS. ROSEN. He likes bad jokes.

(Silence.)

JUDGE. I understand his need to put a case. I understand a concern for Justice...a concern for law. I understand his need to put a German in the dock — a German who would say what no German has said in the dock. I understand that...*(The* JUDGE *pauses in thought.)* I understand his guilt...even so, I would not have done this — would never have done this.
MRS. ROSEN. He's more German than Jewish.

(Silence.)

JUDGE. Why did you do it? *(Silence.)* Haven't you done us more harm than good? Is not what you have said against us that will be remembered?

(Silence.)

MRS. ROSEN. He is an anti-semitic Jew.
JUDGE. *(Gently.)* Hasn't he the right?
MRS. ROSEN. *(Passionately.)* No, he has not the right. *(She shouts.)* After all that has happened, nobody has the right. *(Pause.)* He wanted to go to Calvary, Your Honor. So get out his nails. Take him, part his raiment. Cast your lots. This is the King of the Jews, Your Honor. Offer him vinegar. He wants to be crucified. Let him make his sacrifice. Your Honor, take the old sadist out and stone him. Take the old masochist out and scourge him.
JUDGE. Be quiet.

(GOLDMAN laughs.)

OLD WOMAN. Mr. Goldman, tell me. I was there.

(Silence. GOLDMAN comes out of the booth and goes to the OLD WOMAN and embraces her.)

GOLDMAN. *(Very gently to the OLD WOMAN.)* Sweetheart, you did me. Where's your brains? You're senile. You should never have spoke. Wanted to make some offering for them — something they'd understand. Wanted to let him take me up and swing me north, south, east and west. I wanted when the life was gone, they'd kiss my ass, kiss the turning cheeks of my swingin' ass, kiss my ass and call me sexy. Could I help my own dimensions? Could I help my sense of progress? Me? A messenger of peace. Best thing I ever did was break my glasses. Lost my contacts in a urinal. Should've stayed down there in the toilets.
JUDGE. Take him out. Gently. *(To MRS. ROSEN.)*

(But GOLDMAN kicks at the GUARDS. He turns to the OLD WOMAN again.)

GOLDMAN. *(Grinning.)* Was I bein' too hard on ya, sweetheart? *(He shouts.)* Sweetheart, if not *us*...who else? *(He wheels round to the audience. He looks at them.)* I chose ya because I knew ya. I chose ya because you're smart. I chose ya because you're Jewish. I chose ya because you're the chosen. I chose ya for remembrance. *(*GOLDMAN *begins to take off his shirt.)*
WOMAN. *(Desperately.)* You chose us because you love us.
GOLDMAN. *(Throwing out his arms to the audience.)* Battened down as we were, my brothers, my cousins, shunting from siding to siding, there was time. But after the wire I rode. I rode on Russian horses, on great black Russian horses. Every lamp post in Danzig a gallows. I clawed out their dead eyes with my nails. I rode on Russian horses and we battered Polish castles, we looted museums, we broke, we burned, we raped and we drank. We draped ourselves with gold tapestries, we covered our fingers with golden rings, we arrayed our horses with golden armor and we ate the German boys. We picked them up and ate them. We crushed them, we trampled them, we ravaged them in the snow — the snow that kept on falling. We kicked in their golden heads. We who were German and Jewish. We did that.

(Pause.)

JUDGE. You can leave the court. *(But now* GOLDMAN *goes to the glass booth. He takes the door key and locks himself inside. He takes off the rest of his clothes. The* GUARDS *beat on the door. The* JUDGE *descends from the bench and walks slowly to the naked* MAN *in the booth. But* GOLDMAN *is silent. Silence. Then the* OLD WOMAN *cries in anguish. Silence. Silence. Silence.)* Carry him out of the court.

(The GUARDS *gather round the booth examining it. The* COURT OFFICIALS *join them. For the moment they do not know how to get the man out. The* LIGHTS *fade.)*

Curtain

Teaching Activities

- As a class, read the entire script of *The Man in the Glass Booth* and then read the book. Compare treatments of the story.

- Show *Nazi War Crime Trials*, a documentary that uses 1945 newsreels and filmed footage to look at what happened to such Nazi war criminals as Hermann Goering, former chief of the Gestapo. Next, ask students to identify Nazis who, in their opinions, should have been brought before a court but were not. They might, for example, wish to try Adolf Hitler who avoided capture and trial through suicide. Then, assign students to stage war crimes trials for those individuals they have selected and to create transcripts of the hearings. Students not cast as defendants, prosecutors, witnesses, and judges should form four teams and assume the responsibilities of journalists invited to cover the trials for the media. Team #1 should be from an American news program such as *Sixty Minutes* or *Good Morning, America*. Team #2 should be from the Israeli equivalent of that show. Teams #3 and #4 should be comprised of radio and print journalists from the United States and Israel, respectively. Coverage should be compared based upon the requirements of the particular medium and the national perspective of the journalists.

- The class may elect to do any or all of the segments in this activity. First, provide students with opportunities to research the war crimes trials held at Nuremberg after the Second World War and those related to the more recent conflict in Bosnia. Press them to give particular attention to video and transcript records of these proceedings. Based upon these formal accounts, invite them to investigate the backgrounds of witnesses and to reenact scenes in which these individuals undergo legal examinations. Next, based upon their research and role playing, ask the students to compare these trials. What conclusions do they draw about the nature and application of justice for war crimes? Continuing along these lines, challenge pupils to investigate episodes of other war crimes that have occurred in the past fifty years and to report their findings. As a conclusion to their reports, they should determine if other war crimes trials should be held. If they answer in the affirmative, they should identify who should be charged and why.

- Divide the class into groups and require that each group locate and view at least one film, documentary, or television program that presents an accounting of a Nazi war crimes trial. Some of the fifteen hours of original Nuremberg trial footage, interviews, background reports, and commentary by legal experts shown on Court TV to mark the fiftieth anniversary of the international war crimes tribunal, for example, would be an appropriate choice as would the PBS documentary created by ABC News and PBS, *The Trial of Adolf Eichmann*, which premiered April 30, 1997. Ask each group to report orally upon what they watched. If possible, encourage them to include selected video or film clips in their presentations to classmates.

- Using the Nazi war crimes trials as the basis for this activity, students with access to the Internet should do a web search on that topic. They should contact those institutions holding relevant materials that they find particularly interesting. After data collection has been completed to the students' satisfaction, the class can undertake the creation of a reference or a resource book. Format, content, and similar decisions should be left to the students.

- "The trial of the century" has been used over the years to describe the Nuremberg war crimes trials as well as sensational American criminal trials dealing with kidnapping and murder. Invite students to respond to these applications of this title. Encourage them to formulate and share opinions as to the validity of this description in reference to such diverse events.

- As a writing assignment, instruct students to select one of the following quotes and to respond to it. Have these predictions come true? Require that opinions be supported with research.

> "The Jews in America will suffer for what you have done to me," Ohlendorf told Ferencz.
>> Benjamin B. Ferencz, chief prosecutor in the subsequent U.S. hearings at Nuremberg and SS General Otto Ohlendorf.
>
> "What is frustrating in the last 50 years is to have witnessed these crimes being committed again and again and again," Ferencz said.
>> Lynn Elber, "Short version of Nuremberg trials on tap," *The Saginaw News*, 12 November 1995, A4.

- Holocaust deniers have argued that Jews use the Holocaust in order to be seen as victims and as a device to generate sympathy. Others argue that the Holocaust was not a unique genocidal event and cite such incidences of mass annihilation as the slaughter of Native Americans by white settlers and the deaths of slaves in America. Either orally or in writing, call for students to formulate responses to these arguments.

- Assign students to find a publication in which an article, advertisement, or letter to the editor denies or minimizes the magnitude of the Holocaust. In their own letter to the editor, ask them to respond to what they have read in the publication. Discuss their responses. What did they write and why?

- Students should read aloud Goldman's speech that begins, "One moment, Judge. One moment." Then, working in small groups, they should select one of the following for analysis and report their conclusions to the class.

  > Identify actions taken by the Catholic Church during the Holocaust and later in 1964 and 1965. To what is Goldman referring in the monologue and why does he make these connections?

  > Investigate cult behavior. Argue for or against the notion that the Nazis constituted a cult that Hitler led.

- The Nazi war crimes trial of Maurice Papon in France captured international attention. Invite students to gather information about the defendant and his trial and then to respond to the following:

A legitimate defense for Nazi war criminals is that they were following orders.

To bring Papon to trial is a matter of revenge rather than justice at this point in his life.

- Spur students to study Nazi hunters. How do these individuals or organizations function? How successful have they been in their quests?

- After comparing the trial of Adolf Eichmann to that of Goldman in *The Man in the Glass Booth*, as a class debate the playwright's intention. Is Eichmann a deliberate model for the play's protagonist? If so, in what ways has the playwright engaged in applying dramatic license?

- Critics have given various explanations for Goldman's motivations. As a class, discuss why he might assume a Nazi identity and want a trial held in Israel. In light of their responses, next challenge students to respond to the following: Might it be possible that Goldman is suggesting that had Hitler loved the Jews, they would have loved him in return? Why or why not?

- The Office of Special Investigations filed cases against a number of individuals living in the United States who were suspected of being war criminals. In his book, *Quiet Neighbors: Prosecuting Nazi War Criminals In America*, Allan A. Ryan, Jr. notes the status of these cases as of July 1, 1984. As an individual or group assignment, students might target some of these people for a "Where are they now?" probe. How many have died, been denaturalized, or deported? Outcomes of student inquiries can be reported to classmates.

Name	U.S. Residence
Basil Artishenko	West Brunswick, NJ
Andrija Artukovic	Orange County, CA
Henrikas Benkunskas	Chicago, IL
Antanas Bernotas	Hartford, CT
John Demjanjuk	Cleveland, OH

Name	U.S. Residence
Feodor Fedorenko	Waterbury, CT
Vytautas Gudauskas	Gilbertville, MA
Vilis Hazners	Albany, NY
Anatoly Hrusitzky	Orlando, FL
Jurgis Juodis	St. Petersburg, FL
Liudas Kairys	Chicago, IL
Bronius Kaminskas	Hartford, CT
Juozas Kisielaitis	Boston, MA
Jonas Klimavicius	Kennebunkport, ME
Sergei Kowalchuk	Philadelphia, PA
Bohdan Koziy	Ft. Lauderdale, FL
Reinhold Kulle	Chicago, IL
Juozas Kungys	Clifton, NJ
Edgars Laipenieks	San Diego, CA
Alexander Lehmann	Cleveland, OH
Karl Linnas	Greenlawn, Long Island, NY
Hans Lipschis	Chicago, IL
Boleslavs Maikovskis	New York, NY
Kazys Palciauskas	St. Petersburg, FL
Mecis Paskevicius	Miami, FL
Conrad Schellong	Chicago, IL
Mykola Schuk	Allentown, PA
Vladimir Sokolov	New Haven, CT
Elmars Sprogis	Long Island, NY
George Theodorovich	Albany, NY
Valerian (Viorel) Trifa	Grass Lake, MI
Antanas Virkutis	Chicago, IL

Allan A. Ryan, Jr., *Quiet Neighbors: Prosecuting Nazi War Criminals in America* (New York: Harcourt Brace Jovanovich, Publishers, 1984), 353-361.

A Bright Room Called Day

The Playwright: Tony Kushner

Tony Kushner is best known as the winner of the Pulitzer Prize and the Antoinette Perry (Tony) Award for *Angels in America, Part I: Millennium Approaches*. He is acclaimed as well for the second installment of that mammoth work, *Angels in America, Part II: Perestroika*. *A Bright Room Called Day* is, arguably, his best-known work prior to *Angels*.

Tony Kushner's plays have been produced throughout the United States and in more than thirty countries. In addition to the Pulitzer Prize and the Tony, he has numerous grants and honors to his credit. These include a directing fellowship from the National Endowment for the Arts, the Princess Grace Award, a New York State Council for the Arts fellowship, the Arts Council of Great Britain's John Whiting Award, two Olivier Award nominations, a grant from the American Academy of Arts and Letters, and the Kennedy Center/American Express Fund for New American Plays Award. Kushner's work has been further lauded with the Kesserling Award of the National Arts Club, the Will Glickman Playwriting Prize, and the *Evening Standard* Award. Among his most prestigious accolades are two Drama Desk Awards, the New York Critics Circle Award, the Los Angeles Drama Critics Circle Award, and the 1994 LAMBDA Literary Award for Drama.

Born on July 16, 1956, in New York, Kushner moved as an infant to Lake Charles, Louisiana. His parents were both classical musicians and his mother was also an actress. Kushner credits her performances for drawing him to the theatre. For his B.A. degree, he returned to New York and attended Columbia University. He then continued his education at New York University, earning an M.F.A. degree in 1984. From 1990–91, he served as director of literary services for Theatre Communications Group. Kushner also has been affiliated with the Julliard School of Drama, New York University Graduate Theatre Program, and both Yale and Princeton Universities. The playwright now resides in Manhattan.

The Play

The playwright's misunderstanding of the title of a work Agnes De Mille was choreographing for the Joffrey Ballet led to this play being named *A Bright Room Called Day*. Upon learning that De Mille's dance was actually *A Bridegroom Called Death*, Kushner thought the shift symbolic of the times. He reveals that five personally calamitous events in 1984-85 stimulated the writing of this play: (1) members of the theatre collective of which Kushner was a founding member parted ways; (2) Kushner's best friend sustained serious injuries in an accident; (3) his beloved great-aunt died suddenly; (4) German director, translator, and Kushner mentor Carl Weber prepared to leave New York; and, (5) Ronald Reagan was reelected (Kushner 172-173). These events, having shaped the play, also found their way into it, notably with a plot centering upon a group of friends separating in turbulent times, the character of Agnes being named for De Mille and modeled upon his great-aunt, a different role created in honor of his confidant, and attention directed to similarities in the rise to power of both Reagan and Hitler.

Kushner describes *A Bright Room Called Day* as a play about "morbidity and mysticism in the face of political evil" (Kushner 180). In it, a group of minor artists and activists face a changing Germany as the Weimar Republic yields to the extremely conservative, nationalistic, and violent practices of fascism. This story line is interrupted by the contemporary character, Zillah Katz, who forces didactic comparisons between 1930s Germany and the America of the 1980s and 1990s. (It is worth noting that when the play was produced in London, Great Britain replaced America and Margaret Thatcher appeared instead of Ronald Reagan as the powerful contemporary leader about whom Zillah rants.) By suggesting rather than showing the horror in store for Germany, Kushner intended the play as a warning for contemporary audiences.

A Bright Room Called Day was first performed as a workshop production by Kushner's newly reconstituted theatre collective, now known as Heat & Light. It was seen initially in New York in April 1985. Staging was under the playwright's direction. The Eureka Theatre premiered the play in San Francisco in October 1987. The next year, it was published in *Seven Different Plays*, an anthology edited by Mac Wellman for Broadway Play Publishing. The New York Shakespeare

Festival presented the drama at the Joseph Papp Public Theatre in January 1991.

Information about the Play and the Holocaust

A constitutional democracy was implemented in Germany after World War I. The Weimar Republic, established in 1918, was a parliamentary government. Authority was shared between an elected President and a Chancellor whom he appointed, the nationally elected Reichstag (parliament), and regional parliaments. Despite a German Army High Command attempt to seize power, failed ventures in 1919 by Communists to do likewise, and fascist efforts to topple the coalition-based system in the 1920s, the government prevailed but was largely ineffectual. The Reichstag was repeatedly dissolved and leftist parties like the Social Democratic Party and the German Communist Party were unable to halt the advance of fascism. Under these notably tenuous conditions, the National Socialist German Workers' Party (Nazis) gained control of the legislative assembly. After receiving 37.5 percent of the popular ballots in the 1932 parliamentary elections, the Nazi Party dominated the Reichstag as a voting bloc. Although their popularity began to decline shortly after this, the Nazis were able to secure Adolf Hitler's appointment as Chancellor of the German Reich.

Hitler's appointment on January 30, 1933, marked a "watershed in Germany's political and cultural life" (USHMM diorama). For certain groups, years of acculturation and assimilation would soon give way, whenever possible, to refugee flight. Prior to 1933, Jews made valuable contributions to German life. Eleven of thirty-seven German Nobel Prize winners, for example, were Jewish; after 1933, however, Jews would be seen by many of their countrymen only as threats and liabilities. While Jews certainly suffered, they were not alone. Other groups were forced into exile from Germany as well, including political outsiders, intellectuals, and artists. At gravest risk were those of whom Hitler disapproved. Outcasts included Communists and Social Democrats, pacifists, Catholics, Protestants, those whose artistic and scholarly works were considered dissident, and other individuals or members of various organizations not sanctioned by the Nazis. For those who did not leave, the consequences were often dire. In German concentration camps, for example, eighty thousand Communists died. The Nazis also imprisoned ten thousand homosexuals during the Holocaust of whom half died. For more than a third of the Jehovah's Witnesses imprisoned, incarceration proved fatal.

A Bright Room Called Day is about the last phase of the collapse of the Weimar Republic. The action takes place during the period from January 1, 1932, to November 12, 1933. Notable events during that time were many, as the following chart illustrates.

Dates	Event
January–June 1932	Germany, having suffered defeat and humiliation in World War I, faces severe economic crisis and staggering unemployment.
	Unable to implement stability, the government is ineffective; resulting political fighting among various factions spills into German streets.
April 1932	Hindenburg defeats Hitler in presidential election.
July 1932	To realize the Nazi objective of restoring Germany to its rightful place as a powerful nation, that party advocates rejection of reparations under terms of Versailles Treaty of World War I, unification of pure Germans and exclusion of all others, obedience to leader, defeat of communism, and restoration of German values and national pride.
	Nazis gain majority in parliament by winning largest popular vote (37.5%) they will ever have.
November 1932	Elections give Communists twelve more parliamentary seats; Nazis lose thirty-four seats but remain in control.
November 1932–January 1, 1933	A shift finds Catholic center parties moving to the right.
	Hitler garners support from industrialists, capitalists, military leaders, and middle and lower class citizens, although it is less than he desires; secret deals involving a number of political and government leaders, including Hindenburg, seem the norm.
January 30, 1933	Hindenburg appoints Adolf Hitler Chancellor; he marks his inauguration with violence against political opponents.

Dates	Event
February 27, 1933	The Reichstag burns; Hitler blames Communists and issues decree allowing him to crush opposition. Four thousand Communists and Social Democrats arrested.
	Hitler's decree becomes foundation for police state that lasts until 1945.
March 1933	Election campaign blemished by intimidation, mainly at the hands of the SA (Brownshirts); fifty Nazi opponents killed and others beaten.
	Since only members of the Nationalists, a right-wing political party, and the National Socialist German Workers' Party (the Nazis) are able to run for offices, together they have an elected majority.
March 5–15, 1933	Using purges by Stalin as an excuse, Germany outlaws German Communist Party; this is accompanied by arrests and decisions by some party members to leave the country.
March 15, 1933	Dachau Concentration Camp opens.
March 23, 1933	Enabling Act gives legislative power to Hitler; parliament becomes a rubber stamping body.
May 1–June 22, 1933	The long established German Labor movement disappears without meaningful opposition and the Social Democratic Party soon follows; led by Hitler, the Nazis rule Germany.
May 2, 1933	Abolition of German trade unions.
May 10, 1933	First public book burnings occur; in Berlin more than 25,000 volumes go up in flames.
	Among those Jewish and non-Jewish authors whose books were burned in the spring of 1933 were Franz Werfel, Stefan Zweig, Max Brod, Albert Einstein, Sigmund Freud, Erich Maria Remarque, Heinrich Mann, Bertolt Brecht, Marx, Lenin, Leon Trotsky, Rosa Luxemburg, and Magnus Hirschfeld.
June 1933	During the "Week of Blood," Nazi henchmen kill ninety-one Communists in Berlin.

Dates	Event
July 14–17, 1933	On July 14, all political organizations except for the National Socialist German Workers' Party (the Nazi Party) are banned.
	Period culminates six months of work needed to establish the Third Reich, which then exists for thirteen years.
October 14, 1933	Germany withdraws from the League of Nations and from disarmament talks.
November 12, 1933	Reichstag elections yield a 95% popular consent vote.

As signs of collapse became more pronounced in the Weimar Republic, many liberal-minded artistic and political denizens found it necessary to leave Germany or to go into hiding. Normal daily activities, for them, became exercises in self-preservation. With each new crushing restriction, ban, or toppling of opposition, pressures to escape or to hide mounted. Individual lives and personal relationships, like the Weimar Republic itself, disintegrated as Hitler solidified his power.

Synopsis of the Second Interruption

At the time of Zillah's second interruption, appropriately entitled "The Politics of Paranoia," the characters in pre-war Germany are, like her, experiencing a sense of uneasiness. For them, power that should be in the hands of the common people is being usurped through influential secret deals. Zillah, a contemporary figure who daily writes vitriolic letters to the President of the United States, articulates here her own sense that all is not well with America. She opines that this country could be headed down the path upon which Germany previously descended.

Second Interruption
The Politics of Paranoia

(Lights up on ZILLAH.*)*

ZILLAH. I used to be a normal human being. Like most Americans of my class I would fatten and thrive on governmental scandals, as long as they were relatively infrequent and bloody enough when they occurred to alleviate the ennui of being a citizen in a two-party democracy. Watergate was one of the happiest times of my life, really well-done, dramatic and garish and incredibly funny. Not at all like the bone-naked terror of these days. I've lost my sense of humor. I have become instead a completely convinced, humorless paranoiac. I see elements of profound truth in nearly all the Kennedy assassination theories. If you tell me that Happy Rockefeller, John Paul I and John Lennon were killed by a cabal of lapsed-Catholic anti-Trilateralists, I will believe you. People who don't know that this government survives by the grace of a secret club of trained WASP terrorists are living with their heads in pink clouds. I believe, I do believe it. Hannah Arendt says she escaped from Germany before the war by being more paranoid than her friends. She read detective novels. She believed in conspiracies. They said she was crazy then but Hannah died in 1972 in her own bed and lots of the people who laughed at her.... I believe. I read the histories of Germany. I read the Book of Revelations. I read the *Times*. I sense parallels. Just call me paranoid.

(End of interruption.)

Synopsis of Scene Seventeen

Scene seventeen takes place on March 12, 1933. Agnes Eggling, the central figure in this play and a minor character actress in German films, is sitting for a poster that her friend Annabella Gotchling is creating. Agnes, in her mid to late 30s, lacks the political fervor of her older friend, a Communist artist and graphic designer. Still, she knows that the future does not bode well for either of them given the course of events in Germany. In this scene, Agnes is forced to face issues of hiding, exile, and safety for herself and others when Gotchling asks to use her apartment as a safe haven for fleeing comrades.

Scene Seventeen
Hic Domus dei est et Portae Coelis
(This is the House of God, and These are the Gates of Heaven)

SLIDE: MARCH 12, 1933.
SLIDE: THE FLAG OF THE WEIMAR REPUBLIC
SLIDE: IS ABOLISHED.

(AGNES *is sitting for a portrait that* GOTCHLING *is constructing.* AGNES *holds a red hammer and a carpenter's level.* GOTCHLING *works with a pencil, paper and a variety of assemblage materials. As she works, they talk.)*

AGNES. I don't feel like doing this today.
GOTCHLING. I know. I appreciate it all the more.
AGNES. There's no point to this. No point to making posters, they just rip them down. Don't they arrest people for this?

(No answer.)

I walked to the Studio yesterday. All the way I felt like I was walking through a strange city, not Berlin. That strange sun not the Berlin sun, too bright. I found myself saying an old prayer for protection...
I keep thinking that maybe it wouldn't have been so bad to have been a wise old lady-in-waiting for the Kaiserin. In the films I had lots of well-made objects to handle: a big sturdy clothes brush with stiff bristles, Belgian lace, and there were those silver cases with little enameled hunting scenes on the lids. They were cold but they warmed in your hand and they were heavy. Just holding them made you feel safe. What's so great about democracy?
Want to see a jolly twinkle? *(She twinkles.)*
GOTCHLING. Please, that's nauseating.

AGNES. I know you think I'm a reactionary for feeling this way, you judge everyone all the time but I feel it anyway, I feel...
GOTCHLING. Feel feel feel feel feel. So much feeling. Hold still. Don't feel. Think for a change.
AGNES. There's nothing to think about.
GOTCHLING. There's plenty.
AGNES. Nothing pleasant.
GOTCHLING. Unpleasant then.
We need apartments.

(Pause.)

We need apartments. Belonging to people who are sympathetic.
AGNES. We who?
GOTCHLING. The Party.
AGNES. The Party's been outlawed.

(Pause.)

GOTCHLING. As I was saying. We need apartments. Way stations to the east. Storage rooms...
AGNES. No.
GOTCHLING. Not for storage, then. A way station. There are people hiding...
AGNES. No.
GOTCHLING. Agnes.
AGNES. People shouldn't be leaving. They should be staying. Everyone is going. There should be fighting. Who's going to fight? What are people like me supposed to do if people like you just leave?
GOTCHLING. Some of us are staying. Some can't.
AGNES. Are you leaving?
GOTCHLING. I can't say.
AGNES. You are. I knew you would. For God's sake, Annabella, what is going to happen to us?
GOTCHLING. I don't know.
AGNES. And still you recklessly ask me to...
GOTCHLING. Not recklessly.
AGNES. It sounds dangerous.
GOTCHLING. It is dangerous.
AGNES. Then I won't do it.

GOTCHLING. The Party needs it.
AGNES. There is no Party! There's no more Party! Wake up! You're a painter, not a politician, you always were a painter so start acting like one!
GOTCHLING. How do I do that, Agnes?
AGNES. Leave me alone!
GOTCHLING. No. I've never been that kind of a painter.
Art...is never enough, it never does enough.
We will be remembered for two things: our communist art, and our fascist politics.

(Pause.)

AGNES. I don't understand you, Gotchling. You navigate this. You're the only one. Why is that?
GOTCHLING. I'm much more intelligent than the rest of you.
AGNES. Then why do you bother with us?
GOTCHLING. I enjoy feeling superior.
Listen, Agnes.
I am working-class.
And that really does make a difference. I know what's useful, and what isn't.
I know the price of things,
and I know how to give things up.
I know what it is to struggle —
these tough little lessons
I don't think you people ever learned.
I hold tight, and I do my work.
I make posters for good causes.
Even if they get torn up, I make them,
even though we live in a country
where theory falls silent in the face of fact,
where progress can be reversed overnight,
where the enemy has stolen everything, our own words from us,
I hold tight, and not to my painting...not only to that.
Pick any era in history, Agnes.
What is really beautiful about that era?
The way the rich lived?
No.
The way the poor lived?

No.
The dreams of the Left
are always beautiful.
The imagining of a better world
the damnation of the present one.
This faith,
this luminescent anger,
these alone
are worthy of being called human.
These are the Beautiful
that an age produces.
As an artist I am struck to the heart
by these dreams. These visions.
We progress. But at great cost.
How can anyone stand to live
without understanding that much?

Think it over, Agnes. We need the apartment.

(End of scene.)

Synopsis of Scene Twenty-Three

Scene twenty-three, entitled "Revelations and Farewells," finds Agnes' friends preparing to leave Germany. "Bloody Sunday" (the name given to street battles that left one Communist dead and hundreds wounded), book burnings, and the abolition of trade unions have already occurred and it is clear that Hitler will tolerate no opposition to his will. Paulinka Erdnuss, an actress who once held membership in the German Communist Party (KPD) and Gregor Bazwald (Baz), a homosexual, are bidding Agnes farewell as all prepare to go their separate ways. As Baz describes the children in this scene, he is illustrating how efficiently and totally the Nazi way of life would hold sway over Germany, beginning with the youngest of her citizens.

Scene Twenty-Three
Revelations and Farewells

SLIDE: JUNE 22, 1933.

(AGNES stands near the window, looking out. PAULINKA is dressed for travel. BAZ is in a chair, his coat and valise nearby.)

PAULINKA. The train ride to Moscow will take three days. The trip to Hollywood would have taken a month. So I decided to go to Russia. Well, not really. The Americans found out about my old KPD membership.
BAZ. Remarkable.
PAULINKA. What kind of a world is it where Husz moves to America and I wind up in the USSR? Doesn't that seem...backwards or something?
BAZ. Don't talk about Husz when you get to Moscow. Don't say you knew him. Stay out of politics.
PAULINKA. Easy for me to do.
   There was this woman in wardrobe who used to fold a KPD leaflet very carefully and slip it into the pocket of my costume on the sly. Every once in a while. Then she'd wait for me to find it, and when I did she'd be watching, and she'd wink at me. I hated her. Last week, I guess someone informed on her; they came for her at the Studio. She screamed. But...
   That was it for me. I faked a nervous breakdown, or maybe I didn't fake it, who knows. And so on. The end.
   You're being ominously quiet, Agnes. You could at least wish me a pleasant voyage east.

(Pause. AGNES looks at PAULINKA, then out the window again.)

BAZ. The winters in Russia have a nasty reputation.
PAULINKA. I packed my fur. And I expect a warm welcome in Moscow.
   I, too, have a reputation.
   It isn't so terrible. They do make the best films.
BAZ. Not recently.

PAULINKA. Don't be so morbid, Baz. Put a good face on it.
BAZ. Hard to do.
PAULINKA. Apparently. Not for me. Frightening, isn't it? What an actor does? Assume the mantle of truth, of courage, of moral conviction, and wear it convincingly, no matter what sort of chaotic mess there is inside.
Agnes, you have to say something.
AGNES. You...are going to miss your train.
I wish you'd go now. Please go.

(Little pause. PAULINKA *leaves.)*

AGNES. See? You'd think, when a person goes, a whole person just goes away, it would leave a hole, some empty place behind, that's what I thought, I imagined that, but...it doesn't. Everyone's going but it isn't like the world has gotten emptier, just much smaller. It contracts, the empty places...collapse.
Goodbye.
BAZ. Plans? What are you...
AGNES. Sssshhhh. Goodbye. Please.
BAZ. Do you remember ten years ago, Agnes?
One red word and a streetful of people would come running.
The Revolution.
When I was sixteen, in Leipzig, I joined
a band of young people — we went
off to the mountains,
read Wedekind and Whitman the American,
and Schubert and Mahler the Jew,
worshipped the sun, made a god of nature,
experimented with each other
in all sorts of ways, and then...
We got crazy, we got pregnant, we
discovered urges we wished we'd left alone.
Everyone fled back to Leipzig, back
to upholstered furniture, marriage,
heterosexuality, each
to his or her own prison.
We were too young and too frightened
to see how close we'd come to something
truly free;

knocked on the gates of the Divinity,
only to retreat in terror.

(He stands to leave.)

Today I saw a platoon of children,
younger than we were,
marching to the mountains.
As organized as ants. They wear uniforms.
They plan experiments of a different kind.
They'll dream blood-dreams
of goats rutting and lions killing,
and they'll sing songs about racial purity.
Their revolution, I think, will succeed.
They'd be the future except
they stand as a guarantee
that no future exists.
Only a long, long nightfall,
and then a permanent good-night.

Good night. Paris awaits.

(He reaches in his pocket, takes out an orange, places it on the table.)

Weather this, Agnes. And keep the door locked. *(Exits.)*

(End of scene.)

SLIDE: JULY 14–17, 1933.
SLIDE: ALL LEGISLATIVE AND POLITICAL WORK
SLIDE: NECESSARY FOR THE ESTABLISHMENT
SLIDE: OF THE THIRD REICH HAS BEEN COMPLETED.
SLIDE: THE FASCIST MACHINERY CREATED IN SIX MONTHS
SLIDE: WOULD FUNCTION EFFICIENTLY
SLIDE: FOR THE NEXT THIRTEEN YEARS.

Synopsis of Scene Twenty-Four

In scene twenty-four, Gotchling returns to again plead for the use of Agnes' apartment as a way station. Agnes at first remains reluctant, but Gotchling's persuasive powers prevail.

Scene Twenty-Four
All That Was Fat and Bright Is Perished from You

(GOTCHLING *and* AGNES.)

AGNES. What do you want?
GOTCHLING. That's quite a welcome.
AGNES. I haven't seen you for months. You must want something. I thought you'd gone for good.
GOTCHLING. I have, officially.
AGNES. Officially where?
GOTCHLING. Officially Switzerland.
AGNES. And really where?
GOTCHLING. Switzerland.
AGNES. Lie.
GOTCHLING. You don't want the truth.
AGNES. Lie.
GOTCHLING. It doesn't matter. I need your help. The apartment...
AGNES. I knew it. The answer's no.
GOTCHLING. There's no one else. You have to.
AGNES. I do not. You can't make me risk my life. Risk your own.
GOTCHLING. I am.
AGNES. Good for you. How wonderful. I refuse this honor.
GOTCHLING. Tell you what. We'll make a deal.

(*No answer.*)

You can't save yourself, Agnes. If you make it, you make it, but only because you're lucky.
AGNES. I don't know what you're talking about.
GOTCHLING. You will.

If you say no to this, Agnes, you're dead to me. And we both need desperately to keep at least some part of you alive. Say yes, and I promise to carry you with me, the part of you that's dying now. I can do that, I'm stronger than you. Say yes, and I will take your heart and fold it up in mine, and protect it with my life. And some day I may be able to bring it back to you.

You're very fond of regrets, Agnes, but the time for regretting is gone. I need very much to be proud of you.

AGNES. If I get arrested, Annabella Gotchling, I swear to God I will never forgive you.

GOTCHLING. Three days from now, around six in the evening. Expect her. She says she know you. Her name is Rosa. *(Exits.)*

(End of scene.)

Teaching Activities

- Working in groups, invite students to create collages depicting the events that unfolded in Germany from January 1, 1932, through November 12, 1933. Display the finished artwork in the classroom.

- During the summer of 1996, the Ku Klux Klan staged rallies in several Michigan towns. On July 6, 1996, they staged a rally in Saginaw and returned there in the fall of 1997. The debate that the first visit sparked in the local newspaper raged for days prior to the event. The questions raised were the same questions asked as the Nazis rose to power. Should free speech be denied to certain groups? Is the best response to ignore the event, confront the demonstrators, or stage counter demonstrations? Who should pay for police, clean-up, and the like when hate groups gather? Provide an opportunity for students to discuss these questions and encourage them to support their opinions. Next, ask the students to consider that, when the Klan returned to Saginaw, the community largely ignored the activities. Ask students how they feel about this approach. Is giving a hate group minimal attention better than being prepared for violence and confrontation? Why or why not? If neither approach is satisfactory, what strategies for dealing with such organizations would the class recommend and why?

- The entire class may wish to undertake this task or it may be assigned to only a few students. Ask participants to respond, based upon the scenes from the play that they have studied, to the following quote. Do they agree or disagree with it? What is the basis for their opinion? Do not reveal the speaker[4] until the conclusion of the exercise.

> It is immature, certainly, to write a play which asks an audience, among other things, to consider comparisons between Ronald Reagan and Adolf Hitler. *A Bright Room Called Day* is an immature play (Kushner 172).

---

4. The speaker is Tony Kushner.

As a follow-up activity, ask students to locate and read the entire play and then to again contemplate the quote. Has their opinion or their reasoning changed?

- When students have read scene seventeen, pair them for the following improvisational scenario. After determining casting and setting, ask for volunteer pairs to play the improvisation.

  Who: An ardent Communist and his or her apolitical friend.
  What: The Communist wants the friend to give his or her apartment as a place of safe haven for those fleeing Germany. The personal risk to the friend for doing so is great; however, he or she does not support Nazi rule.
  Where: Germany as the Nazis are gaining control of the country.
  When: 1933.

- Kushner suggests updating Zillah's interruptions to stay in keeping with contemporary political events. Ask students to write an essay describing what Zillah might feel paranoid about today. What social, political, or cultural issues in America might, in her opinion, require action or redress? Answers should be supported and, if students so choose, read aloud.

- In the second interruption, Zillah talks about parallels. Invite students to investigate American life and politics under Presidents Reagan and Bush. Do they find analogies to events occurring during these administrations and those taking place in Germany during Hitler's rise to power and ensuing dictatorship? If so, what do they believe are common events, issues, and/or effects?

- Agnes' friends in the play are artists and political activists. In scene seventeen, her friend Gotchling is creating a political poster. Involve students in research teams whose task is to find examples of both political and non-political art created during the final years of the Weimar Republic. Discoveries should be shared through team generated oral reports that include visual examples. In other words, team members should talk about and show their findings.

- Convert a part of the classroom into a gallery space and using slides, posters, collages, and other works of visual art that the students create, mount an exhibit entitled *Germany: January 1, 1932, through November 12, 1933*. If desired, students can design and produce the exhibition catalogue as well and invite other classes to view the show.

- Jews were not the only group to be discriminated against in Nazi Germany. In this exercise, each student should select an opening line from the options below. He or she then should find a narrative account, newspaper article, diary entry, or similar selection from the period of Nazi domination in Germany, couple it with the opening line of dialogue provided, and adapt all into a complete monologue. These character speeches should be rehearsed and performed for the class. Encourage each student actor to create a costume appropriate to the chosen role. If desired, monologues can be grouped together and staged for other classes.

    Opening Lines

    I am a Communist discriminated against because of my political views.

    I am a Social Democrat discriminated against because of my political views.

    I am a homosexual discriminated against because of my sexual orientation.

    I am a dissenting member of the clergy discriminated against because I speak out against the government.

    I am a trade unionist discriminated against because of my political views.

    I am a pacifist discriminated against because of my political views.

    I am a Jehovah's Witness discriminated against because I refuse to swear allegiance to the state.

I am a Gypsy (Romanie) discriminated against because the Nazis think I am inferior to a pure Aryan.

I am a Slav discriminated against because the Nazis think I come from an inferior race.

I am mentally and physically disabled and am discriminated against because I am seen as a social burden.

- Encourage students to read *The Other Victims: First-Person Stories of Non-Jews Persecuted by the Nazis* by Ina R. Friedman and the full script of Kushner's play, *A Bright Room Called Day*. Compare and contrast the experiences related in the book with those of the characters in the play.

"Voice" in *Remnants*

The Playwright: Hank Greenspan

Hank Greenspan is a clinical psychologist as well as a playwright. Educated at Harvard University and Brandeis University and a member of the Dramatist Guild, he now teaches at the University of Michigan in Ann Arbor. He has been interviewing Holocaust survivors since the late 1970s, and his seminar on survivors' experiences was one of the first of its kind. His scholarly writing on Holocaust remembrance has appeared in numerous journals and collections. Greenspan is the author of the book, *On Listening to Holocaust Survivors: Recounting and Life History*, and has written several plays, including *That Again*, *Slideshow*, and *Call Forwarding*.

The Play

Remnants takes as its subject the human experience of living after the Holocaust and attempting to find meaning in a destruction that defies even articulation. It is the fruit of two decades of conversation between Greenspan and Holocaust survivors. Although not verbatim quotation, the play accurately represents survivors' memories and reflections.

In both his dramatic and scholarly writing, Greenspan follows a method that is very different from most testimony projects. Rather than interviewing each survivor only once, he has talked with the same core group of survivors many times over many years. The result is that the monologues of *Remnants* have an unusual individuality and depth. They reveal what survivors tend to say only after years of personal acquaintance, at moments of special clarity and candor.

Remnants was originally produced for radio by the Michigan Radio Theatre and distributed to National Public Radio stations across the United States. As a stage play, it has been presented at the John Houseman Theatre in New York, the Attic Theater Center of Los Angeles, the Mill Mountain Theatre of Roanoke, and the New Hope Performing Arts Festival in Philadelphia. It also has been used extensively in secondary schools, universities, and Holocaust remembrance programs in the United States, Canada, Europe, and Israel. *Remnants* has been a winner of the Attic Theater Center New Plays Festival, the Henrico National Play Competition, the New Hope Performing Arts Festival, the National Script Competition of the Midwest Radio Theatre Workshop, and the Michigan Public Radio Focus Awards. The play has been translated into French for productions in France, Switzerland, and Belgium.

Information about the Play and the Holocaust

What did survivors live through and how did they do it? Although Germany surrendered in May of 1945, at the beginning of that year there were more than 600,000 prisoners, including Jews, gypsies, criminals, Jehovah's Witnesses, homosexuals, and political prisoners confined to concentration, forced labor, prisoner-of-war, work-education and other types of camps. The imagery of their stories communicates experiences seemingly beyond the scope of human endurance — having only a piece of bread as ration, washing one's face with coffee because there was no water, watching the wounded die because guards would not, in their words, waste bullets to finish the killing mercifully, wearing uniforms of paper dresses that didn't fit, faking death in order to cling to life, seeing piles of dead bodies, watching smoke rise from the crematorium and discovering in that way that families were lost forever, braving cold while standing in line for hours, seeing family photographs destroyed by guards, and hearing shots ring out as some of the doomed tried to escape trains pulling into the death camps. Tattooed numbers on their forearms robbed prisoners of personal identities. Fierce dogs, starvation, disease, beatings, hangings, and shaved heads further dehumanized inmates. To endure such harsh treatment, emotions were suppressed, energy directed solely to tasks at hand, and mourning delayed. Some prisoners were motivated to survive by thoughts of revenge; others found attributes like a sense of humor and an ability to adapt helpful. Seeking assignment to easier jobs, finding support in small self-help groups, and holding onto personal dignity and decency were some of the measures taken by inmates as they attempted to prolong life. For those in the camps, survival hardly ever meant thinking about what one's life would be like after the war. It was a moment-to-moment task lacking the luxury of long-range plans. Survival, like death, was random. Decisions and actions of some saved them when others, following the same courses, were doomed.

At war's end, nearly two million people were in the Allied occupied zone, classified as displaced persons (DPs); of these, Jewish survivors had no homes to which they could return. These camps, administered by the United Nations Relief and Rehabilitation Administration, were often little better than concentration camps. Until the practice met with protest, for example, Jews could be housed with non-Jews, some of whom were anti-Semitic and had collaborated with Nazi captors. Immigration was not always easy either, although by 1952 there were 137,450 Jewish refugees calling the United States home. For others, experiences as DPs led to active work for the creation of the state of Israel.

For those who did try to go home, the stability of a former life was elusive. Too often, survivors never would be reunited with family members. Desperate searches for loved ones proved futile. Death would prevent grandparents, aunts, and uncles from restoring extended families. Possessions or money left in the safe keeping of presumed friends or neighbors might be gone, and it was not uncommon for those so entrusted to deny ever having these valuables. Communities, customs, and cultures that survivors had known before the war had vanished. Those who returned to what had been their homes now lacked material, physical, and emotional resources. The fact that they still could be viewed by countrymen as peripheral to society added to their woes.

Survivors' Holocaust memories are as individual and varied as they are. Time, however, soon will still survivors' abilities to share their experiences directly with others. For this reason, there has been a vigorous interest of late in recording survivor testimony and, among some of those heretofore unwilling, a desire now to share their stories.

At war's end, a number of survivors had a pressing need to talk about their experiences but often found that no one wanted to listen. Some were met with responses of disbelief or ultimately found their own memories too painful to articulate. Others chose to remain silent for fear that listeners who had no experience akin to what they would hear simply would not understand. Perceived indifference or insensitivity could be enough to provoke withdrawal from society at large and to cause movement to a smaller circle consisting of family and those who also had lived through the tyranny. In many instances, survivors are only now beginning to speak out about what they endured — both during the Holocaust and after.

Synopsis

Voice is the opening monologue in *Remnants*. Like the other pieces in this script, it offers not only a survivor's memories of the Holocaust but also personal reflections and insights.

"Voice" in *Remnants*

During the war I lost my voice. I literally lost my voice. I was a little kid at the time, a little *pisher* like we say in Yiddish. I was eight-years-old. And at that time, I lost my voice.

This was in 1943. In the ghetto. It was after one of those *Aktions* — you know, when the SS come in and they kill a lot of people. And they round up the others and they take them to the train. And the train takes them away.

After one of those *Aktions*, I lost my voice. I don't know why. But for two years, I did not speak a single word.

(steps forward)

After the war, my voice came back. Not right away, but very slowly. This was in 1945, in a "D.P. Camp," a camp for "displaced persons," mostly for Jews who had survived the war. During the day in that camp I did not speak at all. But at night, when I was having a nightmare, I screamed. So that was how we knew I still had a voice. Because during the day I was completely mute. But during the night I screamed.

(warming somewhat)

There was a doctor at that camp, a Jewish doctor, who said: "If the girl can scream in the night, when she is asleep, so she can scream in the day, when she is awake. And if she can scream in the day, so she can also sing or cry. And if she can sing or cry, she can speak words as well. The voice can be salvaged. The screams can be refined into cries. And the cries can be refined into words."

So the doctor tried to help me. He took me to run in the hills near that camp. And he had me run with my mouth open, so I could feel the air push up against my throat.

(raises one hand to throat)

And he told me to try to scream with the air in my throat, or to make any sound at all. And soon I did start to scream when I was running. And then I was crying and making other different sounds. And eventually the sounds became a voice. I could speak words again, after two years of no words at all.

(pause; becomes very still as at start)

Today, we have **many** words about the Holocaust. We argue what does it mean? What should we do? What should we have done at the time? We argue for God and against Him. For Israel and against Israel. For reaching out to others and against reaching out to others. We argue and we reflect and we argue some more.

But to me, when I think about the Holocaust, I remember the doctor. And I remember myself, when I was a young girl, running in the hills. Because to me **all** our words, **whatever** we say about the Holocaust, are just so many different refinements of a cry. And the cry is just barely salvaged from a scream. And the scream is just barely salvaged from the silence.

Teaching Activities

- Steven Spielberg, perhaps best known for his film, *Schindler's List*, established the Shoah Visual History Foundation in 1994. Its purpose is to document survivors' stories on film. When completed, the project should have recorded 60,000 interviews as well as catalogued and electronically indexed interviews, maps, photographs, and other supporting materials. Students might contact the Foundation for information related to conducting interviews. Next, ask students to research personal narratives, testimonies, and accounts of survivors' experiences. Working then in pairs, one should assume the role of a survivor and develop a personal story based upon research findings. That student then is interviewed by his or her partner. Follow this by having the students exchange roles. At the completion of the assignment, all interviews could be placed in a school archive or classroom library.

- Smaller in size but similar in purpose to the Shoah Visual History Foundation project is Yale University's Fortunoff Video Archive for Holocaust Testimonies. Invite students to compare and contrast these two endeavors, giving particular attention to financial resources, personnel, and project scope.

- Young people with interest in the Internet could engage in creating an online search project related to retrieving information from the Shoah Visual History Foundation. Online locations are planned worldwide for researchers who, by typing in key words, can get desired data. Furnish students the opportunity to create a list of key terms that they think will be useful for accessing this resource.

- As an assignment related to psychology, students should read the personal accounts of survivors of catastrophes such as natural disasters and war, noting the effects of enduring such experiences. They should then read personal accounts of Holocaust survivors and note the psychological effects that they describe. Findings for both groups should be compared and reported to classmates.

- Using direct conversation with survivors or accounts of their experiences found in literature, students each should write a dramatic monologue modeled upon *Voice*. Prior to writing, however, discuss as a class the process of turning conversation into dialogue for the stage. Follow this by inviting students to memorize and perform their monologues.

- Challenge students to prepare a list of questions that they would like to ask a survivor about his or her experiences during the Holocaust. Then, ask them to imagine that they are Nazi perpetrators and to select roles such as a camp guard or a local cooperating with the Gestapo. They next should develop a list of questions for that character to ask a survivor. How do these lists of questions vary? What, in their opinions, accounts for these differences?

- Imagine having no family photographs or records of loved ones as was the situation for many Holocaust survivors. Working individually or in groups, ask students to brainstorm ideas for other ways to share special memories of loved ones. Follow this by having students select an individual, either living or dead, that they would like others to know and to produce a way of sharing special information about that person. Stipulate, however, that photographs or pictures may not be used to satisfy this assignment.

- Encourage students to read a number of survivors' accounts of their experiences and then to select one that particularly interests them. Each student then should imagine that he or she is that survivor and will be telling the story first to a group of fifth graders and then to a group of high school students. Keeping in mind the importance of tailoring communication to the audience, require students to adapt the story twice and to then present their versions to classmates posing as both audiences. After the presentations, as a group discuss how factors such as the listeners' ages influenced adaptations. Focus attention upon choices related, in particular, to vocabulary and imagery.

Hitler's Childhood

The Playwright: Niklas Rådström

Born in Stockholm, Sweden, in 1953, Niklas Rådström is a noted author who first gained recognition as a poet. His work, *Poems on the Life of Sandro della Quercia*, established his literary standing and was published in 1979. In 1989 and 1992, respectively, he wrote the novels *The Moon Does Not Know* and *While Time Thinks*. Poems and novels, as well as work for the screen and as a librettist, have made him one of his homeland's most distinguished literary figures. His film, *The Mozart Brothers*, was directed by Suzanne Osten. *Hitler's Childhood* is one of many pieces he has written for the stage. In the spring of 1998, the Orion Theatre in Stockholm premiered his most recent play, *Pa vag till havet* (*On the Way to the Sea*). Rådström is a member of the Swedish Playwrights' Union and he divides his time between Stockholm and Oland, a Baltic island. He is married and has two children.

The Translator: Frank Gabriel Perry

Frank Gabriel Perry's versions of contemporary Swedish dramas have been staged throughout the United Kingdom. Among his translations are the Swedish plays *The Tunnel*, written by Par Lagererkvist and produced by the National Theatre, and *Sisters, Brothers* and *The Return of the Convict*, both by Stig Larsson. These have been staged, respectively, at the National Theatre, the Traverse Theatre in Edinburgh, and the Gate Theatre. Perry's translations of Belgian playwright Ignace Cornelissen's *Grace* and Niklas Rådström's *Hitler's Childhood* were both staged by the Oxford Stage Company. *Swedish Drama in the Nineties*, from Methuen, contains four Perry contributions. He is noted for translations of contemporary Swedish literature, including plays, poetry, essays, librettl, and work in film.

A Note on the Translation and Translator's Acknowledgments

Translated in 1984 from the working script of the first production, *Hitler's Childhood* has been revised for this first version to be published in English in line with the Swedish version published by the author in 1985. The translator gratefully acknowledges the financial assistance, encouragement, and support of the Swedish Embassy in London and the Swedish Institute of Stockholm in the preparation of the original translation, and, in particular, the good offices of Kerstin Asp-Jonsson, Barbro Edwards, and Elisabeth Hall. A special vote of thanks must go to the translator's agent, Sarah McNair, at Alan Brodie Representation Ltd. for all of her help with this published version.

The Play

Hitler's Childhood was written in 1983. The world premiere was at Unga Klara, Stockholm's Stadsteater on April 27, 1984, in Stockholm, Sweden. Suzanne Osten directed the original production. The play has since been staged in Lund and Helsingborg, Sweden; Skien and Oslo, Norway; Copenhagen, Denmark; New York, USA; Bern, the Schauspielhaus in Zurich, Switzerland; Stuttgart and Munich, Germany; Ghent, Belgium; Paris, France; Amsterdam, Holland; Vienna, Austria; on tour in Latin America; Peru, Argentina, Bolivia, and Chile; and, with Frank Gabriel Perry's translation, at the Young Vic in London, England, following a nationwide tour of the United Kingdom. The award-winning Oxford Stage Company selected the work as one of three contemporary European plays comprising their program, *Making the Future*, which looked at three different perspectives of childhood through innovative and challenging plays for young people. The play premiered in Britain in September 1995.

In *Hitler's Childhood*, playwright Rådström draws attention to the devastating effects and resultant choices stemming from young Adolf's boyhood in the dysfunctional Hitler family. Raised amidst his father's tyranny and authoritarianism, his mother's grief for her children who had died, and his aunt's madness, the boy's domestic environment is claustrophobic, insecure, and unstable. While this does not generate sympathy for the terroristic acts committed by Adolf Hitler as an adult, it does lay bare the circumstances from which those actions might stem.

Loosely based on the ideas of psychoanalyst Alice Miller, the play came into being through the collaboration of the author and the Unga Klara theatre ensemble under Osten's direction. In her writing, Miller examines the relationship between violence and child rearing. Destructive behavior, she asserts, is reactive and the result of childhood circumstances. Her book, *For Your Own Good*, contains a chapter that specifically addresses the early years of Adolf Hitler, *Hitler's Childhood: From Hidden to Manifest Horror.*

> The connection that Miller wishes to make is between the behaviour of Alois Hitler in his treatment of the boy Adolf in the family situation, and the corresponding behaviour of the man Adolf on the stage of world history. *Through the agency of his unconscious repetition compulsion, Hitler (Adolf) actually succeeded in transferring the trauma of his family life onto the entire German nation.* This refers particularly to the Jewish question. According to this view Hitler's hatred of the Jews stemmed from his father's anxiety that he may have had Jewish ancestry. Further, the persecution and oppression of the Jews under the Third Reich mirrors the situation of the young Hitler, subject to sudden and capricious violence against which there is no protection (*Making the Future Information Pack* 51–52).

Both Miller and Rådström, through their particular treatments of this subject, offer insights into the childhood events that resulted in Adolf Hitler, in manhood, becoming one of history's most heinous monsters. The initial production of *Hitler's Childhood* has become one of the most celebrated works of contemporary Swedish drama and was performed in an adult version as well as in a version especially tailored to a teenage audience. Its dissemination throughout the world attests further to the power of this play.

Information about the Play and the Holocaust

It is perhaps difficult to imagine Adolf Hitler as a child. What boyhood forces could come together to produce someone whose name is synonymous with evil? What early life experiences would mold a man responsible for murdering millions of people? By all accounts, there was little evidence in Adolf Hitler's childhood to suggest the charismatic orator, dictator, and killer he would become. The future *Führer* was, in the early years of his life, more interested in art, architecture, and opera than in annihilation and ruling the world.

In hindsight, it is somewhat easier to see the boy in the man. Hitler's father was a strict and demanding disciplinarian. Like his father, the son ruled Germany with his henchmen by using terror tactics to insure obedience. Alois Hitler seduced and later married the young maid who was Adolf's mother. Adolf, underestimated by both conservatives and left-wing politicians, managed to seduce the entire German nation into allegiance. In terms of financial status and standard of living, he was raised in a family of modest means. As an adult, Hitler found those of the lower middle class like his family among those most willing to adopt his political views.

Hitler was born to Alois and Klara Hitler at Braunau am Inn in Austria on April 20, 1889. The fourth of six children, young Adolf respected his father but did not bestow upon him the same love he felt for his mother. Most likely, this is because Klara fawned over her son while Alois and Adolf more often clashed, usually about the boy's future. Adolf Hitler wished to become an artist but his father would have none of it. He insisted instead that his son follow a career path similar to his own and become a civil servant. When, on January 3, 1903, Alois Hitler died of a lung hemorrhage, the family was left in poor financial condition. With only her husband's pension and some small savings, Klara took Adolf and his half-brother and sister from their home to live in an apartment.

Adolf left school and traditional education behind at age sixteen. Two years later, he applied to the Vienna Academy of Fine Arts with the intention of pursuing his boyhood ambition. Although he passed a portion of the test for admission, he was rejected on the grounds that his artwork was unsatisfactory. This blow was followed by another when, on December 21, 1908, his mother died of cancer. Hitler returned to Vienna where he lived among poor people like himself, painting watercolor postcards and doing odd jobs to earn a living. It was in Vienna that Hitler fervently embraced and crystallized his anti-Semitic views.

He migrated to Germany in 1913. When war erupted, he petitioned King Ludwig III to allow him to join a Bavarian regiment. He served as a dispatch runner for the 16th Infantry Regiment and the List Regiment. Despite being wounded twice, gassed, and receiving the Iron Cross, Hitler achieved only the rank of corporal. His views, however, that in signing a peace treaty the Weimar Republic had betrayed the German army, that Jews in the Weimar government were responsible for this, that war was noble and the German army undefeated on the battlefield, and that all men were not equal, were cemented by his service.

Hitler returned to Munich in 1919. There, he joined the German Workers' Party, which became the National Socialist German Workers' Party, better known as the Nazi Party. Hitler soon became its leader. On November 23, 1923, he and his followers tried to overthrow the government. The coup failed and Hitler went to prison for treason, although he served only nine months before being paroled. While incarcerated, he wrote *Mein Kampf* in which he made clear his political objectives. Upon his release, he pursued political means to achieve his goals. Ultimate success was realized when, on January 30, 1933, President von Hindenberg appointed him Chancellor of Germany. When von Hindenberg died in 1934, Adolf Hitler claimed both the Chancellor's and the President's roles. His iron rule now was complete.

Hitler's Childhood

Prologue

The performance begins with the actors making the audience welcome. One of the actors goes around picking up tear-stained handkerchiefs from the auditorium. Another dries up something on the floor. The actors' welcome is friendly and courteous but they seem a little surprised, as if the audience had arrived early. The actors (and perhaps the stage-hands as well) discuss the subject of the evening's performance with the audience. It isn't, of course, possible to describe fully the substance and intensity of the following conversation.

Commentary

FIRST ACTOR. Adolf Hitler was one of the greatest mass-murderers who ever lived. Can you imagine Hitler as a young boy or a little child? When did he become Adolf Hitler? How does a little child grow up to be a monster? Or are we born evil?

THIRD ACTOR. Parents have a past as well. Alois Hitler was fifty-two when Adolf was born. He was, as far as we know, a very able official working for the Customs and Excise of the Austro-Hungarian Empire. Alois was given the surname Hitler as a present on his fortieth birthday, when he was adopted by a man who might have been his father or his father's brother. Up to that time, his name had been Schicklgruber after his mother, the maid-servant Anna Schicklgruber. We don't know whether Alois knew who his

father was. In any case, Adolf Hitler wasn't sure who his grandfather was.
SECOND ACTOR. Klara was twenty-four years younger than Alois. She was to be his third wife. At the age of sixteen, she became part of his household as a maid-servant. While his wife lay dying, he made Klara, the maid, pregnant. In quick succession, she bore three children who all died of diphtheria in the course of a few weeks, a year before Adolf was born.
THIRD ACTOR. You mustn't forget the three dead children: Otto, Gustav, Ida.

(*The First Actor is left alone onstage.*)

FIRST ACTOR. This is the child.
Nothing exists and everything is coming into being.
One world is all the worlds there are and there are no worlds at all,
for this child as for every child
the world has to be created again.
This is the child, a new-born child,
a fresh spring flowing blindly.

(*In one bound, he becomes a new-born child.*)

SCENE ONE

SCENE: *The stage is in impenetrable darkness. After a while, we hear a child sobbing. The sobs turn to crying. The crying turns to a scream. The door opens but there's no one there. The child starts screaming again. Klara steps over to the cradle and then walks across the stage.*

FATHER. What the hell's the matter with the brat?
KLARA. Go to sleep now, baby. No, I mustn't pick you up, you've got to learn to look after yourself...I could pick you up but you've got no arms to be lifted into and I mustn't take you into mine. Your small feet don't exist and when you've learnt to walk every one of your little steps will just be memories. Thump. Thump. You've got no stomach, you've got no body for me to wrap my arms around. No, I mustn't pick you up. Dinner's waiting on the table out there

but you mustn't have any yet. We must not spoil you. It would be unfair to you. Lean down into the darkness now.

(*Klara exits.*
The child starts to scream.)

FATHER. You don't want for anything, do you hear? (*Kicks the cradle.*) Just you stop all this whining. Klara, you make sure he keeps quiet.

SCENE TWO

SCENE: *Klara is showing the room to the audience. As soon as she approaches the child (onstage), it starts to scream. This is repeated several times.*

KLARA. I do think it's so...it's so important that everything should look nice, everything must look nice. Look at this lovely chair. It's made in the French style, French antique, Louis Cat...t...t...it's nice to have something this lovely in our home, to have the children grow up in a home like this, with a chair like this one. They say the Emperor looked at himself in this mirror. Just imagine...it's so nice to have something like that. To have the chance to look after nice things and to live surrounded by them... and just look at how sturdy this table is. It's got nice legs... Do you know what this way of turning the legs is called? Well, it's a very nice word...I heard it once. When the children are grown up, they can say to themselves — I had a nice home...a fine home...we had this lovely chair there...my parents looked after me so well...and, you know, we had this nice sturdy table. Whenever I looked in the mirror in my parents' home, there was always a sort of noble quality about the look in my eyes. It was such a nice mirror... but...I don't understand why Nuncle can't hang him up...it would be so nice to have him hanging up there on the wall...why can't Nuncle just nail him up there sometime?

Scene Three

SCENE: *Father, Klara, and Adolf in the room. Father is busy getting dressed.*

FATHER. Klara. My collar buttons! Damnation! (*The buttons won't go in.*) There we are. Neatness lends authority to my office. It's important to fulfil the obligations of one's position, to exceed them...go onwards...move upwards...where in damnation... (*He discovers there is a button missing.*) Klara, there is a button missing on this. For God's sake...I can't go to the office without all my buttons...Klara, help me. (*Father is conspicuously afraid of the missing button.*) The button... Klara, look for the button... Don't you understand how important it is that I have all my buttons... Yesterday, I had one of my buttons undone when the Director came in and I thought... Klara, where's the button? (*Father hits Adolf.*) And you can keep quiet. I can do without anyone else working against me. Klara, I must find my buttons. (*Father finds the button.*)

Scene Four

SCENE: *Adolf alone in the room, in bed.*

ADOLF. I'm born. I'm born now. Every day is my birthday. In Austria. In Braunau. A little town, bells, the gloaming, today's page in a calendar, by a river, a house, Bavarian beer-mugs and the river's called Inn. The Inn. Born on the borders of my Mother — thirty years of body-parts, children that can't be identified and potted plants to water. A shoulder, a knee, a head turned-away. EVERYTHING, the child may think. Schicklgruber. Three small coffins and the tears in a handkerchief. It's the custom to exercise the Exciseman. Gigantic and the man in his you-no-form, thousands of buttons. The name on a piece of a paper and two small children dressed in their clothes are walking through one woman towards the next, three girls wrapped in a bridal veil that's marked with crosses. Boy girl, boy girl. Once born, Mother decided I should live. She's always got wet handkerchiefs to lean into. I'm hungry... Hungry... Father has built all the towns with words. All the clothes are sewn by Mother with the panting of her breath. I believe it. I believe in it all. Everything is true. A thousand lantern-slides of every leaf on the ship-wrecked trees. Mother sails in a cloud of handkerchiefs across the sea — decking out the waves. The whole ocean is Mother's thought that the sea exists, with three small boats in a trough in the waves. One measly death, a light at the end of a six-year-long bed, darkness and Paula laughs her way through the whole unbirth. Everything is alive — the chairs are backing down, the table-cloths are being shelved, shoes are pairing off together and the trousers are creasing up. I'm born, everyday is my birthday, all my thousand faces are waiting expectantly for me... I'm hungry...

Scene Five

SCENE: *The Aunt enters and walks over to the bed. She hides behind the bedstead. She starts reciting her rhyme in a monotone — giving dramatic stress to certain words for no apparent reason. She jumps out of hiding every now and again to surprise the boy. At first Adolf thinks the game of Hide-and-Seek is funny, but then it frightens him.*

AUNT JOHANNA. One day Mamma said "Adolf dear,
    I must go out and leave you here.
    But mind now, Adolf, what I say,
    Don't suck your thumb while I'm away.
    The great tall tailor always comes
    To little boys who suck their thumbs;
    And ere they dream what he's about,
    He takes his great sharp scissors out,
    And cuts their thumbs clean off — and then,
    You know, they never grow again."

Mamma had scarcely turned her back,
The thumb was in, Alack! Alack!

The door flew open, in he ran,
The great, long, red-legg'd scissor-man.
Oh! children, see! The tailor's come
And caught out little Suck-a-Thumb.

Snip! Snap! Snip! the scissors go;
And Adolf cries out "Oh! Oh! Oh!"
Snip! Snap! Snip! They go so fast,
That both his thumbs are off at last.

(*The Aunt moves back to the crib and sits on it.*)

Commentary

It's a little known fact that the Hitler family had Johanna, Klara's hunchbacked and mentally ill sister, living with them. It was she who looked after Adolf during the many, long periods when Klara was ill or had a lot to do.

ADOLF. Aunt Johanna's talking between her own legs. That's what she's doing.

SCENE SIX

SCENE: *Adolf is lying alone in bed.*

ADOLF. Why does no one realize I'm hungry? I really am hungry.

(*Heavy blows on the bedstead. The boy jumps with fright.*)

FATHER. You be quiet, bloody little worm.
ADOLF. But...I'm just hungry... (*He cries. The blows on the bedstead are renewed.*)
FATHER. Quiet, I said. It's your duty to be quiet.

(*The boy is silent for a little while.*)

ADOLF. Can't any one be with me? I want someone to be with me. (*He starts crying again.*)
FATHER. This is the bloody limit. (*Father almost chokes him to death.*)

ADOLF. I'm all alone. I feel lonely.

KLARA. Now, my lad, shush. Let's have less of that ugly racket, my ugly duckling.

(*The boy stays quiet for a short while. A last whimper.*)

THE ADULTS. Be quiet!

SCENE SEVEN

SCENE: *Adolf is sitting on the floor, tearing up pieces of paper. Klara enters.*

KLARA. The children mustn't feel lonely. Or abandoned...we have to cherish their memories...Clean the moss away from their stones. Take care of the children's tiny patches of ground...clean rotting leaves away from the soil. Oh, if only I could polish the shiny wood of their coffins. Otto, Gustav, Ida. (*Klara falls asleep...standing up in her sleep.*)
ADOLF. Can you see the water, Adolf —
A dolf. Flod a. A flod — a flood!
You'll come flooding back through your name.
Adolf. Adolf.
Flood, blood, bleed, deed, dead.

Tons of water rushing to the slaughter.
Splish. Splosh. Splash.
KLARA. Stop that.
ADOLF. Adi baddy daddy
Ida hider spider
Ida Adi
KLARA. Get rid of it.
ADOLF. Slurp. Yum-yum, tum-tum
tons of water — yummy mummy,
mother father, father mother. MOTHER!

Scene Eight

SCENE: *Father, Adolf and Aunt Johanna in the room. Father is eating from the biscuit jar. Adolf is hungry.*

ADOLF. I want.
FATHER. Keep quiet, worm. You'll get your dinner soon enough. Until then you'll get nothing. Little worms like you get sick eating between meals.

(There's nothing immediately threatening in the Father's voice and the child continues to show his hunger.)

FATHER. You be quiet now, or else.
AUNT JOHANNA. Well... *(The Aunt takes a biscuit from the jar. She stuffs it into her pants for later.)*
FATHER. So, Johanna's fattening herself up, is she? Perhaps that's for the best. No one's going to want Johanna in their bed without a bit of flesh on her.
AUNT JOHANNA. Noooo...
FATHER. Crayfish tonight! Some people call them pig-food. But Johanna better watch out if she doesn't want to end up as food for the crayfish. I had an old dead granny once who got thrown into the stream to feed the fishes. She wasn't half as plump as Johanna.

(The Aunt vomits. The boy continues begging.)

Bloody hell! Shut up, you hear me! Johanna, tell him.

(Adolf frightened. Runs to the Aunt. She kneels down and speaks to the boy so the Father can't hear.)

The hole in your tum-tum goes boom-boom, empty room. No fishes want to swim in there. Not one single bird, not one berry.

(She starts suddenly.)

AUNT JOHANNA. Ow! Ow! My teeth won't strengthen.

(*The boy is frightened. He sits in silence. The Aunt smiles again.*)

ADOLF. Boom-boom.
AUNT JOHANNA. Empty room.
ADOLF. Empty room.
AUNT JOHANNA. Boom-boom.
ADOLF. Boom-boom.
AUNT JOHANNA (*resignedly*). No food. (*She walks over to the biscuit jar. She's just about to take a biscuit out but stops, looks at the Father, and pulls back her hand. She sits down for a while. She starts as though she'd been hit on the shoulder. She looks up at a spot in the room. She gets up and walks warily over to turn the lid. The boy looks on in silent amazement.*)
FATHER. Does Johanna know how you go fishing for eels?

(*The Aunt looks at the Father, struck dumb.*)

You get yourself a dead body, a dead dog or a cat, a half-rotted sheep or a horse's head maybe and you throw it into the water. After an hour or so you pull it up and out wriggle all the eels. Carrion eaters, you understand, Johanna. You'd better watch out.
ADOLF. Boom-boom.
FATHER (*calls out the door*). Klara! Is that button sewn on yet? Klara?
AUNT JOHANNA. Klara!

(*There is no answer.*)

FATHER. This is the bloody limit.

(*The Aunt checks to make sure that the Father really has gone. Then she stuffs several biscuits into her mouth. The boy laughs. The crumbs spurt from the Aunt's mouth. The game goes on for longer than the boy thinks is funny and, finally, he wants his own biscuit. Sullen and resentful, the Aunt stuffs a biscuit into the boy's mouth. Suddenly, the Aunt shrieks. Then she stuffs another biscuit into his mouth and then another. The boy's being choked rather than fed. The Father appears.*)

What the hell's going on here?... Adi, didn't I say... (*He stops and turns to the Aunt. He points at her in silent question. She points in turn at the boy. The Father turns back to the boy so that they are both pointing at him.*) Bloody little leech! I'll teach you what happens when you give in to desire.

SCENE NINE

FATHER. I rush towards the boy to hit him.
ADOLF. The shape of the high-chair I'm sitting in means I can't really move at all!
FATHER. On the table there are bowls full of words and I keep forcing the boy to eat. Fed up to the teeth.
ADOLF. I try and catch my breath between the words. Fed up to the teeth.
FATHER. I force him to eat word after word. The lad's mad.
ADOLF. I'm being choked. The lad's mad.
FATHER. I'm forcing a spoon down his throat. Spitting image of his Father.
ADOLF. I'm gasping, trying to scream, but I'm being choked. Spitting image of his Father.

SCENE TEN

SCENE: *Adolf standing alone in front of the mirror.*

ADOLF. Hello. Can I be of assistance? No thank you, we won't be having anything. Well now, we're going to be ever so good and eat up our dinner. Hello...Hello...Hello... (*The boy continues in this vein for some time. After a while, the Father enters and catches sight of the boy without his noticing. For a while, the Father stands still, observing the boy with increasing astonishment until he comprehends.*) Hello, my name is Adolf...Adolf Hitler...Yes, that's right. Schicklgruber. Hitler...hello, hello...hello, my name is Alois Hitler.
FATHER. Bloody hell, boy, have you taken leave of your senses? If you're not careful you'll end up like that...You must be out of your mind.

ADOLF. Out of my mind? What does that mean? I'm not outside myself.
I'm right here after all.
Can't be it. He must mean it's me who is the I outside you.
I outside me.
That's it. Me outside you.
I besides you.
No, without me.
Perhaps it would be possible to be me — me, just as a word.
I'm beside myself.
Hello, I'm outside myself...no, beside myself. Not I but me. Where do I come from? I've taken leave of my senses, you see. That's right.
I've come here from out of my mind. That's where I'm from. Beside myself, you see. I'm on a journey. Hello. I'm on a journey outside myself. Hello. Yes, that's right...Out of my mind, that's where I'm from. Hello.

SCENE ELEVEN

SCENE: *Adolf is standing at the table. Father is very neatly dressed in his official uniform and getting ready to go to work.*

ADOLF. Father, where do children come from?
FATHER. What?
ADOLF. Father, where do children come from?
FATHER. What are you talking about, you worm? (*Gives the boy a slap.*) Children don't come into this world to ask nosy questions, but to learn how to do their duty. Understood?
ADOLF. Actually, I'm too little to understand it put like that. Nevertheless, I take Father's reply as an answer. Yes, Father.
FATHER. What did you say?
ADOLF. Yes, Father.
FATHER. I'm ready to go now. I go calling throughout the house, Klara! Klara! I'm going now. Klara! I'm going.

(*He exits. After a while, during which Adolf has been sitting deep in thought, Klara enters. She is doing the cleaning. The boy remains seated, thinking for quite a while before he speaks to Klara.*)

ADOLF. Not why not...I want to know where from. I didn't ask why they don't. Where from. Not why not. I really want to know. (*Adolf turns to Klara.*)

KLARA. What are you talking about?

ADOLF. Where do children come from?

KLARA. What questions you ask, Adi. Does Father know you ask questions like that?

ADOLF (*to himself and the audience*). Yes, Father knows I ask questions like that but he doesn't know I ask questions like *that*! Where from and not why not. (*To Klara.*) What I mean is where from and not why not. (*Klara shrugs her shoulders.*) Mother, where do children come from?

KLARA. Children grow in Mother's body and then they get so big that there's no more room and then they come out. It's terribly painful.

ADOLF. Why does it hurt?

KLARA. So that Mother...to learn all the things her child is capable of.

ADOLF. But how does the child get into the Mother's body? Doesn't that hurt?

KLARA. No...well, yes. Well, no one really knows. It just grows there.

ADOLF. That's strange.

(*Klara does the cleaning feverishly. She ignores the boy. Adolf to himself and the audience.*)

And then Mother starts doing something else. I want to know. I want to know. (*To Klara.*) That's strange.

KLARA. Strange, it's not strange at all. It's not strange that trees grow in the forest and it's not strange that children grow in Mothers. It's been like that for as long as there have been people on earth.

ADOLF. Does Mother have to be on her own when it hurts?

KLARA. Yes...no, no, Mother has a midwife (*pronounced carelessly*) at her side.

ADOLF. What's a mudwife?

(*Klara turns away from him, cleaning feverishly. Adolf to himself and the audience.*)

I don't...and then she doesn't want to again. She always starts doing something else.

ADOLF (*to Klara*). What's that mudwife thing?

KLARA. You see, there's a woman...Most people won't watch when the pain comes but there are some hard-hearted women who are so bold that they dare to watch when it starts to hurt. And just as there are women who wash and dress the bodies of the dead that no one else would touch, there are women who will bring a child into the world in exchange for money. They do it for the money!
ADOLF. I want to watch when a baby comes.
KLARA. Adi! What are you saying? What would *Father* think...
ADOLF. Not for money...I just want to watch...
KLARA. You can go and watch when they're butchering a pig at the neighbour's. Do you remember when their son cut his leg open with an axe and it bled and he had to walk with a splint? That's how badly it hurt. When you've seen that, then you've seen — watch out for the carpet! — What it's like when a child comes into the world.

(*Adolf thinks for a bit. Klara's just about to start cleaning again.*)

ADOLF. How do they know if it's a boy or a girl?

(*Klara turns away from him.*)

KLARA. They don't.
ADOLF (*to himself and the audience*). Don't know. Don't know. Why can't anyone give me a proper answer? Don't know. What about me? They don't know. (*To Klara.*) What about me? Isn't it certain that I am a boy then?
KLARA. Oh yes, that is known. It's something you can...see.
ADOLF. You can see it...How can you see it? (*Klara starts cleaning again. The boy ponders a while.*) Does it have to hurt? (*Klara pretends not to hear him.*) Mother, does it have to hurt?
KLARA. Does what have to hurt?
ADOLF. Does it have to hurt when children are born?
KLARA. Yes, yes...it does. It has to hurt.
ADOLF. Why does it have to hurt?
KLARA. So that Mother's got something to forgive her child.
ADOLF. Mother...

KLARA. Now that's enough. Asking questions like that doesn't make children happy. Children should keep quiet and be happy and play. Just stand still and play now.

(*Adolf sits silently, thoroughly investigating the doll and thinking deeply.*)

SCENE TWELVE

KLARA. It's all so ugly. It's all so unbearably ugly and worthless. This old carpet, this hideous mirror. (*She walks over to the mirror.*) It's hideous. You can't bear to look at yourself in this mirror.

(*Adolf walks forward and looks at Mother in the mirror.*)

ADOLF. Mother looks nice in the mirror. Nice in Mother's mirror.
KLARA. I'm hideous, horrible. Everything is ugly. It's all so revolting and ugly. (*She leaves the mirror.*) All the time, everyday over the same old hideous rickety table. It's unbearable. Everything's so dreary — everything's so dreary when your home's as ugly as this.
ADOLF. Nice chair. (*He points at it.*)
KLARA. Nice. Nice? It's a revolting chair. It's horrible sitting on it. It makes you sick just looking at it. Everything is so revolting and ugly.
ADOLF. Adi is sitting in Mother's lap.
KLARA. Oh yes, I'm good enough for that. Good enough to be a piece of furniture. Good enough to be a chair.
ADOLF. Mother not chair. Mother is Mother.
KLARA. So my little boy doesn't want to sit in his Mother's lap any more, does he? Am I that revolting?
ADOLF. Mother is nice Mother.
KLARA. As hideous as the mirror, as revolting as the chair, as ugly as the carpet.

Scene Thirteen

ADOLF. Little worm, little worm, little Adi baddy worm.
THE JEW. I'm not a worm. (*The voice comes out of nowhere and at first Adolf looks around in surprise. Adolf looks at the Jew.*) Here I am, Adi. I'm here now.
ADOLF. Who are you?
THE JEW. I'm me. You know who I am. I'm the most important of all. I'm the one who's most important.
ADOLF. You don't really exist. (*Adolf hits out at the Jew.*)
THE JEW. Here I am, Adi.
ADOLF. How did you get born? Did it hurt? I hurt Mother.
THE JEW. What are you talking about? I told you I'm important. I've got responsibilities. I'm a person of consequence.
ADOLF. Have you got a uniform?
THE JEW. Can you see a uniform?
ADOLF. No.
THE JEW. Well then, there you are then.
ADOLF. What do you do?
THE JEW. I'm important. I do all kinds of things. I can do anything. I'm the one who makes the decisions.
ADOLF. Me, too.
THE JEW. You, you worm.
ADOLF. Oh yes, I can. I can kill you. I can just sweep you away.
THE JEW. Can you see me?
ADOLF. No.
THE JEW. How do you know I exist then...?
ADOLF. I...
THE JEW. If I don't exist you can't sweep me away, can you?
ADOLF. Yes, I can...
THE JEW. If I do exist and you can't see me, how can you know if I've been swept away when you've done it?
ADOLF. I can say that you exist and then decide that you don't exist any more.
THE JEW. But won't I still exist all the same?
ADOLF. No, because you only exist when I say you can.
THE JEW. If you stop this, I'll tell you a secret.
ADOLF. Tell me.
THE JEW. Come a bit nearer if you want to hear. Mother is two hundred breaths under a sea of cotton wool.

ADOLF. Oooh!
THE JEW. There are thousands of birds in your hair and the buttons on your Father's uniform are the lakes they won't drink from.

(At first Adolf just sits there feeling confused but then his face lights up with happiness.)

ADOLF. Oooh!
THE JEW. Don't you believe me?
ADOLF *(thinks first)*. Oh yes, oh yes.

SCENE FOURTEEN

SCENE: *Adolf, seated, holding Ida's doll.*

ADOLF. Little foot...why are you doing that? Look at the two fishes and that's when the children turn into them. The children are fishes that have swum out of the sea...Maybe the children are longing for the sea...Here comes the doctor. He's going to give you a smack...smack...smack... Why do you do it like that? Don't you want to...little fish...little foot.

(Father enters suddenly. He is angry.)

FATHER. Adi! Adi!

(Adolf immediately hides Ida's doll behind his back.)

Adi, you've taken Ida's doll.

(Adolf looks up at the Father, keeping the doll hidden and shakes his head.)

You've got the doll, haven't you? Own up!

(Adolf shakes his head.)

Mother says you've taken Ida's doll.

(*Adolf continues to shake his head.*)

Adi makes Father feel very unhappy when Adi tells lies. When Adi tells lies, that's the worst thing that can happen to Father. Father gets very sad when Adi tells lies.

(*Father sits down heavily. Father pretends to be very dejected. He sighs heavily.*)

KLARA. I really can't believe the boy is lying, Nuncle.
FATHER. No, no. He wants to tell the truth, of course.

(*Father more and more dejected. Adolf feels very sorry for Father. Adolf walks/crawls over to Father. He shows him the doll.*)

ADOLF. Adi found...
FATHER (*suddenly furious again*). What Adi found was more trouble for himself. Now Adi's going to give the doll to Mother.
ADOLF. Adi wants...
FATHER. No, Adi doesn't want anything. Adi's going to give the doll back.
ADOLF. Father, the child wants to go back to the sea.
FATHER. You will give Ida's doll back.

(*Adolf shakes his head, saying nothing.*)

ADOLF. The child is a fish...doesn't want to see the doctor...doesn't want to see the mud-wife-thing, doesn't want to see the thing...
FATHER. But you do want to give Ida's doll to Mother, don't you, Adi? (*Adolf refuses, saying nothing. He starts to sniffle.*) Adi, I want you to give the doll back to Mother this instant.

(*At first Adolf continues to refuse but then throws the doll at Father's feet.*)

What the...! Are you out of your mind!

(*Klara steps forward to pick up the doll.*)

No, Klara. Don't.

(*Klara steps back.*)

Pick up the doll and give it to me, Adi.

(*Adolf in tears.*)

ADOLF. No. No.
FATHER (*the Father goes and fetches the switch. He shows it to Adolf*). Pick up the doll or I'll beat you with this switch.
ADOLF. No. No.
KLARA. Don't you understand how much it hurts your Father to have to beat you, Adolf? Don't you know how much pain it causes your Father and Mother to see you like this? Do you really want to hurt your Father so badly?
FATHER (*Father picks up the doll and moves to another spot, dragging the boy with him. He throws the doll to the floor and shows Adolf the switch again*). Pick up the doll or I'll beat you with this switch.
ADOLF (*Adolf shakes his head, saying nothing*). Father's giving me a few strokes with the switch.
FATHER. Now will you pick up the doll?

(*Adolf shakes his head. The Father hits him again.*)

ADOLF (*in tears*). Ow! Ow! Ow!
FATHER. Will you pick up the doll now?
ADOLF (*Adolf picks up the doll*). The fish has already swum off...the sea ate the doctor up.
FATHER. There we are then.

(*Adolf rushes over to his Mother with the doll.*)

KLARA. No, Adi. Mother doesn't want anything to do with such a bad boy. Look how you've hurt your Father.
ADOLF (*Adolf looks at his Father. He is confused about which pain is his Father's and which is his own*). Father hurts...

(*The parents turn away from him.*)

FATHER. I'm going out to the bees now.
KLARA. Yes, Nuncle — just go off, why don't you?
FATHER. I thought I'd go and pick some nettles so we could have some nettle soup for supper.
KLARA. If Nuncle wants to go and pick nettles, there's bound to be someone to cook them for him.
FATHER. The nettles do have to be removed from the garden.
KLARA. They don't make more of a mess than anything else.
FATHER. No, but it's not healthy to have them in the garden. This place is like a pigsty as it is.
ADOLF. The whole garden is the sea...but the little fish is in the house eating nettles the doctor gave him...the thing is slowly pouring the sea into the oven...come on, let's eat now...and now we'll mend the shields.

(*Father re-enters.*)

And then Father starts glaring at me...Father's eyes glare at me and at any moment they'll go rushing after the fishes in the room...Father picks up a huge bow, notches an arrow and stretches the bow. In place of the arrowhead, there is a large eye.

Scene Fifteen

SCENE: *Adolf and Klara in the room. They move in a manner that is both controlled and at the same time manically nervous. There is a comic quality to their movements as the audience cannot make sense of them. The boy keeps checking, time after time, that his bed is properly made and he keeps looking in the mirror to see whether he's neatly dressed and keeps moving a chair that's already in the right place. The Mother is doing much the same kind of thing, moving objects that look as though they are already in the right place. Every now and then she stands still and listens out for something.*

ADOLF. What are we waiting for? What are we getting ready for? A party? A visit?
KLARA. Adi, your shirt. Adi, you know what you've been up to. What you've done. You're old enough now to stand on your own two

feet...Adi, don't forget to look Father in the eyes when you thank him.

SCENE SIXTEEN

FATHER. Well then, it's wonderful to come home, to be with my wife, with my family. Now, Klara, tell me what's been happening today.
KLARA. Oh, not much, Nuncle.
FATHER. The office was the same as usual. The same crawlers, the same cowards. Well, they're not worth worrying about...I suppose you've managed to fulfil some of your responsibilities.
KLARA. I haven't cleaned the uniform shirt. I haven't sewn on the buttons. Your pipe fell off...Adi's been playing with his trains.
FATHER. Well, my lad. So you've been controlling the traffic.

(*Adolf nods silently.*)

Haven't you got a tongue in your head? What do you think you are doing? Trains travel on the ground, not in the air. Stop that at once.

(*Adolf is just about to say something but the Father immediately turns his back to him.*)

I showed them how firm I could be today, how strong. No one bullies an Exciseman, I told them. (*Throws himself at the boy.*) On the ground, I said. As if you could lay the rails on to thin air. (*To Klara again.*) And the creeps went and complained to the Director. No one can shake my strength of purpose or my devotion to duty, I told them.
KLARA. So you got what you wanted, Nuncle?
FATHER (*he slaps her*). You be quiet. Don't tease me. (*He walks over to Adolf.*) Don't you understand anything? You're supposed to drive them here. I've never seen anything so stupid. Bloody crawlers.
KLARA. Nuncle...
FATHER (*he looks at Klara as if she were a Doppelganger, a copy of the real Klara*). You keep quiet, you hear. Get out. The bloody crawlers are afraid of everything and then go running to the Director. The Jew, the Jew. They should take a good look in the mirror. That'd show them where the Jew was. (*He rushes at Adolf*

and tears the trains from his hands.) You worm, don't you understand anything? You drive those trains properly now, do you hear?

ADOLF. But the train does fly over the houses...

FATHER. The train has just passed the border and is on its way to the goods depot where the freight has to be declared. Here. The appropriate documents have been filled out. That part of the freight that has been passed by Customs is transferred to the warehouse — over here — and then the train can continue to its next destination, where the same procedure is repeated and so on, ad infinitum. You've got to learn, you've got to learn to do it right. (*He reaches for a walking stick and hits out at the boy, hunting him through the room.*)

KLARA. Nuncle, Nuncle, don't hit him. Don't hit him now.

FATHER (*he aims a blow at her. During the following, Adolf and Klara take it in turns to stand frozen — the other one circling around the figure standing still*). The child has got to learn. The child has got to learn the meaning of fear.

KLARA. But look after him, don't let him get hurt.

FATHER. You're like all the other creeps; any hint of firmness, of thoroughness scares you. Why am I surrounded on all sides by this unparalleled cowardice — this poverty of spirit.

KLARA. He's our flesh and blood...

FATHER. And our blood has to be tamed. I forbid you to cross me.

KLARA. Nuncle...

FATHER. I don't intend to let myself be deprived of my resolve just because some little shrimp is offended by it. It's my duty to use all the means at my disposal to bring the boy up to be tough, to prepare him for the outside world. Go on, get out, all of you. (*Father shakes all over, his face turns blood-red, his eyes stare. He walks to and fro and gradually he calms himself down. A bit shyly, he looks round and takes a peek at the audience.*)

FIRST AND SECOND ACTORS. Alois Hitler had cause to believe his Father was a Jew, a merchant by the name of Frankenberger.

FIRST ACTOR. In accordance with the racial purity laws of the Nazis, every German had to be able to prove his racial purity as far back as three generations.

SECOND ACTOR. There were two exceptions to this law: Adolf Hitler and Jesus.

FATHER. Haven't you noticed how people on the street rush to have a look whenever there's a fight? Toughness is impressive. The simplest man in the street can make an impression through brute strength and ruthlessness. People need a healthy degree of fear. They want something to be afraid of. They want to be frightened and they want something to bow down before in terror. This is true for both men and women and in consequence for children. Children want toughness. They need toughness. (*Calm again.*) It really is wonderful to be back home, to be with my wife, with my family. Adi, come here. You have to learn to do what your parents tell you, don't you?
ADOLF. Yes, Father.
FATHER. If you don't, the Murky Man, the man who lives in the darkness, comes out and he eats the flesh on children's legs.
KLARA (*the Mother seems relieved that Father isn't going to beat the child and she smiles encouragingly at Adolf*). Should I...
FATHER. A civil servant needs his family as a sure foundation, a base from which he can work for the common good. My pipe, Klara. Yes, Adi, he'll come out of the darkness — his teeth are all black — when children are sleeping...

(*Klara takes a pipe from the pipe-rack.*)

Silently and carefully, without his being heard or sensed in any way. Klara, that's the one I had yesterday. You know the one I mean.

(*Klara takes another pipe out.*)

Silently and carefully he eats the flesh from their legs. If the child has just committed a little lie, on waking up he finds that the whole foot and the leg below the knee have turned into a pile of bones, but if it's a big lie what's left of both legs is just a pair of stumps, which the child has to use as crutches. Isn't that right, Klara?
KLARA. Yes it is, and, Adi, there are children who've been totally eaten up.
FATHER. I know of a child who woke up one morning and only his head was left. My newspaper, Klara.

(*Mother fetches it and gives it to Father.*)

Under the blanket there was just a skeleton, just a jumble of damp bits of bone. (*Loses himself in what he's reading.*) This is about Schonerer's new pamphlet. About apes that trample outsiders to death. And what's true of apes must be even more true of human beings. That's the kind of man Austria needs.
KLARA. The Murky Man had left the heart. That's why the boy was still alive...
FATHER. ...but the stomach had gone so the lad starved to death. What's for dinner, Klara?
KLARA. Do you understand now why it's so important to obey your Father, Adi?
ADOLF. Yes, Mother, I do.
KLARA. Well, then thank your Father for going to the trouble of explaining all this to you.
ADOLF. Thank you, Father. Thank you, Father.
FATHER. All right, my lad. Everything's all right now.
ADOLF. Thank you, Father.
FATHER. Well then, what's for dinner?
KLARA. Meat soup, Nuncle.
FATHER. That's food fit for a man. Do you hear, Adi?
ADOLF (*Almost lovingly*). Thank you, Father.

SCENE SEVENTEEN

SCENE. *Adolf in bed. He is frightened and cannot sleep.*

ADOLF. The Murky Man. Where are the footsteps? Dark as the darkness, so I can't hear them. He's as black as the dark. He comes in and goes out in the darkness. Ow! Ow! Ow! No, I am just pretending. All I can do is pretend. I've got to pretend to be asleep when I'm pretending not to be. Pretend that I'm not waiting and the footsteps are black as pitch. The Murky Man? He eats...he eats boys. Just talk, all of it. He's an eater. He can eat up me...you. Me? You, you mean.

Scene Eighteen

SCENE. *The Aunt enters from the darkness and walks over to Adolf's bed.*

AUNT JOHANNA. Listen, Adi. He's coming now. The rays enter here in my back, you see. (*She points at herself.*) Here in my back and then they move down into my leg, here. And some in my arm. Look, look here. (*She slaps herself.*) It's love, Adolf. He's fallen in love with my body, which is why he wants to be inside me. Like that, the ray is here now. (*She slaps the boy.*) It is important to look him in the eyes the whole time. In the eyes, Adolf. Look at him in the eyes. If you fail to look him in the eyes, you lose your ability to move. If you fail to look him in the eyes, you get your mouth sewn shut. Here, through the back of the head, the rays. If you just look him in the eyes, you get back your ability to move. Look, they're dancing with him.

Scene Nineteen

SCENE. *Night. Adolf is lying in bed. Through the door, we hear the parents' voices.*

FATHER. Come here, come here — my girl.
KLARA. Nuncle, help me hang him up now.
FATHER. I've got the nail here.
KLARA. You need a bigger nail than that.
FATHER. Show me the spot. I'll do the nailing. You dolt, sometimes I think all you've got between your ears is fat. Fat between your ears and syrup between your legs.
KLARA. You'll have to get a bigger nail if you're going to get him into place, Nuncle.

(*Adolf sits up in bed, terrified.*)

FATHER. It'll have to wait. I can't be bothered banging in nails tonight.
KLARA. He's got such a gentle face.
FATHER. Weak and puny, that's the Jew. They've got no resistance.
KLARA. There's a lovely kind of purity in his suffering face. He's no Jew. He's an Aryan. Jew, yourself!

FATHER. Well then, stop nagging! I'll be banging in bigger nails tomorrow.

SCENE TWENTY

THE JEW. No more sleep is there, Adi?
ADOLF. No, no there isn't.
THE JEW. Why doesn't sleep come back to haunt us?
ADOLF. Who are they going to nail? Who's the one they're going to nail?
THE JEW. No one who exists, but they're going to kill him because he does. They've decided it.
ADOLF. Who do they want not to exist?
THE JEW. Not a Jew. You heard them say so yourself.
ADOLF. Not a Jew who is allowed to exist.
THE JEW. Not me in any case.
ADOLF. Yes it is, me. Me.
THE JEW. Just how many small boys are there in the house?
ADOLF. Yeah, yeah.
THE JEW. Perhaps, it's just a lark.
ADOLF. No, it's definitely a Jew they're going to be nailing up. But it's not me.
THE JEW. Another Jew.
ADOLF. Yes, but who am I?
THE JEW. Well, don't ask me. You're not a Jew, are you?
ADOLF. No, you're you. You're the one. Not me. (*Pause.*) Listen you, are you there?
THE JEW. Yes, I'm here. There's no sleep, any more.
ADOLF. Why do they have to nail the boy? Why do they have to?
THE JEW. He has to suffer for their sins.
ADOLF. Is he going to,,,
THE JEW. He's going to bear their guilt.
ADOLF. And I'm not the one.
THE JEW. And you're not the one.
ADOLF. Are you sure?
THE JEW. There isn't any sleep.
ADOLF. Are you sure?

Scene Twenty-One

SCENE: *Morning — Adolf lying in bed.*

KLARA. Adi darling, rise and shine. It's a lovely day today and you can go out and play. So rise and shine. Mother's so tired.
AUNT JOHANNA. Hey! Didn't you hear what she just said? Get out of bed. Oh Adi, not again. What a dirty little child you are. Who do you think is going to deal with this? How can your Mother be expected to love a dirty little child like you? What are we going to do with you, my little lad?
ADOLF. I can't help it...it wasn't me...
AUNT JOHANNA. Oh yes, my lad, it was you all right. Now, you'll just have to lie there and wait until we've found someone who can help you. Perhaps that awful old woman down the street can deal with it.
ADOLF. I don't want to.
AUNT JOHANNA. Klara!
ADOLF. Mother!!!
KLARA. Mother's so tired and...then my boy goes and makes a filthy mess like this. We have to pay someone to clean something like this up. And you know what your Father thinks about wasting money.
ADOLF. I just woke up and...I didn't mean to...I didn't know.
KLARA. We'll just have to ask Aunt Johanna to clean you up.
ADOLF. Oh no!
AUNT JOHANNA. Klara doesn't want to have anything to do with a dirty little boy like you. When you're washed and clean, you can go to Mother. Did they send you down to the piddle-cellar then? Did you fetch up buckets from the piddle-cellar? Hey, diddle diddle. The cat ate the fiddle. Fiddle, piddle. Fiddle, piddle — let's cut it off!
ADOLF. No, no.
AUNT JOHANNA. So who is it who empties the buckets in the bed, then?
ADOLF. ...the Jew.
AUNT JOHANNA. The Jew. The Jew he says! Klara!!! Auntie's got one hand in heaven and one in the deep blue sea and that's when you don't wet the bed. Auntie owns all horses. Come on then. We'll clean and trim your little wick.
ADOLF. Mother! Mother!

KLARA. What are you talking about? No, of course, there isn't anything strange about her. She's not a hunchback...Aunt Johanna does not exist!

SCENE TWENTY-TWO

ADOLF. Mother...Mother...
KLARA. Adi, Adi...I can't cope. I'm tired. I can't cope with you at the moment. I'm so tired. Mother has to rest. You've got to let Mother rest now.
ADOLF. Can't you go and lie down then, Mother?
KLARA. No, oh no, I'm not up to it.
ADOLF. I think you should go and lie down and get some rest.
KLARA. No, no, I'm not tired. I'm not tired.
ADOLF. But you said you were tired, Mother.
KLARA. No, I feel wide-awake. I'm wide-awake, yes, I am. I'm too worn out to rest.
ADOLF (*stays sitting in confusion. Starts again*). Mother...Mother...
KLARA. Adi, Adi, I can't cope. I'm tired. Well then, why don't you go and lie down. But that's what I've been saying. Mother's got to rest. You've got to let Mother rest.

(*Now they can hear the Father coming.*)

SCENE TWENTY-THREE

SCENE: *Father enters in silence.*

FATHER. Klara, my pipe wasn't where it's supposed to be.
KLARA. But you've got it now, Nuncle.
FATHER. Yes, but I had to go hunting for it. I haven't got time for that kind of thing. How am I supposed to put up with being undermined like this?
KLARA. But, Nuncle, you don't like it when I touch your pipes.
FATHER. They're supposed to be in their proper place.
KLARA. Since you don't like me touching your pipes, Nuncle, I don't touch them. You must have put your pipe in the wrong place yourself, Nuncle.

FATHER. Me? Me? It's always me who...The home is Klara's domain. Anyway, at the Customs House everything has its proper place.
KLARA. How did you get on with the promotion, Nuncle?
FATHER. Klara, you shouldn't...Well, Klara, you don't get the chances I do. Perhaps that's why you can't keep this place tidy.
KLARA. But to get the chances and not to take them...
FATHER. That pipe has its proper place. That's where I should be able to find it. That's your job, Klara.

(*Adolf is cutting up bits of paper.*)

It's dirty in here. Did you do the sweeping, Klara? Adi, you'll get dirty. Have you swept in here, Klara?
KLARA. Yes, I did.
FATHER. Give me the broom and I'll do it.
KLARA. I have done the sweeping. If you'd only wipe your shoes, Nuncle, when you...
FATHER. The broom, Klara. We'll get this place spick and span.

(*Klara opens a window to air the room.*)

Klara, do you want to let every bloody flying pest in the whole county indoors?
KLARA. The only things out there are your bees, Nuncle.
FATHER. Adi's cold. Do you have to air the room when it's raining cats and dogs?
KLARA. It's just drizzling.
FATHER. The window frame will be ruined.
KLARA. The window frame is already ruined.
FATHER. From all the bloody airing. (*The Father sweeps the floor, making no real effort. What little he sweeps up has just been moved from one spot on the floor to another.*) I thought we could take the whole family out on Sunday.
KLARA. You're always out, Nuncle, anyway.
FATHER. We need to move about, get to meet...The children need to have a look round.
KLARA. I don't want our children running around at night.
FATHER. A Sunday outing.
KLARA. Well, then in that case, I suppose I should start the cooking right now.

FATHER. The boy needs to get out in the fresh air.
KLARA. You can never get rid of grass-stains. You've no idea, Nuncle, how long it takes to...
FATHER. You can stay home and sleep, Klara.
Everything lovely she makes ugly. Everything ugly becomes life's entirety, if she so desires. The place for a pipe loses its meaning, its soul, if it's not part of order itself but just a soulless object that cleaning's brought to light. If you can't understand these values, you can't understand anything.
KLARA. Talk about order. Talk about things in their right place but not be able to see where you've ended up yourself. Everything in the room's ugly, but it's been cleaned.
FATHER. Klara, this place looks bloody awful.
KLARA. It looks nice in here. It's been cleaned.

(*Klara rushes out. The Father remains behind in the room.*)

Scene Twenty-Four

FATHER. Well, Adi, what are you up to?
ADOLF. Building, Father. Town. The whole world. Braunau.
FATHER. It's a great thing to be creative, Adi. To create the truth.
ADOLF. Building, Father. Town.
FATHER. A true town, a true home. That's something worth creating, that is, Adi.
ADOLF. Yes, Father. Braunau.
FATHER. You're a good boy, a hard-working boy to be able to build like that. Like the bees. They take what's best from Nature and make out of it a society that we humans can appreciate and make use of.
ADOLF. Bzzz. Bzzz.
FATHER. They're nice towns the ones the bees have, Adolf. Bee-cities.
ADOLF. Beebraunau, Breebraubee.
FATHER. Well, Adi. Enough of that. (*Silence for a while.*) It's the bloody limit that we should get Jew-weather like this today. When it's this wet the bees can't find any nectar. Bloody Jew-weather.
ADOLF. It's raining, Father. Plip. Plop.
FATHER. And it's not something to joke about. How are the bees supposed to gather the honey and build their hives in weather like this?

ADOLF (*to himself*). Sunny honey.

(*Adolf goes on building. Father waits for something.*)

FATHER. Adi, you're creating things. You're building them. They're true towns, aren't they, my boy?
ADOLF. Hives and industries.
FATHER. Adi, it's not a subject to poke fun at.
ADOLF. Towns, roofs, Braunau.
FATHER. That button! Building and preserving, Adi. Being part of it all. That's what's true, Adi. The Customs House is built like that — a true society, a real truth. Everything has its place there. It's not a house of cards, not a dreamworld. True, Adi. The spotless desks, all those goods being weighed and measured, assessed for duty. The crooks get caught out and honest traders can get on with their business. That's where you'll find true creation.

(*Adolf listens with interest to Father's description of his place of work.*)

At the Customs House, the least little thing is of importance. The true contents of everything are listed — every piece of paper, every little button. Look at my face, Adi. Look at me.

(*Adolf looks at Father.*)

The whole of my being gains substance from my position. My mouth, my eyes, my nose and cheeks — it all has to be carefully constructed. It's all part of a larger creation.

(*Adolf looks at Father. He's very impressed.*)

That's right, Adi. Creation, creating yourself.

(*Father stays sitting for quite a while, stretching nobly upwards. Then his nose starts to tickle and he grimaces to stop sneezing. His whole trunk seems to cave in as a result of his ridiculous grimacing. Adolf starts building again. Father gets bored sitting down. He looks out through the window at the rain.*)

Build strongly. Build to resist.
ADOLF. Yes, Father. Strong Braunau for the beeses.
FATHER. Bees.

(*Adolf goes on playing. Father seems restless with nothing to do.*)
ADOLF (*to himself*). Bloody Jew-weather. Build over the Jew-weather, build round the Jew-bee, the Jew-beeses.

(*Father's got nothing to do.*)

FATHER. You are building properly, aren't you?
ADOLF. Yes, Father.
FATHER. Really true. Truly real.
ADOLF. Yes, Father.
FATHER. Building on the firm foundation of the truth.
ADOLF. Yes, Father.

(*Adolf finds his Father a bit tedious.*)

FATHER. I've heard you don't always do that, Adi.
ADOLF. Yes I do, Father. True Braunau.
FATHER. There's so much tittle-tattle goes on, you know.
ADOLF. Yes, Father.
FATHER. Don't you want to know what your Father has to tell you?
ADOLF. Yes, I do, Father. I do.
FATHER. Well, that's what you say, is it? You're building on the truth.
ADOLF. Yes, Father.
FATHER. Lying's not right, is it?
ADOLF. No, Father.
FATHER. All the same, didn't I hear that you sometimes...
ADOLF. No, Father.
FATHER. Don't interrupt me. You don't know what I'm going to say.
ADOLF. No, Father. Yes, Father.
FATHER. Your Mother says you don't always do what you say. Your Mother says you don't always say what you do.
ADOLF. No, Father...I mean, yes, I do...
FATHER. No, I really can't believe that you'd want to keep anything from your parents.
ADOLF. No, Father.

FATHER. Well then, there we are.

(*Adolf stays sitting. He's confused and a little afraid.*)

Go on building. Build your true town.

(*Adolf hesitates a bit, but then starts playing again warily.*)

Houses built on false foundations don't last long.
ADOLF. No, Father.
FATHER. Truth goes under so many guises. It's not nice to be told that your own son sometimes accepts other truths than those that are truly true.
ADOLF. Father, I haven't...
FATHER. Lied. No, you haven't lied. How could anyone who doesn't know what's true be able to lie? No, you haven't lied, but if you can't see what's true, your whole self becomes a lie.
ADOLF. Yes, Father...I...
FATHER. If you have a think about it, you'll soon see what I mean.
ADOLF. No. Father.
FATHER (*laughing*). My boy...you can't hide from yourself just by saying no to your Father. You've told the lie, whatever you do.
ADOLF. Yes, Father...No.
FATHER. There you are. You see, I knew you'd understand what I meant. A lie cannot be based on truth's firm foundations.
ADOLF. Father, I don't understand...I haven't...
FATHER. Haven't, of course not. But am, Adi, am!
ADOLF. Father, please Father, could you tell...
FATHER. If you look inside yourself, you'll find what I'm talking about. Look inside yourself and you'll find the lie sitting there next to shame, the two of them sitting there inside you like two crows in the rain.

(*Adolf silent.*)

You do understand that with that kind of lie you can't build anything that's true, don't you...or do you want to do your creating with shame?
ADOLF. Father...

FATHER. Doesn't it feel better now you know that I know? Doesn't it feel nicer not having to bear your shame alone? To share the shame with your Father. Isn't it a wonderful feeling to know that I'm helping you with it?

(*Adolf stands in silence.*)

Well?

ADOLF. Yes, it does, Father.

FATHER. Well, then. You know how much I feel for you, my boy. What are we to do with a liar like you? How's he going to bear so much shame?

ADOLF. I don't know, Father.

FATHER. Don't know. Don't know. What kind of nonsense is that? You're stepping in your own lies, treading in them, standing and sitting in them. You eat and shit in your lies and your shame. You sleep in it. It's the whole of you. That's what the whole of you is... (*Father laughs.*) Well then, my lad. Now, I'm going to show you how to bear your shame. Look at this. (*Father writes the word SHAME in huge letters on a piece of paper.*) There you are, you see — I have built a house for you. Now, wherever you go you'll always be reminded of your shame and lies. I can't punish you for that kind of thing. Punishment can't set you free from it. Your lie belongs to you and you have to chastise it yourself. The shame is yours alone, no one else's. You have to bear it on your own. Aren't you glad that I'm helping you with all this?

ADOLF. Yes, oh yes, Father. Thank you, Father.

FATHER. Well, let me have a look at you then. Let me see. (*Father forces the boy to walk backwards and forwards across the room, squaring his shoulders.*) Yes, that's good...that looks splendid.

(*Laughing, the Father forces the boy to prance about. Klara enters.*)

KLARA. What fun you're both having. I could hear you laughing. What are you up to?

FATHER. I'm playing with the boy's shame.

KLARA. I see. Are you having fun, Adi? (*Without waiting for the boy's answer, she gets what she came in for.*) Can't we please hang him up now, Nuncle? I want so much to see him up on the wall.

FATHER. All this bloody Jew-nagging. All right. I'll see to it. Yes, all right. I will. Where do you want him?
KLARA. Here, Nuncle, in this room.

(Father sighs and follows Klara out of the room. Adolf stays standing with his placard. At first, he seems paralyzed. Then he walks over to the town he built.)

ADOLF. Here comes the rain. It's raining now — Jew-weather. Braunau is over here. Beebraunau and Breebraubee and Braunau. They're all drowning. There's a gigantic amount of water falling down and the dams are bursting. The water is reaching the High Street. The High Street and now the alleyways. Over here the rain is falling in the houses and all the honey is flowing away. The water has reached the Town Hall now and they're all drowning. At the Customs House, the courtyard is turning into a lake and the houses are collapsing into it. They're dying all of them and disappearing into the rain. The rain has reached our house now. In the window Mother is screaming, Father is on the chimney. Angela and Junior are locked in the cellar. And here is Adi...Adi...

(Darkness.)

Scene Twenty-Five

ADOLF. The Jew intrudes...the Yid comes unbidden. *(Adolf at the mirror. He looks at himself in the mirror.)* The Yid comes unbidden...from the midden, hidden. Forbidden, hidden. A worm, hidden under the hide, unbidden and forbidden. Here comes the Yid, pest-ridden, hidden.

(The Jew steps out of the mirror.)

THE JEW. ...unbidden.
ADOLF. From the midden... unbidden, ridden and hidden... the Yid is bidden... forbidden... forbidden... unbidden... but bidden... he's ridden... the Yid is bidden... the Yid is bidden.

Scene Twenty-Six

SCENE: *Klara and Adolf enter.*

KLARA AND ADOLF. Father's on his way home now. He seems very upset but he is managing to control himself. He might just be a bit tipsy. There's the smell of being offended hanging around him.

(*Father comes in through the door and dances over to the boy — his way of moving is very gentle. He bends over the boy and "lifts" him from the bed just like in a dream when a reflection rises from the surface of the water and turns into flesh. The Father doesn't ever touch the boy and the whole time they move in a happy dance, face to face — like one another's reflections. The Father suddenly grabs at him and starts to beat him.*)

FATHER. You bloody little worm. I'll turn your face into a hole — your disgusting body into a pile of flesh. I'll bury you in your own arsehole. You bloody worm. No point in beating a creature like you. All anyone's got to do is throw you up into the air and you'd fall and hurt yourself.

(*The stage in darkness, strokes of the switch.*)

ADOLF. Father loves me. Father loves me. Father loves me.

Scene Twenty-Seven

SCENE: *Adolf alone.*

ADOLF. I'm going to bash the whole table onto your head. Thump. The table is the whole world flattened out and your head is where it's going. Then when you're lying there trying to get up on one hand — I'll knock your arm off with the poker. Pow! And the poker'll bend itself around your arm like a handcuff and cut into the flesh to surround the bone in your arm. And then the poker will eat its way like a snake into your bone-marrow. Just like that. And then if I've got ten thousand tons of rocks, I'll bury you under them and

I'll build a big castle around you and you'll have to run all around the walls because the ground is always catching fire in your footsteps. Every time your feet touch the ground, the flames will rise and you'll never be able to stand still. You're living in a volcano and in the flames live red men who shit burning embers onto your legs and stomach. And then I'd throw down a...I'd get a...a wild animal, a lion, to eat you up, bit by bit. Maybe he'd eat your legs first, or your arms or the whole of your head apart from the eyes — he'd save them so that you could see yourself...and because he thinks they are delicious. He wants to save them up. And then he'd start to feel full up and lie down and sleep, perhaps just have a bit of a rest. The ground isn't on fire any more except right there where you are standing. And while the lion is having a rest, I'd let three thousand women look at you. They'd just look at you the whole time and then they'd eat something. They'd eat biscuits and they'd go on just looking at you. And instead of legs, they'd have arms and with them they'd dry up the blood flowing out of you. They'd dry up all the blood and then they'd pour it all back into you. And the whole time they'd talk about someone else and when you sang for them they'd just laugh at you. And then I'd take a pair of scissors and hack you in the head. And then I'd point the end into your ears...because...the lion was so full, he vomited up your head and then I'd stuff your eyes back in only the wrong way round...looking inwards...so that you could see right inside yourself and then you'd be boiling in the castle's cauldron but you wouldn't be able to see the flames, just inside you and there you'd see your blood starting to boil...and then...and, then...no, then, the lion would wake up and be hungry again...

THIRD ACTOR. And a whole people would then stand ready,
to help the child fight its way free.
Millions would recognize the wrath of the child,
millions would raise their arms to battle,
millions would long for the boots
that could step over seven-league lives.
In all Germany, millions of wronged children would
recognize Adolf's cry of vengeance for their murdered lives.

Scene Twenty-Eight

SCENE: *Adolf is sitting in the room. After a while the Father enters carrying his perennial newspaper — he sits down and starts reading. The boy is drawing on a huge piece of paper he's got in front of him.*

ADOLF. This is where you sit...and then we have to light the fire and this is where it's snowing...hello, Mother...we're cleaning the windows...here comes Father with that same old newspaper...yes, there are flowers in the snow...silently, the bird stands still in the sky.

(*Adolf is drawing a house. Father seems to be slightly disturbed by the boy mumbling to himself. Father puts his newspaper down.*)

FATHER. Come here, Adi. What are you up to?
ADOLF. Drawing...Father.
FATHER. Come here. Let me have a look.

(*Adolf pushes the paper over to the Father.*)

Well, what's this supposed to be then?
ADOLF. House, Father.
FATHER. A house. Does this look like a house, Adi?
ADOLF. House. Mother's doing the washing up in the window.
FATHER. I can't see any window. Is this a window, Adi? Is this supposed to be a window?
ADOLF. Bird, Father, a bird that's gone to pieces in the grass.
FATHER. A bird that's...and this, Adi? What's this supposed to be?
ADOLF. Father, Father. Father.
FATHER. What are you talking about?
ADOLF. Father. Father going. Father going to pieces...Father going into the bird's pieces.

(*Father sits in silence for a while.*)

FATHER. You have to learn to do things the right way, Adi.
ADOLF. Right house, Father, drawing house the right way.

FATHER. Does this house look right? Is this a real house? There isn't even a door. Yes, there is, here...is this supposed to be the door?
ADOLF. Cat, Father. Cat swimming in the rain.
FATHER. Bloody hell, boy. Don't you play games with me, do you hear? What kind of mess is this —
ADOLF. Ants, Father. Cloud-ants eating the smoke from the chimneys. Bird feeds them.
FATHER. What sort of disgusting? Are you dreaming about disgusting things like this? Are you, Adi?
ADOLF. Dreaming...?
FATHER. If you keep on like this your brain will rot away and you'll end up in a home with the other idiots. We'll have to leave you out in the forest.

(At first, Adolf is a little frightened. Then he plucks up his courage and points to a place on the paper.)

ADOLF. Forest, Father. Where the ant sleeps.
FATHER. Give the pen here. Give me the pen.

(Adolf gives the pen to Father. But first Father takes hold of an eraser lying on the table and rubs out part of the drawing.)

I'll show you a house. Look, like this, straight lines. Have you ever seen a house as crooked as the conk on a pawnbroker? What kind of wickedness have you got inside that makes you dream up things like this?

(The boy says nothing and at first looks on with interest as Father draws, as if he thought Father really was going to help him. But he soon realizes that Father is just spoiling the picture.)

This is where the door should be. Have you ever seen a house without a door? How could you get out of a house without a door?

(Father tries to draw a door but it obviously goes wrong. He rubs it out and tries again.)

Oh, this is hopeless and this blotch here, what good is that? What did you say it was? A broken cat?
ADOLF. Bird in pieces.
FATHER. Don't play games with me. I might just as well get rid of the whole mess. There isn't any path to the house on this, you know.

(*Adolf tries to show him that there really is a path.*)

That mess.

(*Father rubs it out. Then he tries to draw something.*)

Like this. This is how you do it.

(*It doesn't work. Father throws pen and paper away in anger.*)

You'd ruined it already. You'd already ruined the whole thing. There won't be any house. All you've done is just make a bloody mess of scribbles.

(*The boy looks at the paper.*)

Anyway I've tried to save something at least. But you can't do much against the sick ideas children get. You can just pray that they grow out of the sick things. All you've ended up doing is destroying a sheet of paper. Revolting.

(*Father goes off, leaving the boy on his own.*)

SCENE TWENTY-NINE

ADOLF (*imitating Father*). Why is the bird in pieces? — The bird fed too many ants with smoke. (*Imitating Father.*) I see...are the ants sleeping in the forest now? — No, they died. (*Imitating Father.*) I see.
THE JEW. I could almost touch the bird. It was such a good one.
ADOLF. Don't talk rubbish. I don't want to hear any more about that mess. Do you know who says things the biggest in the whole world?

THE JEW. No.
ADOLF. Don't you? You're sick, you are. You have to know that. It's no one, isn't it? When it hurts the most, that's when you're no one, and then you can say things the biggest in the whole world. There are things Father says that are as big as Yes and No. You can say things as big as that. Big as nothing. Sometimes I have to eat what Father says, even the things that are so big. They can be gigantic. I have to eat them anyway.
THE JEW. Can you? Only no one can eat things that big.
ADOLF. I'm going to be nobody who can eat everything as big as nothing.
THE JEW. You, Adolf. Jewdolf. Jewdolf and Adieu. Adolf and the Jew. Jewdolf.

(*They laugh.*)

I can say something big as nothing. You is big as nothing.
ADOLF (*simultaneously with the Jew's next line*). You. Is it that big?
THE JEW (*simultaneously with Adolf above*). You is gigantic. It's actually much bigger than me. Me is little. (*The Jew exits.*)
ADOLF (*alone*). You and me.
THE JEW. You is so big because no one can't say you. I must say it.
ADOLF. I. I...I...

SCENE THIRTY

SCENE: *Adolf alone in the room. He's got nothing to do. He pulls up a chair to take a biscuit from the jar but he drops the jar. He's terrified. He puts the chair back in its place and walks anxiously to and fro.*

ADOLF. Oh, what have I done? Oh, oh, oh what shall I do? I shouldn't have wanted to steal. You should have kept an eye on me. You should have kept me away. No one must know. No one must know. How could they find out? What would happen? How could they not find out? Just as long as no one sees. They will see. Oh, if only I could die. What you did was done by me. I'll have to take the consequences. I'm the only one who knows. If the others find out it'll be your fault. It was you that saw. It'll be my fault if they find out. Your...you, you...me. Oh...

(*Klara enters and interrupts him. He tries to act as if nothing has happened.*)

KLARA. I see you've made your bed already. That's good. You're a very good boy.

(*Adolf is silent.*)

Well, aren't you?

(*Adolf is silent. He nods unwillingly.*)

Well then, get on with your playing until your father comes home.

(*Klara starts the cleaning.*)

Just don't get dirty. Stand still and play. Did you make the bed properly?

ADOLF. Yes, Mother.
KLARA. That's all right then.
ADOLF. Thank you, Mother.
KLARA. Come here and I'll give you a biscuit.
ADOLF. No. No thank you, Mother.
KLARA. Don't you want... (*Her hand is already in the jar and she can feel the broken lid.*) But Adi, what's all this?
ADOLF. Mother...Mother
KLARA. Why do you do these things to me?
ADOLF. Mother...
KLARA. I can't cope...I can't cope...What will your father say?
ADOLF. Oh, Mother...I...
KLARA. I can't cope...Well, we won't talk about it anymore. It'll have to wait until your father gets home. Do make the bed. It looks dreadful in here. And what do you think you look like? You're an ugly, mean boy, Adi.

(*Adolf is silent.*)

Adi, your shirt. Just look at you. You must keep clean and tidy. You really should understand how important that is. I can't cope. You'll have to manage on your own now. I wash my hands of you.

(*They can hear Father in the hall. He's yodeling.*)

Your father's already here. There's nothing I can do. (*She walks towards the door but hesitates before exiting.*) Adi, don't forget to look your father in the eyes when you thank him.

(*She exits. Adolf remains behind in terror. He stands still as if he were paralyzed.*)

Scene Thirty-One

SCENE: *Father enters, followed by Klara. Both parents look at the boy carefully. It's a while before anyone says anything. Father measures the boy with his eyes.*

FATHER. Hello, Adi.
ADOLF. Hello, Father sir.
FATHER. Well, how are you?
ADOLF. Good, Father sir. Good.
FATHER. Did anything special happen today?
ADOLF. No, Father sir.

(*Father snaps his fingers and points to a spot on the floor close by, just as if he were ordering a dog to come to heel. Adolf comes over to the father.*)

FATHER. Adi, I know you're suffering.
ADOLF. No, Father.
FATHER. Are you contradicting me?
ADOLF. No, Father.
FATHER. Are you going to lie to me as well?
ADOLF (*confused*). No, Father...No. (*Adolf laughs nervously.*)
FATHER. Well, Adi. Calm down now. A child as sick as you can't afford to get excited.

(*Adolf nods.*)

Adi, I know what you're suffering from. I know what's wrong with you. It all depends on you. Otherwise you'll go on suffering, laying awake at night and talking to yourself and no one will want to have anything to do with you. And your skin will turn black like a fly's.

ADOLF. Yes, Father, I didn't mean to. I don't want to be a fly.

FATHER. And you won't have to be one either if you feel remorse. But it has to be real remorse, not false pangs of conscience. False pangs of conscience are the worst things on earth. They are weakness itself. Weakness has to be hammered away.

ADOLF. Yes, Father.

FATHER. Well then, go and fetch the switch. You know where it is.

(*He gestures to the boy as though he were a dog being ordered to fetch. The boy brings the switch.*)

You'll get your punishment this evening. Until then you should marshal your strength and acknowledge your weaknesses.

ADOLF. Yes, Father sir.

FATHER. I know...I know that I have to be a hard taskmaster, a harsh disciplinarian. Being hard is something I have to take upon myself. I have to be cruel. We have to learn to be cruel with a good conscience. The strong have the right before God and the whole world to impose their will. Adi, we have to force ourselves into greatness if we are to fulfil our duties, take our rightful place in history. Harshness is the sacrifice I make. Are you listening?

ADOLF. Yes, Father.

FATHER. Well then, go and hang the switch on the wall over there. That will be the altar on which we offer up your weakness.

(*Adolf hangs the switch up in a central location on the stage.*)

Now get out of my sight, you worm.

(*Adolf rushes to the door, but is stopped by Klara, who has been standing looking on anxiously the whole time. She looks at him with some tenderness but there is a demand in her eyes. Adolf walks back to Father. He looks up at him, straight in the eyes.*)

ADOLF. Thank you. Thank you, Father sir.

SCENE THIRTY-TWO

SCENE: *Klara in the room. Behind a door the boy is being beaten. Klara tries to make noises to cover the sound of the blows.*

KLARA. There we are. We have to keep everything nice here. It'll be spring soon and time for the spring cleaning. Outside and beat the carpets. Yes, we'll have to beat...hit the dust out of the carpets. No, polish...the silver has to be shiny clean and bright. Spring flowers for the children's graves. Small flowers on the little graves. I've got to look after the little ones. Flowers and then the bulbs come up. The crocuses look like little children's fingers coming out of the earth.

(*The sound of blows stops. Adolf, in a serious condition from the abuse, enters.*)

ADOLF. I got thirty-two strokes from Father.
KLARA. The children mustn't feel abandoned in their graves. We've got to look after their little graves. They mustn't feel lonely in that silent graveyard...
ADOLF. Thirty-two strokes and I didn't make a sound, not one.

(*Klara smiles nervously.*)

That's how to behave...I didn't make a sound. Not a hint of childishness.
KLARA (*breaking down*). Those little lives. I mustn't forget to clean the glass on their photographs. Nice and clean. You've got to look after your own, take care of their graves.
FATHER. Adolf!

(*Father enters, throws the whip to Adolf who is to hang it up.*)

Scene Thirty-Three

SCENE: *Father and Klara are dancing together in a very formal way as though their relationship belonged in an operetta.*

FATHER. Well, Klara. Am I going to get my evening tipple today, my girl?
KLARA (*dancing*). Of course, nuncle. (*She fetches him the bottle and a glass.*)
FATHER. Now, you come on over here, my girl.

Scene Thirty-Four

ADOLF. Stop, Stop it. I'm dying. I'm a child. Ask the grass and it will say my name. I'm a child. It's a child they're persecuting here. Stop! The trees are writing my name across the skies. The mountains will say that my name can speak.

(*Silence.*)

Not even the grass can tell a child. A child? What is a child? A child doesn't exist. I'm not a child and the trees are illiterates. Only strength, rock and hardness are there to build from.
Keep all the voices quiet. Quiet, all of you. Get out! I choose for my path the path I've chosen. I'm me, no one else. I'm me, no one I've become. You can't fool me. Quiet, all of you. Get out!

Scene Thirty-Five

THE JEW. Who are you angry with?
ADOLF. Angry? I'm not angry. It's all right now.
THE JEW. I've been dressing words in clothes.
ADOLF. Words in clothes?
THE JEW. Oh, yes. Jewdolf, Adieu. Take a ickie, Badolf. Another jickie, Bew? Words in clothes. Clords in wothes.

(*Adolf laughs.*)

Go on augh, Ladolf. Jagh at the Lew. You take a word and put clothes on it. You are a biscuit, Badolf. I'm not here. The Hew isn't jere.

(Adolf laughs. The Aunt walks across the stage.)

ADOLF. Aunt Johanna.
THE JEW. Aunt Johanna's got a screw loose, needs new juice..."talks between her legs"...Jaunt Hanna balks between her tegs.
ADOLF. Father.
THE JEW. Father's uniform. Of course he's uniform. The uniform is Father's home, the whole of his world. Father is uniform. Un is fatherform. He walks around dressed in fatherform. Must find my buttons. Must bind my futtons.

(Adolf laughs and then suddenly becomes serious.)

ADOLF. Oh, please be quiet. It hurts to laugh at Father. I don't want to laugh at Father. I don't want to be able to laugh. Laughing is like dying. It's like not being able to keep things in the right place.
THE JEW. Any word can be dressed up in whatever clothes you like. Everything can be said.
ADOLF. No. Not everything. Not all of them.
THE JEW. Oh yes, every single one.
ADOLF. No rage.
THE JEW. Age, Rudolph?
ADOLF. Rage hasn't got any clothes. Rage is naked. I'm not naked.

SCENE THIRTY-SIX

SCENE: *The Aunt enters carrying eggs, frightened by Adolf.*

AUNT JOHANNA. Big and little. Old and young. This little one wanted to be hanged. This one wanted to be king. Defeat and victory. Dumb and...and dumb. The big and the little. Gain and pain. Thee and thine. This and that. Morning and night. Good night, good night.

(A little laugh from Adolf.)

ADOLF. Yes, I am laughing as well. She's mad.
THE JEW. Lonely.
ADOLF. She's mad, crazy, kaput!
THE JEW. Too crazy.
ADOLF. Too crazy.
THE JEW. Lonely.
AUNT JOHANNA (*lines up the eggs on the floor*). This piggy was a noble one. His hands were going two. Then he hanged them up in a three. What did he want the bullets in his rifle four? To stay afive?

(*The Jew laughs at her play on words. Adolf laughs at her madness.*)

ADOLF. She's disgusting.
THE JEW. ...Lonely...
ADOLF. She's revolting. She's nasty...
AUNT JOHANNA. Nasty game, always the same.
THE JEW. Lonely.
ADOLF. Disgusting. (*Adolf breaks an egg underfoot.*)
AUNT JOHANNA. Ah!
ADOLF. Look at how disgusting she is. Look at this. Johanna. Come on now. It's time to feed the crayfish.

(*The Aunt is frightened out of her wits.*)

Listen now, Johanna. Time to feed the crayfish. Time to fish for eels now. Are you ready, Johanna?

(*She's frightened out of her wits.*)

(*To the Jew.*) Just look at her. She's disgusting.
THE JEW. She leads a lonely life.
ADOLF. That's not a life. It's a non-life.
THE JEW. But...
ADOLF. Why should I have to bother with this kind of thing? Why should I?
THE JEW. You're afraid of her, aren't you?
ADOLF. Johanna, Johanna, Johanna. Stand up, Johanna, stand up.

(*The Aunt gets up.*)

Johanna, down! Down! Stand up! Sit down! Stand up!

(*Turns back to the Aunt. Gives her a newspaper.*)

That's enough for now.
AUNT JOHANNA. Thank you for having me.
ADOLF. Nuff!

Adolf sets fire to the newspaper. Aunt Johanna exits with the burning newspaper. A scream is heard.

SCENE THIRTY-SEVEN

SCENE: *Klara and Adolf in the room. Adolf has just come back from school.*

KLARA. Well, Adolf, just stand still now. Stand still.

(*Adolf stands still.*)

Look at this. Look at the floor. Look what you've dragged in with you.
ADOLF. Mother, the buds have come on the trees. I saw them today.
KLARA. Yes, yes, but the dirt. Along with the buds, the sunshine, and the spring comes the dirt.
ADOLF. At last, the snow is melting away. At last sorrow's melting away. At last, we can move freely again.
KLARA. Oh, my dirty little boy. You see it and you know what it means already, don't you? The snow melting. The trees in bud. Get changed now. We'll have to start the spring cleaning soon. We'll do the airing today.
ADOLF. Father wants things cleaned but he doesn't want to see the cleaning being done.
KLARA. Let's get the cleaning done. (*They stand for a while in silence.*) I don't understand why you say... (*She cuts herself off when she hears Father in the hall. She looks quickly at the clock.*) So soon. (*To Adolf.*) We'd better...Get changed now.

Scene Thirty-Eight

SCENE: *Father enters with muddy boots.*

FATHER. Bloody slush. Good evening, Klara.
— Oh, you're home already, nuncle?...Yes, I see you're home. Well, am I going to get any dinner today?
— Yes, nuncle...
At last the shroud is vanishing, at last...
And you, my lad, how did your day go?
— Good, Father. The water is babbling in the brooks.
I don't mean that kind of thing, Adi...Schnapps, bread...I'm sure you know very well the kind of thing I'm talking about.

(*The boy is slightly confused.*)

I mean at school, Adi.
ADOLF. Yes, Father.
FATHER. I think you understand perfectly well that I'm talking about school.
ADOLF. Yes, Father.
FATHER. Well then, how did things go?
ADOLF. Good. Everything's going well, Father.
FATHER. Really?
ADOLF. Yes, Father.
FATHER. I met your teacher today, Adi. He seemed to be of a very different opinion.

(*Adolf is silent.*)

Yes, he said that your schoolwork left a great deal to be desired. What do you think we should do about it?
ADOLF. Father, I learn the things I'm supposed to...
FATHER. You mean you learn the important things and forget what isn't that important?
ADOLF. Yes, Father. That's right.
FATHER. That's the right thing. You can't drag all that mental clutter around with you.
ADOLF. No, Father. No.
FATHER. So you mean you're the one who decided what's important?

ADOLF. Yes, Father.
FATHER. And you think you're man enough to know things like that?
ADOLF. Yes...I don't know, Father.
FATHER. No, you don't know, do you? And all the same, you're the one who decides what's important.
ADOLF. Yes, Father.
FATHER. Well, that's evidence of firmness, anyway. The question is, is it the right kind of firmness?

(Adolf is silent.)

You do understand that a career civil servant has to have a broadly based educational foundation?
ADOLF. Yes, Father.
FATHER. Well then, don't you have to learn what your teacher tells you? Even if you think some form of knowledge is unimportant, you've got to be taught that it's your duty to learn it, haven't you?
ADOLF. Yes, Father.
FATHER. There must be some kind of schoolwork you're good at.
ADOLF. I don't know, Father.
FATHER. Don't know, what's that supposed to mean? A man knows what he's capable of, doesn't he?
ADOLF. Yes, Father.
FATHER. There you are then.

(The boys stays silent.)

What's your maths like?

(The boy looks down at the floor in embarrassment.)

I see, not that then. Well, I hope at least that you're learning to obey your teacher. God knows obedience is something I've tried to drum into you.
ADOLF. Yes, Father.
FATHER. And how about composition, then?

(The boy says nothing.)

Nothing is more important than caring for our German language. Our language is a monument to our strength. This is the bloody limit, boy. Aren't you good at anything? What does your teacher say?

(*The boy says nothing.*)

Even an idiot is capable of doing something well.
ADOLF. He liked a drawing I did.
FATHER. A drawing?
ADOLF. It was a dog. A big Alsatian and a kennel.
FATHER. So you got good marks for something you'd drawn?
ADOLF. Yes, Father.
FATHER. Do you think a drawing can help you as a civil servant?
ADOLF. No, Father...but...
FATHER. What use to you is being able to draw?
ADOLF. I don't know.
FATHER. Do you think it might be the kind of skill you could put to good use?
ADOLF. I don't know, Father.
FATHER. You've never thought of becoming an artist, have you?
ADOLF. No, Father. I...
FATHER. Perhaps being an artist isn't so bad. There are many great German artists.
ADOLF. I don't know...
FATHER. Well, an artist, eh? Why not? Do you want to be an artist?
ADOLF. No — well, I...
FATHER. It's something you could try...

(*Adolf feels encouraged.*)

ADOLF. I...perhaps, I...
FATHER. An artist! One of those Jewish bunglers who walks the streets selling postcards. Is that what you're thinking of?
ADOLF. No, Father, I...
FATHER. I see, an artist...and you think that's a future for a man?
ADOLF. I...no, Father, I didn't mean...
FATHER. You make a mockery of your Father with ideas like that. Have you ever heard the like! A painter? An artist? There's always been something wrong with you, but now you've completely taken leave

of your senses. What is it in that bad blood of yours that makes you want to be an artist? An artist — over my dead body.
ADOLF. Father...I didn't mean...
FATHER. Don't you contradict me. I told you, don't you contradict me. I'll show you an artist. (*He takes the switch down from the wall. At the end of every sentence, he gives the boy a blow.*) This is my brush. This is my tool, my art. Now I'll show you how to paint a man of duty. This is what you do. First, you brush a line through weakness, then one through cowardice, then through laziness, then over frailty, and one through indolence. And finally, one through all that's unnatural, through everything that's against nature. All the dirt, all the sniffing around, and all the false rumors.

(*At the end, the boy is lying on the ground. Father turns away from him and leaves the room. He laughs contemptuously.*)

Klara. Klara — do you want to hear something funny? Do you know what Adi said?
ADOLF. Help...help.

(*The boy is left alone in the room. He's not, in fact, crying but walking backwards and forwards like a caged animal. The Aunt enters to fetch the Father's glass.*)

AUNT JOHANNA. There isn't any help. No one will listen to you.

SCENE THIRTY-NINE

Commentary

THIRD ACTOR (*every time the Actor says the word "Jew," Adolf says "child"*). I can't really say when I heard the word Jew [child] for the first time. At home with my parents, I can't ever remember hearing the word Jew [child] while my father was alive. But whenever there's anything shameless or rotten going on to do with family life, there's bound to be at least one Jew [child] involved. If you lance a boil carefully, you find — just like a maggot in a rotting corpse — a little Jew [child], often quite dazzled by the sudden light. The Jew [child] is a principle. The Jew [child] is evil, Jewishness [childishness] pure and simple. Once you've succeeded in awakening order and devotion to duty through consistently revealing the presence of the Jew [child], the rest goes very quickly.

SCENE FORTY

THE JEW. Jewdolf, Jewdolf, it's Adieu. I'm coming from out of my mind.
ADOLF. I'm too tired to go on playing...
THE JEW (*simultaneously with Adolf's next line*). A gate to escape through. A window.
ADOLF (*simultaneous with the Jew above*). A window to flee through. I want to escape through the window. I have to escape.
THE JEW. Where will you escape to?
ADOLF. I don't know. I'll go to me.
THE JEW. To me. That's right. You can keep yourself safe there.

(*They start building.*)

Jewdolf, you're making the window too small.
ADOLF. Be quiet. You don't know anything about being shut in.
THE JEW. Adolf, don't make the window so small that your name runs away from you. Don't deny that you have a name blowing in the wind out there. Your name is friends with the grass.
ADOLF. No, no, it's not true.
THE JEW. Adi, don't deny that the grass knows your name. Don't deny that the grass has spoken.
ADOLF. No, no, it's not true.
THE JEW. In the end you'll have to deny everything that knows your name and you'll have to look for your name in everything, Adolf, and then deny that anything ever spoke to you. In the end you'll have to deny to every tree, every rock, and all the blades of grass that they ever spoke to your name.
ADOLF. No, no. I don't want to know it's true. Shut up. You be quiet.
(*Adolf goes on building.*)
THE JEW. Adolf, aflood. Flowed, Adolf...Make your window bigger.
ADOLF. Be quiet. I don't want to listen to you.

THE JEW. Adolf, it's over now. No one will have spoken to your name. You're walling yourself in.
ADOLF. Stop!
THE JEW. What are you doing?
ADOLF. This is the way it is. You see? You could suffocate.
THE JEW. Jewdolf...Jewdolf...
ADOLF. Adolf. Adolf. Do you hear? My name is Adolf. (*Adolf drowns the Jew.*)

Scene Forty-One

ADOLF. You're falling down into the darkness now and I'm the one who pushed you. You were standing at the very edge and the blind women who led you there had already returned to their cocoons. I've broken the steps to bits and burnt up the rope. You're falling now. I'll stamp on your hands when they try to catch hold of the grass. I'll keep kicking you in the face till no one will want to say your name any more. And while you're falling, I'll have kept a part of you back and tied it to a tree-root and when you're falling, you'll unwind out of yourself and you'll hang down into the darkness like a bloody rope down into the abyss. And at the very bottom of the rope your tongue will be fluttering, trying to say the name of every child, but that's when I'll cut it off.

Scene Forty-Two

ADOLF/ACTOR. Adolf Hitler, at the age of eleven, tries to escape through the narrow window. He takes his clothes off above the waist and manages to get part way out but is stopped by his waistband. He crawls back and tears off his trousers. He throws the clothes out through the window in front of him and then tries to climb out after them. He's left his shoes behind in the room and has to rush back to get them. Just as he's about to run to the window, he hears his Father at the door. He grabs a towel to shield his naked body.

Scene Forty-Three

SCENE: *Father enters, followed shortly by Klara. Adolf looks at Klara. She laughs at the boy. Father shows Adolf up onto a stool. The boy stretches. The father points to the boy's penis with his stick. All three laugh as if they'd all quite suddenly entered into a secret agreement. Adolf climbs down from the chair. He's still laughing a little. When he speaks, he does so as an adult. While laughing, he keeps his hand in front of his mouth the whole time.*

ADOLF. It took me a long time to get over this particular episode. But now, of course, I understand...now I can laugh at that kind of thing...Father called me an ascetic and a child of god at the same time as he took the switch down from the wall and Mother just stood there laughing helplessly. You have to understand that I did look funny standing there naked. All children have read adventure stories, haven't they? They're always imagining things. I always remember Mother as being so beautiful when she laughed. Once, I made up my mind not to make a sound at the next beating. I had read somewhere that it was a sign of courage not to show pain. My mother must have been beside herself with worry, waiting outside the door. The things children imagine. All of life has to be bought with blood. It starts with being born. No one listens if the grass is speaking. It's the most natural thing, the most ordinary. (*He laughs.*) Well, I had to laugh. With Father pointing at... well...and then he said we have to clean the good fruit of the wicked worm. Father could sound harsh but there was a good heart hidden under that sometimes rather stern exterior.

ACTOR. Only a few short weeks after the annexation of Austria, Hitler had the parish of Dollersheim and its surrounding area turned into a military testing range. His father's birthplace and his grandmother's gravestone were razed to the ground.

(*Adolf stops as if someone had asked a question.*)

ADOLF. There were only me, my father, mother and my brothers and sisters in my childhood home. So much gossiping goes on among the grass and the trees write such rubbish. There's nothing living in the rocks. The midge gets eaten by the dragonfly which gets eaten by the bird. Everybody eats everybody and the idea of eternity is based on that. The Devil only knows. Why this should be so is not something I need to bother my brain with. Our most important task is, after all, to keep Germany free from tainted blood.

ACTOR. Under the name of Operation Euthanasia, all the mentally ill and the retarded in Germany were put to death after the Nazis came to power.

ADOLF. It goes without saying that if you make the same plea as the grass makes, then silence becomes a necessity. The green words of the grass poison the brain and stop you thinking clearly. Grass doesn't exist and the trees fumble emptily across the paper of the skies. There aren't really any trees and I forbid everyone to listen to them. Rocks are nothing but firmness; no one's story is carved on them. Just the firmness of the law. The law of necessity. (*Adolf gives a little laugh.*)

ADOLF. I must have looked absurdly funny when I was hanging the switch back on the wall. If grass did exist, even grass would have laughed like Mother. The grass would have seen what kind of game was being played in front of Father's five short letters. But grass doesn't exist and everything is as I know it to be. One short moment and I'm free of it all. Father's always been right. Everything tells lies. You can't trust anything. That's why my body has to be on fire all the time. Nothing must put my body to shame. No one is allowed to put my body to shame. You can't see me naked. No one must see me naked.

Part Two 277

Teaching Activities

- Before reading the play, have students think about what they know of Adolf Hitler and write a description of his childhood as they envision it. After reading the play, ask them to compare their idea to the description offered by the playwright.

- If they like, students may work in teams to research biographical facts about Adolf Hitler. Encourage them to give particular attention to his childhood. Then, either orally or in writing, provide an opportunity for them to expand upon the content offered in the "Information about the Play and the Holocaust" section of this chapter.

- Students may wish to work in groups to define what, in their opinions, constitutes a dysfunctional family. Once defined, ask each group to identify ways in which Hitler's family, as portrayed in the play, is dysfunctional. If interest merits, continue this exercise by having groups investigate the adult Hitler's relationships with women as well as his apparent appetite for decimating property and people. How does their definition of "dysfunctional" apply to these aspects of his life?

- Study family communication, child and adult psychology, and the biography of Adolf Hitler. What factors related to these studies do students believe might have shaped the Nazi leader's personality?

- As a class, survey the characteristics of charismatic leaders as well as those attributed to people who join cults. Based upon this information, call for students to argue in favor or against the notion that the Nazis were a cult led by Hitler.

- The technical elements of scenic and costume design in a play communicate its message and meaning visually. Using characters of their choice and the interior of the Hitler house for this assignment, direct students to create designs that reveal information about the character(s) and the location. Offer them an opportunity to explain their renderings to the class. Guide their thinking so that they address the following: (1) have they used symmetrical or asymmetrical balance and why did they make this choice?; (2) why did they select particular colors?; (3) what mood did they wish to convey by their design choices?; (4) did they employ symbolism and, if so, where and how?; (5) both in terms of the artistic elements of design and historical accuracy, what research did they find necessary for this task?; and (6) how have they coordinated their scenic and costume designs to produce a unified effect?

- As a follow-up to the previous activity, encourage students to build scale models of their sets or to actually construct costumes from their renderings. If possible, costumes could be worn and the classroom arranged as represented in their settings for dramatizations of selected scenes from the play.

- A chart large enough to be displayed in the classroom should result from students' efforts in this activity. They should combine historical inquiry and their reading of the play. Next, they should identify content in the play that has a parallel in Adolf Hitler's adult life. The former should be inserted into the column on the left and the latter into the column on the right. An example follows.

Play Content	Parallel or Result
Hitler has a mentally ill and hunchbacked aunt care for him.	Hitler condones extermination of mentally and physically challenged on the grounds that they are a burden on society.
Hitler's own heritage is unclear.	Under the Nazis, laws make it necessary that a person be able to prove racial purity for at least three generations.

Some speculation may be necessary in making these associations and students should be able to support their choices.

- In creating a role, actors determine what they share in common with, as well as how they are different from, a character. They also look for clues in the script that reveal characterization such as: (1) what the playwright says about the character, (2) what other characters say about the character, (3) what he says about himself, and (4) his actions. Using these guideposts to develop the role of

Adolf Hitler in this play, challenge students to write a role analysis. Those who wish might perform a portion of the script in which they demonstrate applying their analysis to the role in performance. This exercise may be repeated for other characters as well and scenes staged in the classroom.

- Using the investigative techniques described above, charge students to analyze (1) the relationship between Adolf and Klara and (2) the relationship of Adolf and his father. Students may wish to work on this assignment in groups. Their descriptions should be reported and validated by dialogue and action in the script.

- Each student should read a book that gives a biographical portrait of the dictator, such as Albert Marrin's *Hitler: A Portrait of a Tyrant*, and follow the reading with an oral book report.

- In programs for theatrical productions, sometimes the director of the show will include notes to help the audience better understand the play. Invite students to imagine that each is directing a production of *Hitler's Childhood*. What would each pupil include in his or her "Director's Notes"? How would this content assist viewers in comprehending this complex play?

- Humor, often taking the forms of satire, burlesque, or defiant laughter, has been both a mechanism for coping with dire circumstances and a tool for resistance. Consider the comedy of Charlie Chaplin and others and then pose the following thought questions to students. "Might any of the characters in this play be portrayed with exaggerated humor? If this were done, which characters should be portrayed this way? Why? What would be the result of this interpretation?" Be certain that students understand that there are no "correct" answers but that what is important is the reasoning they use to support their ideas.

Part Three

Bibliography

Bibliography

"Adolf Hitler's Childhood: From Hidden to Manifest Horror." *Making the Future Program.* Oxford: Oxford Stage Company, 1995.
Anesi, Chuck. "The Horst Wessel Song: Words and Music." Online posting. http://www.brainlink.com/ ~ Anesi/horstw.htm. 1997.
Baltimore Area Theatre Schedule. "The City Paper Theatre Critics' Top 10 for 1996." Online posting. http://www.interactiveads.com/trademkr/shows/cptop10.html. 1998.
Barnsdale, David. "Fall of the Weimar Republic." Online posting. http://www.barnsdle.demon.co.uk/hist/tyra.html. 1997.
Bauer, Yehuda. *A History of the Holocaust.* New York: Franklin Watts, 1982.
Behrendt, Ed. "Reach and Teach: Worldwide Holocaust Education." Online posting. http://home.att.net/ ~ edsdanzig/index2.html. 1998.
———. "Train Children of the Holocaust (The Kindertransport Story)." Online posting. http://home.att.net/ ~ edsdanzig/train.html. 1998.
Bezdek, Michael. "Did Only Nazis Kill Jews?" *The Saginaw News,* 7 July 1996, sec. C, p. 5.

Block, Gay and Malka Drucker. *Rescuers: Portraits of Moral Courage in the Holocaust*. New York: Meier and Holmes Publishers, Inc., 1992.

Bolkosky, Sidney, Betty Rotberg Ellias, and David Harris. *A Holocaust Curriculum: Life Unworthy of Life*. Farmington Hills, MI: The Center for the Study of the Child, 1987.

Bolkosky, Sidney M., Anya Verkhovskaya, Joanne Rudof, Henry Greenspan, and Joan Ringelheim. "Holocaust Oral Histories: Controversies and Concerns." United States Holocaust Memorial Museum and the Social Science History Association Panel Discussion. Washington, DC: United States Holocaust Memorial Museum, 16 October 1997.

Brecht, Bertolt. "Fear and Misery in the Third Reich." In *The Stage in Action*, eds. Helen Manfull and Lowell L. Manfull. Dubuque, IA: Kendall Hunt Publishing Company, 1989.

Brennecke, Fritz. *The Nazi Primer: Official Handbook for Schooling the Hitler Youth*. Trans. Harwood L. Childs. New York: Harper and Brothers Publishers, 1938.

Brown, Jean E., Elaine C. Stephens, and Janet E. Rubin. *Images of the Holocaust: A Literature Anthology*. Lincolnwood, IL: NTC Publishing Group, 1997.

Browning, Christopher R. *Genocide in Yugoslavia During the Holocaust* (pamphlet). Washington DC: The United States Holocaust Memorial Museum, n.d.

Carmean, Karen and Georg Gaston. *Robert Shaw: More Than a Life*. Lanham, MD: Madison Books, 1994.

Dadlez, Anna. Letter to author, 14 November 1997.

Dalglish, Darren. "*Kindertransport* at the Vaudeville Theatre." London Theatre Guide—Online posting. http://www.londontheatre.co.uk/reviews/kindertr-vaud96.html. 1998.

Draper, Paula J. *Holocaust Resource*. Willowdale, Ontario: Holocaust Education and Memorial Centre of Toronto, 1985.

Dwork, Deborah. *Children With a Star: Jewish Youth in Nazi Europe*. New Haven, CT: Yale University Press, 1991.

Eden, Thea. *A Transported Life: Memories of Kindertransport, The Oral History of Thea Feliks Eden*. Edited by Irene Reti and Valerie Jean Chase. Santa Cruz, CA: HerBooks, 1995.

Elber, Lynn. "Short Version of Nuremberg Trials on Tap." *The Saginaw News*, 12 November 1995, sec. A, p. 4.

Electronic Mail & Guardian Daily. "Jews, Truth, and the Spotlight." Online posting. http://www.mg.co.za/mg/art/reviews/97april/17apr-theatre1.html. 1998.

Feingold, Marilyn B. "Problems Related to Knowledge Utilization in Elementary and Secondary Schools." In *Studies in Judaism: Methodology in the Academic Teaching of the Holocaust*, eds. Zero Garber with Alan L. Berger and Richard Libowitz. New York: University Press of America, 1988, 275-300.

Fischer, Klaus P. *Nazi Germany: A New History*. New York: Continuum, 1995.

Friedman, Ina. *The Other Victims: First Person Stories of Non-Jews Persecuted by the Nazis*. Boston: Houghton Mifflin Company, 1990.

Gill, Anton. *The Journey Back from Hell: An Oral History — Conversations with Concentration Camp Survivors*. New York: William Morrow and Company, Inc., 1988.

Greenspan, Hank. *Remnants*. Unpublished, 1991.

Grobman, Gary. *The Holocaust: A Guide for Pennsylvania Teachers*. Millersville, PA: Millersville University, 1990.

Guernsey, Otis L., Jr. *Curtain Times: The New York Theater, 1965-1978*. New York: Applause Theatre Book Publishers, 1987.

Gutman, Israel, ed. "Belgium." *Encyclopedia of the Holocaust*. New York: McMillan Publishing Company, 1990.

———. "Odessa." *Encyclopedia of the Holocaust*. New York: McMillan Publishing Company, 1990.

———. "Riga." *Encyclopedia of the Holocaust*. New York: McMillan Publishing Company, 1990.

———. "Rovno." *Encyclopedia of the Holocaust*. New York: McMillan Publishing Company, 1990.

Hilberg, Raul. *Perpetrators, Victims, Bystanders: The Jewish Catastrophe, 1933-1945*. New York: HarperPerennial, 1993.

Hirschfeld, Gerhard. "Great Britain and the Emigration from Nazi Germany: An Historical Overview." In *Theatre and Film in Exile: German Artists in Britain, 1933-1945*, ed. Günter Berghaus. Oxford: Berg Publishers Limited, 1989, 1-14.

Kaye, Ephraim. "Use of Survivors Testimonies as an Educational Tool in Teaching the Holocaust to Various Age Groups." n.p., December 28, 1995.

Kesselman, Wendy. *I Love You, I Love You Not*. New York: Samuel French, Inc., 1988.

Koch, H.W. *Hitler Youth: The Duped Generation*. New York: Ballantine Books, Inc., 1972.

Kraus, Joanna H. *Angel in the Night*. Woodstock, IL: Dramatic Publishing, 1995.

Kuperstein, Isaiah, Henry Hausdorff, and Doris Gow. *Witness to the Holocaust: Study Guide*. New York: CLAL–The National Jewish Center for Learning and Leadership, 1986.

Kurth, Joel and Fred Kelly. "Klan, Foes, Police Map Strategies." *The Saginaw News*, 6 July 1996, sec. A, p. 1–2.

Kushner, Tony. *A Bright Room Called Day*. New York: Theatre Communications Group, Inc., 1994.

Landau, Elaine. *Nazi War Criminals*. New York: Franklin Watts, 1996.

Langer, Lawrence R. *Holocaust Testimonies: The Ruins of Memory*. New Haven, CT: Yale University Press, 1991.

Lank, Barry. "Play 'Kindertransport' Brings Home Echoes of the Holocaust." Shamash—The Jewish Internet Consortium online posting. http://www.shamash.org/jb/bk/bk960105/bnplay.htm. 1998.

Lord Russell of Liverpool. *The Scourge of the Swastika: A Short History of Nazi War Crimes*. 1954. Reprint, London: Corgi Books, 1970.

——. *The Trial of Adolf Eichmann*. London: William Heinemann Ltd., 1962.

Making the Future Information Pack. Oxford: Oxford Stage Company, 1995.

Milton, Sybil. "Statistics of the Holocaust." Washington, DC: United States Holocaust Memorial Museum, n.p., 1996.

Morin, Isobel V. *Days of Judgment: The World War II War Crimes Trials*. Brookfield, CT: The Millbrook Press, 1995.

Morrow, Lee Alan. *The Tony Award Book: Four Decades of Great American Theatre*. New York: Abbeville Press Publishers, 1987.

Other Side of Faith, The. Produced by Sy Rotter. Film and Video Foundation, 1990. Documentary.

Partisans of Vilna. Produced by Aviva Kempner. Directed by Josh Waletzky. National Center for Jewish Films, 1987.

Pazniokas, Mark. "Holocaust Tape Project Expands." *The Saginaw News*, n.d.

Rådström, Niklas. *Hitler's Childhood*. Trans. Frank Gabriel Perry. Solna, Sweden: Folmer Hansen Teaterförlag AB, 1984.

Robinson, Alice M., Vera Mowry Roberts, and Milly S. Barranger, eds. *Notable Women in the American Theatre*. New York: Greenwood Press, 1989.

Rosenberg, Maxine B. *Hiding to Survive: Stories of Jewish Children Rescued from the Holocaust*. New York: Clarion Books, 1994.

Roskies, Diane K. *Teaching the Holocaust to Children*. Hoboken, NJ: KTAV Publishing House, Inc., 1975.

Rückerl, Adalbert. *The Investigation of Nazi War Crimes, 1945-1978: A Documentation*. Trans. Derek Rutter. Hamden, CT: Archon Books, 1980.

Ryan, Allan A., Jr. *Quiet Neighbors: Prosecuting Nazi War Criminals in America*. New York: Harcourt Brace Jovanovich, 1984.

Samuels, Diane. *Kindertransport*. New York: Penguin Group, 1995.

Scher, Linda. *The Holocaust: A North Carolina Teacher's Resource*. Raleigh, NC: The North Carolina Department of Public Instruction, Council on the Holocaust, 1994.

———. *South Carolina Voices: Lessons From the Holocaust*. Columbia, SC: The South Carolina Department of Education, Council on the Holocaust, 1992.

Schwartzman, Roy. "'Telogogy' as a Rhetorical Basis for Holocaust Education." Paper presented to the National Communication Association, Hilton Towers, Chicago, November 1997.

Shaw, Robert. *The Man in the Glass Booth*. New York: Samuel French, Inc., 1968.

Shea, Christopher. "Debating the Uniqueness of the Holocaust." *The Chronicle of Higher Education*, 31 May 1996, sec. A, p. 6, 7, 12.

Soble, Frieda. *An Overview of the Holocaust*. Revised edition. Dallas: Dallas Memorial Center for Holocaust Studies, n.d.

Stableford, Sandra and Laurie Barnett. *Anne Frank and Us: Insights into Cruelty, Discrimination and Hope*. Flint, MI: The Flint Cultural Center, 1997.

Stephens, Elaine C., Jean E. Brown, and Janet E. Rubin. *Learning About...The Holocaust. Literature and Other Resources for Young People*. North Haven, CT: Library Professional Publications, 1995.

Steven Barclay Agency. "Tony Kushner." Online posting. http://www.barclayagency.com/kushner.html. 1997.

Stringer, Virginia. *Can You Hear Them Crying?* Colorado Springs, CO: Contemporary Drama Service, 1998.

Tampa Bay Holocaust Memorial Museum and Educational Center Academic Symposium, Tampa, Florida, January 1996.

Torres, Robert. "Adolf Hitler." Online posting for NSDAP Museum. http://www.mtg-cards.com/museum/se/in/hitler.htm. 1997.

Trosky, Susan M., ed. *Contemporary Authors: A Bio-Bibliographical Guide to Current Writers in Fiction, General Nonfiction, Poetry, Journalism, Drama, Motion Pictures, Television, and Other Fields.* Vol. 133. Detroit: Gale Research Inc., 1991.

United Jewish Appeal. *Network* 2, no. 2 (summer 1996): A, D.

United States Holocaust Memorial Museum. *Permanent Exhibition Collection.* Washington, DC: United States Holocaust Memorial Museum, 1997.

———. *Resistance During the Holocaust.* Washington, DC: United States Holocaust Memorial Museum, 1996.

———. *Teaching About the Holocaust: A Resource Book for Educators.* Washington, DC: United States Holocaust Memorial Museum, 1996.

———. *Update* (newsletter). Washington DC: United States Holocaust Memorial Museum, winter 1995–96.

Verberg. Steven. "Klan Leader Softens Message of Hate for Broader Appeal." *The Saginaw News*, 5 July 1996, sec. A, p. 1.

Volavková, Hana, ed. *I Never Saw Another Butterfly.* Expanded Second Edition by the United States Holocaust Memorial Museum. New York: Schocken Books, 1993.

Willmott, Kevin and Ric Averill. *T-Money & Wolf.* Woodstock, IL: Dramatic Publishing, 1994.

Witnesses to the Holocaust. Narrated by Miles Lerman. The United States Holocaust Memorial Council, 1996. Audiocassette.

Zamichow, Nora. "'Nazi Ideas' Written in MENSA Bulletin Outrages Members." *The Saginaw News*, 11 January 1995, sec. A, p. 4.

Appendices

Appendix A

Plays, Playwrights, and Publishers

Can You Hear Them Crying?
by Virginia Burton Stringer

Contact:
Meriwether Publishing Ltd.
Permissions Dept.
885 Elkton Drive
Colorado Springs, CO 80907

Angel in the Night
by Joanna H. Kraus

Contact:
The Dramatic Publishing Co.
PO Box 129
311 Washington Street
Woodstock, IL 60098

Kindertransport
by Diane Samuels

Contact:
Plume, a division of Penguin Books USA, Inc.
% Penguin Books
375 Hudson Street
New York, NY 10014

Published in Britain by:
Nick Hern Books
14 Larden Road
London W3 7ST
England

T-Money & Wolf
by Ric Averill and Kevin Willmott

Contact:
The Dramatic Publishing Co.
PO Box 129
311 Washington Street
Woodstock, IL 60098

The Man in the Glass Booth
by Robert Shaw

Contact:
Samuel French Inc.
45 W. 25th Street
New York, NY 10010–2751

A Bright Room Called Day
by Tony Kushner

Contact:
Theatre Communications Group
355 Lexington Avenue
New York, NY 10017

"Voice" in Remnants
by Hank Greenspan

Contact:
Hank Greenspan
The University of Michigan
Residential College
Ann Arbor, MI 48109-1245

Hitler's Childhood
by Niklas Rådström, translated by Frank Gabriel Perry

Contact:
Alan Brodie Representation Ltd.
211 Piccadilly
London W1V 9LD
England

Appendix B
Resource References

The following is provided to assist in locating resources pertaining to the study of plays in this anthology.

Books

Holocaust Study Guide for *Can You Hear Them Crying?*
This is a kit that is packaged for use with the play.
Contact:
Meriwether Press Ltd.
Contemporary Drama Service
PO Box 7710-TT
Colorado Springs, CO 80933
Phone: (800) 937-5297

*I Never Saw Another Butterfly: Children's Drawings and Poems from
    Terezin Concentration Camp 1942-1944*
Hana Volavková, Editor
This expanded second edition includes additional drawings and poems from the State Jewish Museum in Prague and was published by

Schocken Books (New York) to coincide with the opening of The United States Holocaust Memorial Museum. The paperback was published in March 1994. A hardcover edition is also available.
Contact:
The United States Holocaust Memorial Museum
100 Raoul Wallenberg Place, SW
Washington, DC 20024
ISBN: 0805210156

    This book was originally published in 1959 for the State Jewish Museum in Prague (Státni Zīdouské Museum). McGraw-Hill published an eighty-page version in 1964.
Contact:
The McGraw-Hill Companies, Inc.
1221 Avenue of the Americas
New York, NY 10020

Hitler: A Portrait of a Tyrant
by Albert Marrin
Published in 1987
Contact:
Viking
375 Hudson Street
New York, NY 10014-3657
ISBN: 1558034013

The Man in the Glass Booth
by Robert Shaw
    Although the novel is out of print, some bookstores are willing to try to special order used copies. Published in 1967.
Contact:
Harcourt Brace Jovanovich, Inc.
6277 Sea Harbor Dr.
Orlando, FL 32887
ISBN: 9997408160

For Your Own Good: Hidden Cruelty in Child-Rearing and the Roots of Violence
by Alice Miller
   The third edition was published in 1990 and is available in paperback.
Contact:
Noonday Press
19 Union Square
New York, NY 10003
ISBN: 0374522693

Rescuers: Portraits of Moral Courage in the Holocaust
by Gay Block and Malka Drucher
Published in 1992
Contact:
Holmes & Meier Publishers, Inc.
160 Broadway
E Wing 9th Floor
New York, NY 10038
ISBN: 0841913234

The Other Victims: First-Person Stories of Non-Jews Persecuted by the Nazis
by Ina R. Friedman
Published in 1990
   Offers first-person accounts as well as a useful listing of additional books of interest to the reader.
Contact:
Houghton Mifflin Company
222 Berkeley St.
Boston, MA 02116
ISBN: 0395502128 (hardcover)
ISBN: 0395745152 (paperback)

CD/Audio Cassette

Dos Elnte Kind (*The Lonely Child*)
Lyrics by Shmerke Kaczerginske and music by Yankl Krimski is found on both the compact disc and the cassette tape, *remember the children: Songs for and by Children of the Holocaust*.
Contact:
Aligned Audio
151 22nd Street
Brooklyn, NY 11232-1119

Movies
Four Little Girls
Directed by Spike Lee
This Academy Award nominee for best documentary premiered February 23, 1998, on Home Box Office as part of Black History Month.
Contact:
Home Box Office
A Division of Time Warner Entertainment Company
1100 Sixth Avenue
New York, NY 10036
Phone: (212) 512-5249
Fax: (212) 512-5598

The Man in the Glass Booth
Directed by Arthur Hiller
1975
117 minutes
Not available on video.
Contact:
Cinevision
Released by AFT Distributing Corp.

Nazi War Crime Trials
(documentary)
Contact:
Video Images
Box C
Sandy Hook, CT 06482
Phone: (800) 243-0987

Plays

I Never Saw Another Butterfly (full-length script)
by Celeste Raspanti
Contact:
The Dramatic Publishing Company
PO Box 129
311 Washington Street
Woodstock, IL 60098

I Never Saw Another Butterfly (one-act cutting)
by Celeste Raspanti
Contact:
The Dramatic Publishing Company
PO Box 129
311 Washington Street
Woodstock, IL 60098

Goodbye Marianne
by Irene Kirstein Watts
Published in the United States by.
Anchorage Press
PO Box 8067
New Orleans, LA 70182
Phone: (504) 283-8868
Fax: (504) 866-0502

Television

Nuremberg trial footage, interviews, background reports and commentary by legal experts
Court TV aired programming to mark the 50th anniversary of the international war crimes tribunal.
Contact:
Court TV
600 Third Avenue
New York, NY 10016

The Trial of Adolf Eichmann
(PBS documentary)
Contact:
Corporation for Public Broadcasting
901 E Street, NW
Washington, DC 20004-2037
Phone: (202) 879-9600

Theatre

Seem-To-Be Players
% Ric Averill
PO Box 1601
Lawrence, KS 66044

Video Archives

Shoah Foundation
PO Box 3168
Los Angeles, CA 09978-3168

Fortunoff Video Archive for Holocaust Testimonies
Sterling Memorial Library
Yale University
PO Box 802840
New Haven, CT 06520-8240
Phone: (203) 432-1879

Video

The Other Side of Faith
Contact:
Film and Video Foundation
1800 K Street, NW
Washington, DC 20006
Phone: (202) 429-9320

In addition to the above, teachers and students may wish to view the following.

Hitler: The Whole Story
1989 documentary
Directed by Joachim C. Fest and Christian Herrendoerfer
Contact:
NDR International
Hitler Offer
PO Box 68618
Indianapolis, IN 46268
Phone: (800) 423-8800

Heil Hitler! Confessions of a Hitler Youth
HBO 1991
Contact:
Zenger Video
PO Box 802
Culver City, CA 90232-0802
Phone: (800) 421-4246

The Courage to Care
Directed by Robert Gardner
  Academy Award nominee in 1986 for best short documentary film.
Contact:
Zenger Video
PO Box 802
Culver City, CA 90232-0802
Phone: (800) 421-4246

Partisans of Vilna
Directed by Josh Waletzky
1987
Contact:
Zenger Video
PO Box 802
Culver City, CA 90232-0802
Phone: (800) 421-4246

Schindler's List
Directed by Stephen Spielberg
1993
Contact:
Amblin Entertainment
MCA Universal Home Video
Universal City, CA 91608

Appendix C

Other Works by Contributors

Students interested in other works by contributors to this anthology might consider the following. Unless otherwise indicated, the title denotes a play.

Virginia Burton Stringer

Holocaust Study Guide for *"Can You Hear Them Crying?"* (curriculum guide)

Joanna H. Kraus

The Tall Boy's Journey (novel)
The Ice Wolf
The Kimchi Kid
Remember My Name
Sunday Gold
Mean to be Free
Circus Home

Tenure Track (with Greer Woodward)
The Last Baron of Arizona
The Shaggy Dog Murder Trial
Ms. Courageous: Women of Science
Sound and Motion Stories (book)
The Dragon Hammer and the Tale of Oniroku

Diane Samuels

The Life and Death of Bessie Smith (with Sara Milne and Homerton Youth Theatre)
Frankie's Monster (adapted from the novel *The Monster Garden* by Vivian Alcock)
Chalk Circle
Salt of the Earth
The Bonekeeper
Watch Out for Mister Stork
Turncoat
How to Beat a Giant
One Hundred Million Footsteps
two together (BBC radio play)
Frankie's Monster (BBC radio play)
Watch Out for Mister Stork (BBC radio play)
Kindertransport (BBC radio play)
Swine (BBC radio play)
Hardly Cinderella (BBC radio play)
Doctor Y (BBC radio play)
Forever and Ever

Ric Averill

Alice in Wonderland
The Bremen Town Musicians
Alex and the Shrink World
Reliable Junk
Trickster Tales from the Melting Pot
The Seem-To-Be Just So Stories

The Seven Voyages of Sinbad the Sailor

Kevin Willmott

Shields Green and the Gospel of John Brown (screenplay)
Captive (screenplay)
Ninth Street (screenplay)

Robert Shaw

The Man in the Glass Booth (novel)
The Hiding Place (novel)
The Sun Doctor (novel)
The Flag (novel)
A Card from Morocco (novel)
Cato Street
The Pets (teleplay)
The Florentine Tragedy (teleplay)
Situation Hopeless but Not Serious (screenplay)

Tony Kushner

Yes, Yes, No No
Stella (adaptation from Goethe)
Hydriotaphia
The Illusion (adaptation of Corneille)
Widows (with Ariel Dorfman)
Angels in America: A Gay Fantasia on National Themes, Part One: Millennium Approaches
Angels in America: A Gay Fantasia on National Themes, Part Two: Perestroika
Slavs!: Thinking About the Longstanding Problems of Virtue and Happiness
The Good Person of Setzuan (adaptation of Brecht)
The Dybbuk (adaptation of Ansky)

Hank Greenspan

On Listening to Holocaust Survivors: Recounting and Life History (book)
That Again
Slideshow
Call Forwarding

Frank Gabriel Perry

Sisters, Brothers (translation of a play by Stig Larsson)
The Tunnel (translation of a play by Par Lagererkvist)
The Return of the Convict (translation of a play by Stig Larsson)
Grace (translation of a play by Ignace Cornelissen)
Swedish Drama in the Nineties (collection of plays)

Niklas Rådström

Poems on the Life of Sandro della Quercia (book)
The Moon Does Not Know (novel)
While Time Thinks (novel)
The Mozart Brothers (film)
Pa vag till havet (*On the Way to the Sea*)

Index

A Bright Room Called Day, 191, 192, 194, 207, 210, 295
Allied occupied zone, 212
American Alliance for Theatre and Education, 22, 49, 122, 123
Angel in the Night, 5, 49-52, 92, 293
Antoinette Perry (Tony) Award, 170, 191
Aryan, 26, 124-125, 210
Auschwitz, 11-16, 22, 30, 35, 40, 41, 45, 46, 96, 97, 166
Austria, 8, 10, 11, 218, 220, 275
Avenue of the Righteous Park, 53
Averill, Ric, 122, 294, 302, 306
Belgium, 11, 14, 211, 218
Bermuda Conference on Refugees, 13

Britain, 15, 98, 99, 171, 192, 218, 294
British, 97, 121, 171
Can You Hear Them Crying?, 5, 21-23, 46, 48, 293, 297
cast, 38, 91, 120, 164, 170, 186
Catholics, 193
character(s), 4-6, 17, 47, 90-91, 93, 96, 118, 164, 170, 174, 192, 196, 197, 209, 210, 216, 277-279
choral reading, 47
collaborators, 172, 173
Communists, 9, 193-195
concentration camp, 9-11, 15, 22, 41, 47, 174, 195, 297
costume(s), 47, 92, 209, 277, 278
curriculum, 5, 21, 305
Czechoslovakia, 10, 24, 41
death camp, 12

309

death march, 13
Denmark, 11, 13, 218
deportation, 12, 15, 166, 172, 173
dialogue, 4, 90, 209, 216, 279
Displaced Persons, 7, 172, 212
Drama Desk Award, 191
Einsatzgruppen, 11
England, 96-99, 119, 121, 170, 218, 294, 295
Final Solution, The, 4, 6, 12
France, 11, 13, 14, 171, 188, 211, 218
Führer, 9, 22, 124, 219
gas(sed), 8, 11, 15, 45, 46, 97 98, 171, 220
genocide, 6, 7, 12, 163, 173
Germany, 6-15, 43, 46, 96-99, 118-121, 124-125, 163, 172, 192-197, 201, 207-209, 211, 218-221, 276
Gestapo, 9, 24, 124, 125, 186, 216
Ghetto, 6, 11, 13, 22-25, 26, 28-30, 36, 44
Goebbels, Paul Joseph, 10
Goering, Hermann, 171, 186
Great Britain, 99, 171, 192
Greece, 11
Greenspan, Hank, 210, 295, 308
Gypsies, 6, 8, 9, 11, 12, 15, 211
Himmler, Heinrich, 9, 26
Hitler, Adolf, 7, 123, 186, 194, 207, 218-222, 241, 274, 277, 279
Hitler, Alois, 219-221, 241
Hitler, Klara, 220
Hitler Youth, 9, 10, 124, 164, 303
Hitler's Childhood, 217-219, 221, 279, 295

Holland, 11, 218
Holocaust, 3-7, 11, 12, 14-17, 23, 43, 47, 48, 50, 51, 92, 96-98, 120, 123, 165, 166, 171, 188, 193, 210-213, 215–216, 219, 300, 303
Holocaust deniers, 4, 188
homosexuals, 6, 9, 193, 211
Hungary, 13
I Never Saw Another Butterfly, 22, 38, 46, 297, 301
immigration, 172, 212
improvisation, 46, 208
International Red Cross, 22, 34
Israel, 7, 9, 99, 121, 166, 171, 173, 174, 186, 189, 211, 212
Jehovah's Witnesses, 9, 194, 211
Jew(s), 3, 5-15, 22, 24, 26, 44, 46, 50, 51, 90, 91, 92, 97, 118, 119, 123, 125, 163, 165, 173, 188, 189, 193, 209, 211, 212, 219, 220, 241, 299
John F. Kennedy Center, 123
killing centers, 16
Kindertransport, 95-100, 118-121, 294, 306
Kindertransport Association, 121
Kraus, Joanna H., 49, 293, 305
Kristallnacht, 10, 118, 163
Kushner, Tony, 191, 295, 307
League of German Girls, 124, 164
Lift up the Flag, 121
Man in the Glass Booth, The, 169-171, 174, 186, 189, 294, 298, 300, 307
Mein Kampf, 8, 221
mentally impaired, 6
Miller, Alice, 218, 299

monologue(s), 120, 162-164, 188, 209, 211, 213, 216
National Socialist German Workers' Party, 193, 195, 196, 220
Nazi(s), 3, 4, 6, 8-10, 12, 14, 15, 22, 25, 30, 34, 35, 46, 50, 51, 90, 93, 96, 97, 121, 123-125, 163, 167, 170-174, 186-189, 193-196, 201, 207, 208, 209, 210, 212, 216, 220, 241, 276-278, 299, 301
Nazi hunters, 125, 189
Netherlands, 14
Norway, 11, 218
Nuremberg, 14, 125, 167, 171, 172, 186-188, 302
Nuremberg Trials, 125, 171
Office of Special Investigations, The, 189
open-ended story, 119
pacifists, 193
Palestine, 7, 15
pantomime, 47, 93
perform, 47, 164, 216, 279
performance, 22, 47, 120, 163, 169, 221, 279
perpetrator(s), 3, 7, 90, 125, 172, 216
Perry, Frank Gabriel, 217, 295, 308
physically challenged, 6
play(s), 4-6, 16, 17, 22-23, 42, 47-50, 90-93, 95-97, 99, 118-123, 163, 164, 169-171, 182, 191, 192, 193, 197, 207, 208, 210, 211, 217-219, 277-279, 293, 297, 301, 305, 306, 308

playwright(s), 4, 16, 17, 23, 49, 50, 95, 96, 122, 169, 189, 191, 210, 217, 218, 277, 278, 293
Poland, 10-12, 29, 50, 90, 92
Poles, 6, 92
political enemies, 6, 9
Protestants, 193
psychological effects, 7, 99, 215
psychology, 5, 171, 215, 277
Pulitzer Prize, 191
Rådström, Niklas, 217, 295, 308
readers theatre, 47, 163
Reichstag, 9, 193, 195, 196
Remnants, 5, 210, 211, 213, 295
rescue(r), 51, 97, 98, 121
resistance, 4, 13, 51, 90, 279
role, 35, 163, 164, 186, 192, 209, 215, 278, 279
Samuels, Diane, 95, 96, 294, 306
Serbs, 6
Shaw, Robert, 169, 294, 298, 307
Shoah Visual History Foundation, 215
Social Democratic Party, 193, 195
Soviet Union, 11, 171
SS (Security Police), 9, 10, 172, 188, 213
Star of David, 11, 118
stereotyping, 5
Storm Troopers, 8-10
Stringer, Virginia Burton, 21, 293, 305
survivors, 3, 5-7, 52, 98, 118, 120, 172, 174, 210-213, 215, 216, 308
Theresienstadt, 22-24, 26, 29, 32, 34, 36, 38, 39, 41, 44, 46, 47

Third Reich, 7, 97, 123, 124, 164, 166, 196, 219
Treaty of Versailles, 7
T-Money & Wolf, 5, 122, 123, 126, 294
United Nations Relief and Rehabilitation Administration, 212
United States, 12, 15, 97, 163, 166, 171, 172, 174, 186, 189, 191, 196, 211, 212, 301
United States Holocaust Memorial Museum, 8, 17, 42, 298
victim(s), 3, 5, 6, 15, 23, 38, 48, 125, 166, 172, 173, 188, 210, 299
videography, 166
war crimes, 14, 166, 167, 171, 172, 174, 186-188, 302
war criminals, 171-173, 186, 189
Warsaw ghetto, 13
Weimar Republic, 8, 192-194, 196, 208, 220
Willmott, Kevin, 122, 294, 307
World Jewish Congress, 12
World Movement for the Care of Children from Germany, The, 97
World War I, 7, 193, 194
World War II, 3, 6, 10, 14, 50, 92, 99
Yad Vashem, 50, 52
Yale University's Fortunoff Video Archive for Holocaust Testimonies, 215
Yugoslavia, 11

About the Author

Janet E. Rubin is a professor of theatre at Saginaw Valley State University. In addition to her accomplishments as a theatrical director and teacher, she is a respected scholar of youth theatre and arts educator. She has authored numerous publications and has collaborated on several books on using the arts in education. Two collaborative works led her into specialized research involving the use of plays in teaching about the Holocaust.

Voices: Plays for Studying the Holocaust contains a selection of plays and play excerpts about the Holocaust designed for classroom use, with additional activities and materials for teachers. In connection with this work, Rubin was named to the Visiting Fellows program of the Center for Advanced Holocaust Studies at the United States Holocaust Memorial Museum in Washington, DC.

Articles by Rubin have appeared in several communication, speech, and theatre journals, as well as publications developed for teachers of drama, theatre, and English. She also has made numerous national and international presentations. Rubin has served in residence at the University of Mysore (India) and at Ballarat College of Advanced Education (Victoria, Australia).

The author received her B.A. degree form The Pennsylvania State University, her M.A. degree from The University of Connecticut, and her Ph.D. from Ohio State University. She is the 1997–98 recipient of the Earl L. Warrick Award for Excellence in Research. This award is presented to an SVSU faculty member whose scholarly activity during an extended amount of time has been of the highest quality. In 1998, she also was named Saginaw Valley State University winner of the Faculty Association Award for Scholarship.